TALK YOUR WAY TO SUCCESS

TALK YOUR WAY TO SUCCESS

by
Lilyan Wilder

Foreword by John Naisbitt

Eastside Publishing
New York

Published by Eastside Publishing, New York, 1991

First published in 1986 by Simon & Schuster as *Professionally Speaking*
Fireside trade paperback published in 1987 by Simon & Schuster as *Talk Your Way to Success*

Text designed by Carla Weise/Levavi & Levavi
Printed in the United States of America

ISBN: 0-9629260-1-9
(Previously ISBN: 0-671-63956-0)
Library of Congress Catalog Card Number 91-71430

We have made every effort to trace the ownership of all copyrighted material and to secure permission from copyright holders. In the event of any question arising as to the use of any material, we will be pleased to make the necessary corrections in future printings. Thanks are due to the following authors, publishers, publications, and agents for permission to use the material indicated.

American Broadcasting Company: from "Nightline." Courtesy ABC News, copyright 1983, 1984, and 1985 by American Broadcasting Companies, Inc.

The Art Institute of Chicago: *American Gothic* by Grant Wood, 1930, oil on Beaver Board, 29⅞ × 25, Friends of American Art, 1930, 1934. © The Art Institute of Chicago, all rights reserved.

ARTnews: from Ansel Adams, "The Last Interview," interviewed by Milton Esterow, Summer 1984. Reprinted by permission of Milton Esterow and ARTnews.

Beacon Press: from *Reconstruction in Philosophy* by John Dewey. Reprinted by permission.

Chappell/Intersong Music Group: from "My Funny Valentine" by Richard Rodgers and Lorenz Hart. Copyright © 1937 by Chappell & Co., Inc. Copyright renewed. International copyright secured. All Rights Reserved. Used by permission.

(continued at the back of the book)

To Irving

ACKNOWLEDGMENTS

Of the many experiences I have had in writing this book only one was more surprising than the overall exhilaration and satisfaction. And that is, I have learned what it means to have the support and attention of friends.

Some old friendships deepened and some new friendships were made in the sharing of insights with the people who helped me with this book: Jean Carper, Mark Estren, Harriet Englander, Mary Esch (who did the diagrams for voice and articulation), Gilroye A. Griffin, Peter Herford, Donald Hutter, Linda C. Jones, Noel Katz, Margaret Loft, Laurie Lister, Elizabeth Martin, Lawrence McQuade, Maureen Orth, Ray Price, Catherine Shaw, Sandra Sheppard, John Striker, Grant Tate, Alma Varvaro (whose impeccable fashion sense is a continuing inspiration), and Paul Wilson. I am very grateful.

In the Rodgers and Hammerstein musical *The King and I,* one of the song lyrics underscores my own discovery—that if you become a teacher, you'll be taught by your students. And so, to my students, for all the lessons I have learned from you, my heartfelt thanks.

I wish that I could repeat the names of the generous people, named and unnamed in this book, who gave of their time and experiences in interviews. They have contributed greatly.

And thanks, too, to Dennis Hawver of The Hawver Group, who did the research on, and provided the survey of, middle managers.

Finally, and from the beginning, two very special people gave consistently of their intelligence, talent and soul to the life of this book. Katherine Kormendi and Priscilla Shanks have my enduring appreciation.

CONTENTS

7

PART TWO: ALL YOU NEED TO KNOW TO GET YOUR MESSAGE ACROSS: THE LILYAN WILDER PROGRAM (STEPS ONE–THREE)

PART THREE: HOW TO SOUND YOUR BEST: THE LILYAN WILDER PROGRAM (Step Four)

FOREWORD

Many say we are becoming a civilization of illiterates. But our concept of literacy is also radically changing. That's what this book is about. It's more than about how to speak successfully; it's a plea for a new literacy of the human voice, with instructions from a skillful teacher about how to achieve a new competence in oral communication so necessary for survival in this revolutionary age of information.

Literacy, according to most dictionaries, is a static term: the ability to read and write. But today's literacy is dynamic and must be measured by an ability to handle the language currency of the day. And the definition of who is literate and who isn't—or who will be—is undergoing shock-wave changes as the old industrial society falls away and the new society founded on the ability to process and transmit information takes over.

It is true there is a crisis in traditional literacy. Some recent national reports condemn the products of our educational system. According to one, 28 million Americans are functionally illiterate—unable to read, write or handle the language. The Carnegie Council of Policy Studies in Higher Education recently reported that "because of deficits in our public school system, about one third of our youth are ill-educated, ill-

13

employed and ill-equipped to make their way in American society." For
the first time in history, youngsters graduating from high school are less
skilled than their parents. There is a generation gap in traditional literacy.

At the same time, the prospects for a new literacy are exhilarating.
Just think, we have invented a whole new literacy in the last decade—
the computer word, peculiar to our generation alone. And coupled with
that is a revival of our oral tradition, the first in five hundred years,
since it was squashed by the invention of the printing press. Virtually
everyone recognizes the emergence of the high-technology literacy, the
ability to manipulate the language of the computer. As I noted in *Megatrends*, those without such computer literacy will be condemned in the
future to wandering around the library of knowledge without a Dewey
decimal system, card catalogue or librarian to guide them—denied access to the very information that underlies their society.

On the other hand, almost totally ignored is the emergence of a
counterpoint to the new computer literacy that is just as important to
making our way in the informational new world: the ability to communicate effectively in the oral language. If one side of the new literacy
coin is the computer word, the flip side is the spoken word. That they
are coming into prominence together should not be surprising.

High technology—in this case computers—always brings with it a
counterbalancing human response, what I call the "high touch" response.
The more high-tech, the more high-touch. Without the high-touch reaction, the high technology will be rejected by society.

What could be a more logical "high-touch" counterpart to the cold,
steely voice of the computer than the human voice? We find it all around
us: oral communication, the most compelling way to reach one another.
Surely, the prime examples are radio and television. The endless spoken
word. And although many complain that the message is empty, it need
not be that way, nor is it likely to continue that way as television matures,
becomes more decentralized and video capabilities fall into everybody's
hands (as is already happening with the wide distribution of home video
equipment). In business and politics, too, decentralization brings confrontation on more personal levels, where human speech carries the
message. Conference calls are becoming more common, for example,
and major political decisions are increasingly being made at community

meetings. In the "global village," as in real villages, people will be thrown closer together, where they will be forced to communicate more effectively. It has even been predicted that our preoccupation with materialistic consumption of goods may give way to a nonmaterialistic consumption of human relationships requiring more intimate interactions.

So it's hardly such a shocking prospect to get back to talking to each other—instead of primarily writing to each other. After all, our oral tradition is of much longer duration than our printed tradition. The printing press, the invention that brought reading and writing literacy to the masses, is only five hundred years old, compared with untold centuries of oral communication.

As the movie *Quest for Fire* made clear, the humanizing of the race came with oral language. The language we grew heir to, for hundreds of thousands of years, was oral—grunts, sounds, words, sentences, whole epic poems passed from generation to generation by great storytellers. The tales of Homer were centuries old before they were "written down." The ancient Egyptians dictated to scribes. In medieval England the definition of literacy was to recite in Latin. Poetry, mostly silent today, was originally conceived for the ear. And when the printing press overthrew the long history of oral communication, the scholars of the day mourned and decried the destruction of literacy. What would happen to human memory, they asked, when ideas could so easily be transferred to paper for everyone to read? It's somewhat the same way the high priests of the written word are rising to protect today's traditional literacy against intrusions by computers and television.

But the new literacy is unstoppable, and those who understand it and grasp it will be the winners of the future. It is a skill necessary for survival and success in the new informational society. And just as the language of the computer must be learned, so must the forgotten language of the spoken word. Few of us do it very well. We are out of practice. And unfortunately, most of us think we cannot learn. We believe that our voices, our speech patterns, our ability to communicate are natural, as immutable as our fingerprints. We mistakenly think that actresses and actors and "great communicators" in business and politics were born with the voices and abilities to get across their messages.

Those of us who have studied with Lilyan Wilder know that is not true. We know that the voice is subject to enormous changes in tone and volume and warmth. We know that our thoughts need not only to be written down but to be thrown out there with force, wit, sensitivity and meaning, so that they can be picked up by other human beings. We also know that these skills are not merely for a select few. The measure of the new literacy is that everyone will need to acquire it.

There are many teachers of computer science but few teachers of human communication and speech. Lilyan Wilder is unquestionably one of the most notable. She has long privately taught some of the best communicators in the country. By putting her years of experience, sensitivity, secrets and advice into a book, she is providing everyone with access to the new literacy of the future, where the human voice is fully as important as the computer voice.

JOHN NAISBITT,
author of *Megatrends*
July 1985

INTRODUCTION

My whole method consists of enabling students to have an experience. I try to plan for them things to do, things to think about, contacts to make. When they have had that experience well and deeply, it is possible to point out what it is and why it has brought these results.

The real laws of art, the basic laws, are few.

—Kimon Nicolaides
The Natural Way to Draw, 1941

Thursday, September 27, 1984. The phone rings. "This is Vice President Bush's office," said the voice at the other end of the line. "The vice president is inviting you to a rehearsal of his debate with Geraldine Ferraro this Monday." I had nine appointments scheduled for Monday. I asked if the rehearsal could be videotaped so that I could critique it from New York. The woman at the other end said she would call back. Twenty minutes later the phone rang again. "There will not be a videotape made. The vice president would like you to attend the

17

rehearsal. You will have fifteen minutes with him afterward." I said I would be there.

I had been working with George Bush since late 1978 when he decided to throw his hat in the ring for the presidency in 1980. He had come to my office at the insistence of a close associate who knew how important it was to sharpen communication skills before a political campaign began. George, however, was not sold on the idea of working with a communications consultant. He was resistant to the idea of being "made over." He wanted to win, but he wanted to win because of who he really was and what he had accomplished; because of his intelligence and strength of character; and the authority he'd acquired through a lifetime of private achievement and public service as president of his own oil company, congressman, ambassador to the United Nations, ambassador to China, and director of the CIA. Besides, the demands on his time were fierce; his skills as a public speaker seemed good enough to him already.

In fact, back in 1978 George Bush was an adequate speaker. He came across as a man of intelligence and authority. He had strong convictions about what he was saying, as well as a winning, natural warmth. He felt comfortable before large crowds.

All this became clear to me during our first visit, as he practiced the speech he was to give to the Republican Booster Club in New York City. And the first thing I did when he had finished was to point out his intrinsic strengths as a communicator. I reassured him that I didn't want to make him over. I wasn't in the market for grafting cosmetic images onto real people. What life and experience had already given him were the most precious resources he had as a communicator. All I wanted to do was to teach him to use these assets more fully, to help him bring his own unique self more to the fore, so that the connection he made to an audience was strong, positive and personal. At present he wasn't doing himself justice.

As we went over the practice videotape I'd made, I pointed out that his ideas could have been structured to come through more clearly. Excess verbiage and abrupt, unnecessary gestures were getting in the way of his message. A slight New England twang interfered with the warmth and vitality behind his words.

I could see George's mind start to click. He began to catch a glimpse of the kind of speaker he could become, of how much more effective *and true* the videotape speech could have been with the changes I was suggesting. This kind of work was worth a serious investment of his time. He was convinced.

As our sessions progressed we tackled his verbal skills. I tape recorded some of George's speeches and transcribed them verbatim. He was amazed to note the sea of words on each page and began to fix the problem almost immediately. I then showed him how to mark a text so that key words and thoughts would stand out for him as well as the listener. We also worked at refining his body language. He had a tendency to point his finger and hit the lectern for emphasis. Videotaping convinced him of how distracting these gestures were, and he began to substitute smoother movements.

As we continued to work on particular skills, not only did the personal and professional strengths of which George was already aware come through more and more clearly, personal qualities ("colors") he'd either been unaware of or had dismissed as unstatesmanlike—his low-key humor and boyish charm, for example—began to emerge. And the more sure he became of himself as a communicator, the freer and more spontaneous he became as well.

George Bush, who had been so skeptical, turned into a committed, enthusiastic student of oral communication. Whenever I sent him a written critique of a particular speech or TV appearance, he responded with a handwritten memo. Now, six years of hard work were to culminate in what would perhaps be the most critical speaking engagement of his career. He was to debate Geraldine Ferraro, the vice presidential candidate on the Democratic ticket, on national television.

This debate was of crucial importance to both Bush himself and to the presidential campaign. President Reagan had not done well in his recent debate with Walter Mondale—it was said, among other things, that Reagan's age had been noticeable—and it fell to George Bush to rally support and solidify the Republican ticket. Adding to the pressure was the growing popularity of Geraldine Ferraro. As the first woman nominated for vice president on a major party ticket, she was drawing large crowds everywhere. Hungry for campaign dramatics, the news media had built this debate into a major confrontation.

When I arrived at the Old Executive Office Building next door to the White House for the first rehearsal, I was directed to a small auditorium.

His closest advisors waited for the vice president's arrival. When at last he walked in, it was clear that he was exhausted. I was shocked to see how thin and gaunt he had become. Campaigning in two or three states a day was obviously taking its toll. He was clearly overworked and had not yet been able to take the time to prepare for this event. Some of his answers to the tough, hostile questions fired off by four people acting as reporters lacked impact. His interactions with Mrs. Ferraro's stand-in were sometimes defensive and at other times aggressive.

After the rehearsal, I met with Bush in his office and he asked for my comments.

"Number one," I said, "don't think of Ferraro as an opponent. In a debate you've got to be gracious and noncombative because hostility works against you." I had been making notes for him on 3×5 cards, and I handed one to him on which I'd written an oriental proverb: "If you wish your merit to be known, acknowledge that of other people." "What is it about Ferraro that you admire?" I asked. He thought a moment and said: "I really admire the closeness that she has with her family." "Good," I said. "Let that positive feeling take root in you, and on the day of the debate your warmth toward her will come through, and your delivery is bound to be more confident and affable.

"Number two: even though you're preparing for a debate, which by its nature requires that you be spontaneous, you should prepare as you would for a speech. Your responsibility is the same for both occasions. You must get your facts crystal clear in your mind. Then put them in your own words and rehearse that language out loud. Find the time, somewhere between Arkansas and North Carolina, to prepare.

"Number three: be ready to bridge to the point you want to make after answering a question. That way you can control the content of the material to some degree.

"Number four: the facts that you prepare, the answers to questions you think you'll be asked, and the body of information you want to get across form the basis of the 'minispeech'—the technique that we've worked on all these years. Etch that format in your mind.

"Number five: you have the opportunity to work on your conclusion. You will be given [three] minutes air time. Know your closing remarks by heart, and truly believe what you're saying. Prepare and practice."

That first rehearsal proved to be very valuable. It focused the vice president's attention on the issues he wanted to concentrate on. He had the technical aspects of the debate under control, so that during the event itself he'd be free to focus on content.

On October 11, 1984, millions of radios and TV sets were tuned into the Bush-Ferraro debate. That night, George Bush gave himself to the fight. He really wanted to win, and that competitive spirit motivated him to harness all his technical skills and use himself in a real way. As he told me afterward, "As soon as I realized that Mrs. Ferraro wasn't twenty feet tall, I was okay."

Bush kept up the momentum and made sure that he communicated his firsthand experience of Central America and the Soviet Union, and his knowledgeability in the area of terrorism. He fielded tough questions on abortion and nuclear war, and at one point he had the self-confidence to take issue with a reporter who asked: "Was it right for your administration to pursue policies which required those at the bottom of the economic ladder to wait for prosperity to trickle down from those who are much better off?"

"It's not trickling down," Bush asserted, "and I'm not suggesting there's no poverty. I am suggesting the way to work out of poverty is through real opportunity." He went on to discuss the various programs where spending was up and supported his assertions with facts and statistics. Throughout the debate, his voice varied in volume and nuance depending on the content of his words. Bush's energy and ardor were in marked contrast to Geraldine Ferraro, who displayed an uncharacteristic reserve on this occasion.

Of course, there were moments when his performance was not perfect. Occasionally there escaped a spontaneous phrase uncensored by his better judgment. An attempt at humor backfired, and at one point he corrected his own misstated statistic. But these were minor slips that actually served to humanize him. They didn't diminish his competence and commitment.

The vice president spoke with fervor from his heart. This was what moved people: that he was real, and that he cared. He cared about what he was saying, to whom he was saying it and the larger picture, the vision the administration had in mind for America.

A *USA Today* poll of 586 debate watchers gave Bush a 19 percent point margin, 48 percent to 29 percent over Ferraro.

"I really felt it was George Bush who was seemingly more forceful, more committed, more enthusiastic," said James Ungar, director of the National Forensics Institute, Washington. "I think George Bush really needed to win one for the Gipper, and he did that tonight." "Whatever Reagan lost, Bush got back!" agreed a South Florida Democrat.

Six years ago the vice president had come to me with the same intelligence, insight, and strength of character that had so impressed the nation during the debate. Now, however, he had the confidence to tap deep into the real feelings within himself and share them with an audience of thousands. And, as I have learned from teaching an entire spectrum of students, from politicians to broadcasters to major executives, this and only this will make an otherwise adequate communicator truly outstanding.

For communication is an exchange of life, a dynamic encounter between human beings. If I truly communicate with you, I must move you, stimulate you, arouse your interest, draw you in toward me. I must share myself. Words alone will not achieve it.

Whether I am pleading with you to do something about an urgent situation, describing a technical innovation, or cataloging goals and plans for the future, I must first believe in what I am saying, believe that it matters and speak from my own sense of urgency about the situation or excitement about the innovation. Secondly, I must make a personal connection to you, as one human being to another, whether you're an audience of one or one thousand.

During the 1968 presidential campaign, Robert F. Kennedy paid a visit to a day nursery outside Indianapolis. "Most of the children were from broken homes. 'Two little girls,' wrote David Murray in the *Chicago Sun-Times*, 'came up and put their heads against his waist, and he put his hands on their heads. And suddenly it was hard to watch, because he had become in that moment the father they did not know. . . . You can build an image with a lot of sharpsters around you with their computers and their press releases. But lonely little children don't come up and put their heads on your lap unless you mean it.'"

At its best, communication can be a totally involving experience for both speaker and listener—emotionally, intellectually and physically—provided the speaker reaches out with everything he has within him: his own physical vitality, his desire to be seen as he truly is and his deepest feelings about what he is saying, what it means to *him*. He gives information and inspiration to his listeners, who respond and stimulate him in return. This sense of true communication is what separates my method from any others that I know. It is the core of my process, both as I teach it one-on-one and as I've laid it out in the chapters to follow. It's what I've come to call "being real." Here is a brief summary of the Lilyan Wilder Four-Step Program.

First, you organize your thoughts and develop your own style of expressing them.

Second, you design your road map, a visual guide to help you emphasize key words and thoughts.

Third, you learn how to practice out loud to prepare for the delivery of your message.

Fourth, you develop your personal sound to express yourself in a voice that truly reflects you. It is your first and lasting impression.

To put these four steps into practice, you learn how to handle the important and difficult communication problems in your nine-to-five day, whether it is selling your ideas to senior management, conducting a staff meeting or dealing with an intimidating boss. You find out how the media works and how to make it work for you.

Finally, you acquire five handy pocket guides. They prepare you for any speaking situation you might face in the next thirty minutes, six hours, six days or six weeks. You also get a four-step guide for media preparation.

This method grows out of a lifetime devoted to communication. It started in the 1940s when Alvina Krause, then the head of the Drama Department at Northwestern University, took me on as her personal assistant when I was still an undergraduate. I assisted in the running of her speech labs and later, after earning an M.A., I began my teaching career at Northwestern with her help. Soon I moved on to Chicago's Teachers College and then to New York City, where I continued my work as an instructor in Voice, Articulation and Public Speaking at Brooklyn and Hunter colleges. I also worked for a year at the New York Hospital for Speech Disorders, where I deepened my understanding of remedial therapeutic techniques.

In 1956 I began my own speech practice. My clients included children with speech defects, executives who wished to sharpen their speaking skills, and actors and actresses. I also designed communications programs for major corporations around the country, including IBM and RCA in California.

During this period, roughly from 1956 to 1969, I also studied singing with Emmy Joseph and worked as an actress in Broadway and off-Broadway plays and on television. The work I did in theater, and especially my studies with Lee Strasberg, fed and enriched my teaching techniques. Strasberg taught me how to delve into my psyche and use my real self as a performer. It is this philosophy that forms the foundation of my program.

In 1969 my work took a new turn. I was teaching Voice and Articulation at the Strasberg Theater Institute when a call came from ABC asking if anyone was interested in coaching an ex-athlete who had been hired as a sportscaster at WFIL-TV (now WPVI-TV) in Philadelphia. Working with Bill White, the former St. Louis Cardinal baseball player, was my entree into a new career as a talent coach to broadcasters. I went on to work with WFIL's chief anchor Larry Kane, and then with the station's affiliates in New Haven, Connecticut, and Buffalo, New York. Soon I was consultant to stations in New York, Boston, Washington, Minneapolis, Denver, Dallas, Los Angeles, San Francisco and other cities across the country.

Currently I work with the three major networks and their stations and affiliates, designing programs tailored to individual needs. In addition, I have private clients, among them talk show hosts, media personalities, authors and politicians. I also work with numerous Fortune 500 corporations, coaching high-profile executives and designing group-training programs for managers and salespeople.

Occasionally, I have returned to academia. In 1972 and '73 I taught on-air delivery techniques to minority students at the Columbia School of Journalism under the auspices of the Michelle Clark Foundation Program.

My book contains information and exercises that are widely applicable, yet I intend it primarily for people in the business world. The broadcasters and politicians who seek my services know that their visibility makes it imperative that they communicate well. The executives who come to my office generally want to prepare themselves for an isolated event—an important speech or an appearance on television. Some want fast results, a quick fix. Others know that to make sense out of the new information age takes effort and commitment to communication skills.

It seems important to return again to the example of George Bush. At first he resisted the idea of a time-consuming program of self-improvement, reasoning that his speaking skills were perfectly adequate. Learning to communicate better gave him the ease and self-confidence to reach into himself and share his feelings with the people listening to him. To persuade and convince, you must reach inside yourself, and that takes more than learning some tricks. That takes real commitment. George Bush took an unsparing look at how he communicated, and he decided to work for change.

With the help of this book, you too can embark on that same rewarding journey. You may not be headed for high political office, but there is no telling how far you can go or how much you can contribute to your organization, your profession and your community, when, like George Bush, you make communicating with excellence a priority in your life.

PART ONE

WHAT IT TAKES TO BE A SUCCESSFUL COMMUNICATOR

Chapter One

THREE
OF
THE BEST

As a kid I went to a concert by Paderewski. . . . I had seats in about the third row. There were two girls sitting next to me with the score. When Paderewski came out, everybody just stood. No clapping, nothing, everyone just stood. He turned a pale, ashen color. . . . Then there was the sound of thousands of people sitting down. And he was obviously very moved; you could see it. He was going to play a Mendelssohn sonata. Well, these girls had their score open, and he saw them. He looked over and said, sort of sotto voce: "You will not find it there, my dears." Boy, they closed that score. And then he proceeded to play.

—Ansel Adams
"The Last interview"
ARTNews, Summer 1984

"The surfer does want to ride the wave to the beach, yet he waits in the ocean for the biggest wave to come along that he thinks he can handle. If he just wanted to be beautiful, he could do that on a medium-sized wave. Why does the surfer wait for the big wave? . . . because he values the challenge it presents. . . . The more challenging the obstacle he faces, the greater the opportunity for the surfer to discover and extend his true potential . . . Note that the surfer in this example is not out to prove himself . . . but is simply involved in the exploration of his latent capacities."

You can experience the same heightened awareness as that of the surfer described by W. Timothy Gallwey in *The Inner Game of Tennis* when you communicate successfully. The difference between *adequate* communication and the *art* of communication is the difference between riding the medium-sized wave and taking on the big wave.

How can I get you to imagine what communication is like when it's an exhilarating experience? The best way I know is to show you three superb communicators in action: Lee Iacocca, Millicent Fenwick and Ted Koppel. I chose them because they are individuals whose enormous success in business, public life and the media literally cannot be separated from the masterful use of the spoken word. And their examples are widely applicable. Each of these great communicators faces the kind of challenges that you as a professional person face in everyday life.

CHALLENGE #1: WINNING THE BATTLE

Imagine this: You've been put in charge of a major account; handed one of your company's most important departments to reorganize; or entrusted with the campaign of the season to handle as you will. Take your pick. But choose something that could make or break your career.

Now imagine this: Things have gone terribly wrong. Yet you believe the situation is salvageable. You know that given one more chance you could turn it around 180 degrees, bring enormous profit to your company, and save your own neck. But no one else does. Your subordinates are demoralized. Your superiors are impatient to cut their losses, admit defeat, and put the whole thing in someone else's hands. Your credibility is shot. How do you convince everyone involved not simply to go along with yet another scheme you can't prove will work, but to give you more time, more money, and even a bigger chunk of total corporate power?

• • •

When Lee Iacocca took over the chairmanship of the Chrysler Corporation, he stepped into a position experts said would bring him to his doom. The company was reeling under billion-dollar losses. To escape bankruptcy, billions more would be needed to rebuild its gas-guzzling, out-of-date fleet from the ground up. And who wanted to give Chrysler a second chance? "Let Ford and GM take over the market," grumbled some; "Chrysler's too small to compete, and a bailout will only postpone the inevitable." Angry creditors and suppliers were banging on the door; they'd had enough. So had many thousands of Chrysler workers already fuming at massive layoffs and wage and benefit cutbacks. Why should they pay another penny for management's mistakes?

Unfazed, Iacocca launched a one-man communication blitz to rally the company, the financial sector and the nation to his side. He went to Washington and persuaded Congress to guarantee Chrysler a $1.7 billion loan. He charmed, bullied and dazzled suppliers, local governments, private lenders and the UAW into believing that Chrysler could pull through and was worth saving. Then he proceeded to negotiate huge concessions out of every one of them. He persuaded dealers all over the country to carry Chrysler's line despite past failures. He awoke a new team spirit within the mass of remaining Chrysler workers, persuading them to give their all in spite of salary and benefit cutbacks. He raised their morale, made them feel involved in a great cause, and brought new vitality to the company. Finally, he launched a flurry of press conferences and a $200 million TV advertising campaign featuring none other than Iacocca himself extolling his new K-cars, offering $50 to anyone who would test-drive a Chrysler, daring the viewer to prove him wrong: "If you can find a better car, buy one!" The American public was hooked. Rooting for Iacocca all the way, they bought Chrysler stock and Chrysler cars.

Time and again, Iacocca got his message across loud and clear: "Chrysler must be given a chance." He made you believe you had a personal stake in Chrysler, made what mattered to him matter to you.

He won confidence.

He won loyalty.

He won.

And he did it all because, like the understudy who wins front-page raves the day after the star falls sick, he was ready when his moment came.

• Iacocca has known all his life that good communication isn't icing on the cake. It's the meat and potatoes of his profession. "To motivate people you've got to communicate with them," he says. "Otherwise why be in business? Top management should always be reaching out to help the people they're working with, getting them involved, giving them direction, plugging into their needs. Just because you get involved and excited and tear into things doesn't mean you'll die of hypertension next week." Iacocca begins a story: his eyes light up and he rears into action like a race car driver taking the wheel. *He's devoted to communicating 100 percent.* And he loves doing it.

• Whenever Lee Iacocca gets up to speak, he knows just what he wants to achieve and what points he must make to a particular audience. And no matter what questions are thrown his way, no matter how "chatty" or "casual" the occasion, he never goes off track. *He speaks purposively.*

Appearing before Congress to argue for a loan, Iacocca answered questions, but he also scored the points he wanted to make.

"The Treasury Department had estimated that if Chrysler collapsed, it would cost the country $2.7 billion during the first year alone in unemployment insurance and welfare payments due to all the layoffs. I said to Congress, 'You guys have a choice. Do you want to pay the $2.7 billion now, or do you want to guarantee loans of half that amount with a good chance of getting it all back? You can pay now or you can pay later!'" He got his loan.

Though Iacocca was up against the wall in 1979, he communicated like a winner, going straight for what he wanted, focusing attention on those issues he wanted discussed, putting facts into perspective.

• *He knew what he was talking about.* Keeping track of government regulation of the auto industry over the past decade, for example, he could accuse Congress of having acted irresponsibly and support his position with hard facts.

Knowing all there is to know about auto design and market dynamics, he was in a position to persuade all involved that his schemes for putting Chrysler back on its feet were worth investing in. And once the K-car and minivan began to roll off the assembly lines in Detroit, Iacocca was able to sell them convincingly because he knew the value of each design feature, each technical detail, knew what the competition was offering and how it compared to his products. Iacocca's vast pool of information gave him statistics, examples, and illustrations to draw upon at will to bolster his arguments.

• *Well-honed verbal skills* opened his listeners' ears to these arguments, and captured their imagination. Iacocca's style is unequivocally direct, outspoken, bold. It's the style of a man who is strong, honest, gutsy, gritty, real. He describes things with down-to-earth, sensual imagery—the K-car as Chrysler's "gold standard," small cars as "puddle jumpers," the minivan's seat as "fanny-high." His words play on our imaginations. We started seeing Chrysler's cars with Iacocca's eyes, feeling his excitement, saying "yes" to his vision.

He also draws us in with humor. When he appeared on the "Donahue" show and the host asserted: "You're trying to recapture California" with the minivan, he answered: "You're darn right we're trying to recapture California!" Later, returning playfully to that theme, and alluding to Donahue's casting him in the role of the aggressive salesman, he joked: "We'll sell it for $1,000.00 less in California without windows. They go for that out there." After Iacocca had praised the minivan at some length, Donahue interrupted: "Ten minutes for this commercial!" Iacocca retorted: "Well, you let me go on, and I figured since this was a free one I'd take advantage. Usually we only get 30 seconds and we have to pay through the nose!"

• Iacocca works to *cut through* whatever *barriers* exist between him and his listeners by meeting them where they are. During the crisis, he let his workers know how much it grieved him to accede to massive layoffs. "My heart bleeds for those guys," he said, and they believed him. By showing awareness, respect, even sympathy for their position, including their bitterness and disappointment with management, Iacocca *made a strong personal connection* to his workers and forged a new relationship between them, based on mutual trust and understanding. They began to think of him as part of a "we" rather than as an object of suspicion or animosity.

• It's probably obvious by now that Iacocca sold everyone on Chrysler because he sold everyone on himself. Says Maryann Keller, a portfolio manager at the brokerage firm of Vilas/Fischer: "I wouldn't doubt that people have bought a Chrysler car just because they wanted Iacocca to make it." And Ron DeLuca, vice chairman of Kenyon Eckhardt, the advertising company behind Chrysler's TV campaign: "Iacocca has gone from being a corporate spokesman to somewhat of a folk hero." Vince Williams, a Portland, Oregon, auto salesman, opened a Dodge rather than a Pontiac dealership solely because of Iacocca. "All of us at Chrysler believe in the man," says St. Louis plant manager John Burkhardt. "I worship the guy."

The basis of this self-sell is confidence. Iacocca has great self-assurance, even under fire. When he speaks, he does so with such clarity and such a sense of knowing what he's talking about that his listeners have to take him seriously. "With Lee it's almost impossible to win a debate," said one colleague at Chrysler. "He commands you to follow, and you're afraid not to."

• *He's real.* When he says the minivan is "coming on like gang-busters," he means it. He speaks from having assessed his situation as it really is, not as he might wish it to be. If he's up against the odds, he doesn't sugar-coat. Asked if the state Chrysler was in when he took over was as bad as he expected, he says: "You're darn right it was. Worse. It was an absolute mess!" At the same time, he believes in himself and in his product. And he expresses his belief in a way that is more than just "honest." He formulates answers, arguments, explanations in terms that are personally meaningful to him. Describing the Chrysler minivan on "Donahue" he begins: "We're really proud of it. I spent eleven years developing it together with another engineer." This is the real, personal basis of his own belief in the minivan.

He doesn't adopt one voice for addressing the public, another for his workers, and another for government officials, financiers or labor leaders. He may vary the content of his presentations, true, but he always says what he means and does so in the colorful, blunt language that is Iacocca's own. To an audience of college students he said: "You know what? It breaks my heart that I can't say to you today that you've got the world by the tail." To a group of disgruntled managers, it was: "Don't give me any crap!" He connects to each person in a real, flesh-and-blood way, without being either too formal or condescending. And he can do all this, mean what he says, use words that are real to him, relate to others, because he trusts himself.

CHALLENGE #2: MAXIMIZING YOUR CAREER

Are you adept at putting your ideas into words? Do others turn to you to be their spokesperson? Is your voice heard in your organization? Good communicators don't restrict themselves to speaking when spoken to; when they see a point that will make a difference they speak up, never excusing silence with the cop-out that they weren't hired or trained to give opinions on that matter.

Initiating discussions, throwing out thought-provoking suggestions (you don't have to have all the answers), voicing a sharply honed critique: the more actively you enter into the exchange of ideas, formally at office meetings, informally at business lunches, the more valuable you will be. Your stature will increase. Your involvement in business will expand and diversify, and you can build a career that has the shape and scope you choose. In time you may even find yourself explaining company policy to boards of directors, stockholders, the general public or the media, areas you cannot now imagine being open to you.

If this seems like fantasy to you, just take a look at what Millicent Fenwick achieved, largely on the basis of her outstanding skill as a communicator.

An ex-model and associate editor of *Vogue* magazine, Mrs. Fenwick had no professional background in community service or politics when she decided to run for a seat on the Borough Council of Bernardsville, New Jersey, in 1958. As a concerned member of the community and a single parent, however, she had also been involved in local educational reform as a member of the Board of Education. Once on the council, she quickly became a major voice in the community, using her verbal skills to rally support behind a wide range of projects, civil rights causes and prison reforms in particular.

Though she was born into a long-established New Jersey family and educated in exclusive girls' schools, Mrs. Fenwick communicated her concern and compassion so successfully to the underprivileged (seeking them out in person, discussing their needs and problems) that she won the right to represent them. She reached out to the people for whom she fought. And she reached out to the public at large, convincing others to join her in her battles. She made people feel as strongly as she did about these issues.

In 1969 she was elected to the New Jersey State Legislature. Her reputation grew, as did her public profile. (A campaign to provide migrant workers with portable toilets—she was successful as usual—earned her the nickname of "Outhouse Millie.") Elected to Congress in 1974, Fenwick's gifts as a speaker won her influence in excess of that usually afforded a Washington newcomer representing a relatively small district.

Turning her seat into a "bully pulpit," she launched a passionate campaign against governmental corruption. She forced her colleagues to look at both themselves and her in a new light and won a new nickname:* "The Conscience of Congress." Her strong moral sense won Fenwick the ear of the press as well as her colleagues. Said Zbigniew Brzezinski: "She's just damned good. We need a lot more like her."

At the same time, she began to speak out about a broader range of issues. Most dramatically, by speaking on foreign affairs, Fenwick cut a path into that inner sanctum and pinnacle of government power, Foreign Policy. (The achievement could be compared to that of a Johnson & Johnson marketing executive in charge of all the Tylenol accounts for the northeastern United States, daring to discuss international policy with the company's board of directors, and being asked to join the board!) She asked basic questions: How do we choose whom we give aid to? Do we make the politics of a nation's government determine whether or not we let its people starve to death? She spoke so cogently on these points that she was given a seat on the Foreign Affairs Committee (in addition to those she already held on Education, Labor and the Select Committee on Aging), in which she became one of the most active and valuable members.

During debates both in committee and on the floor, Fenwick enhanced the scope and quality of discussion by tossing out new ideas and sharing her thoughts about problems that troubled her. Something in her manner allowed people to discuss explosive issues without exploding. She reminded her fellow legislators of the larger implications of their actions.

*This was actually Walter Cronkite's phrase.

To get people acting and thinking on this level of awareness is leadership of the most creative form.

She was accessible. Her number was published in the Bernardsville directory and she answered calls at all hours of the day and night. She motivated people to be aware of their responsibility as citizens and to make their opinions known on everything from Social Security to U.S. intervention in El Salvador. As Henry Kissinger said: "The task of the leader is to get his people from where they are to where they have not been. The public does not fully understand the world into which it is going. Leaders must invoke an alchemy of great vision."

Millicent Fenwick was reelected to Congress four times, each time by larger and larger majorities. Then, in 1982, after her unsuccessful bid for the Senate (a traditionally Democratic state, New Jersey had gotten caught up in the national reaction against Republican ascendancy in 1982), President Reagan appointed her American ambassador to the United Nations Food and Agricultural Agencies, based in Rome. Millicent Fenwick's abilities were considered simply too valuable to let lapse into disuse.

Her new position is perhaps the most personally fulfilling of Fenwick's career. Through it, she is able to devote herself entirely to the largest and most ambitious of her goals as congresswoman: redressing inequity—hunger, poverty, technological backwardness—on an international scale. It has also opened the door to active involvement in areas of the world she has not yet explored.

As one pictures this indomitable elderly lady kneeling down to comfort an African woman whose baby lies dead of starvation at her feet, or traipsing through a remote village in Ghana, discussing alternative methods of irrigation with a local chief, one feels that Mrs. Fenwick's strength as a communicator will again prove one of her most valuable assets.

From humble beginnings on the school board to world issues at the United Nations! How does she do it? Where does she find the energy and the courage?

• The energy grows out of her belief in *the importance of communication*, of taking a stand, and the exhilaration, for her, of doing what she believes in. "Voice your opinions," she says. "Speak up! The weaknesses of human nature . . . fester and grow in . . . silence and anonymity.

Starting at home, children should hear their parents express anger at violent deeds, pity and shame for the violators of peace and their families." We must speak up, she says, because only then do we have a chance of creating a just and virtuous society.

• Fenwick's courage derives from a strong *sense of purpose.* She never speaks up without having something to say that she feels needs to be said, bringing out a vital consideration another speaker has neglected, shifting the focus of discussion from a peripheral issue to the heart of the matter, arguing with passion when she sees that something must be done. She dares to step forward and interject, interrupt, demand that attention be paid to the injustices she sees: "the [Cambodian refugee] children are so famished they must be fed intravenously before their bodies can accept food." Her purpose is to force us to confront the reality of human suffering and take action.

• Like Iacocca, Fenwick has *an ample body of material* at her command. Whenever possible, Fenwick investigates a topic exhaustively. Before proposing a massive attack on public housing, she did in-depth research to find out why previous housing projects failed. She conferred with architects and met with inhabitants in their homes to find out what they wanted and needed. She personally gathered illustrations of their plight, such as that of an elderly woman climbing up fourteen ice-covered stairs to get home.

Exploring the tragedy of Soviet Jewry, she read personal accounts of their suffering, spoke with their relatives, even traveled to Russia to speak with those involved, both the persecuted and the persecutors.

She has a vast reservoir of facts, anecdotes, quotes and illustrations, an understanding of current events and the nature of government. A voracious reader, Fenwick can quote with ease from history, literature and philosophy. But more importantly, she zeros in on everything around her with a communicator's eyes and ears. Finding the right example to make a point, to persuade your listener, doesn't necessarily come from a reservoir of study, but from a facility for observing and thinking about what you experience. Fenwick's experiences remain etched in her memory, stored up for future use.

• As for her *verbal skills,* they are superb. Her love of words, her years of reading have given her speech a graceful simplicity, an easy eloquence. "I have never seen or imagined such human suffering. The first thought that comes to mind is 'stop the killing.'" She remembers Rabbi Gershon Chertoff quoting to her from *The Wisdom of the Elders*: "Remember, you may never arrive at the solution, but you are never absolved from the responsibility of trying." This, she says, means that "success is not the measure of a human being, effort is."

She can also be earthy. About what she anticipates doing in Africa: "Once you get to a village you go to find the top banana, often some old geezer. You talk to him. You ask him: 'What do you need?' He says, 'Irrigation.' You ask him, 'Where do we start?' He says, 'That field over there.'"

And gritty. "Look around this place [her lawn]. There's not an inch that doesn't have my sweat in it."

Like Iacocca, she has a strong sense of imagery: "The power of the purse, the power of the legislative fist—these are blunt instruments for the delicate operation of diplomatic interchange. It's like trying to open a china box with a crowbar, or untie a knot with your foot."

• Mrs. Fenwick listens to and *identifies with her audience*. She acknowledges that her listeners' thoughts are valuable, and she sincerely believes that opposite views have grounds for common interest. If a speaker communicates in a way that suggests she has all the answers, she doesn't leave space for audience participation or response. The listener feels left out. He may be moved, but he's not moved to action! Fenwick's clearly stated interest in points of view other than her own, her eagerness to learn from others, enables her to reach a lot of people who may not completely agree with her priorities or particular solutions but do agree that the issues are important, that the problems burn. She considers that a triumph. "A good communicator is one who makes you think!"

• Fenwick is *sure of herself as a communicator* because she's not really concerned with herself. The magnitude of what she's striving for lifts her beyond her own situation, helps her focus on what she's saying and why she's saying it. That gives her voice power and authority. Fenwick becomes a sort of medium through which the force of the beliefs that drive her get channeled out to the public.

When you feel this kind of force and power, when you are focused so completely on what you are doing that you almost become it, everything comes together. Losing consciousness of technique, you become like

Yeats' dancer, at one with the dance, or the Zen archer who thinks of nothing but his target, picks up his bow and shoots a perfect shot. The right words just come. You find images, examples, analogies and hit the nail on the head without looking. You soar.

This is what happens to Fenwick, but only because the communication skills she has honed over the years are now so strong that she can forget about them, yet still have them work for her.

• Mrs. Fenwick always *speaks from the heart*. She enjoys her own sense of humor, her stories and quotations. That's why she's able to move her listeners, who can see the sparkle, the indignation or the tears in her eyes. She always begins her presentations with either a personal anecdote or a personal statement, such as "Mr. Speaker, members of the House, we have heard today eloquent statements concerning the barbaric assassination of the former prime minister, the head of his party in a free country. I have family in Italy and this matter is very close to my heart. We should have spoken, too, when the poor policeman in Milan was shot in the back getting into the bus on his way to work."

She talks directly to our senses, our imaginations, our hearts. She shocks us. Touches us. Tickles us. And she feels free to laugh at what tickles her. Once, she made a speech in the New Jersey Assembly proposing an equal rights amendment for women. One of her colleagues rose "with real anguish in his voice, you could tell he was addressing a subject close to his heart, and said: 'I just don't like this amendment. I've always thought of women as kissable, cuddly and smelling good.' [I replied] 'That's the way I feel about men, too. I only hope for your sake you haven't been disappointed as often as I have.'"

She forms an image so strong and evocative that Gary Trudeau used her as the model for his character Lacy Davenport in his "Doonesbury" cartoon. Yet she refuses to romanticize herself. When her campaign manager, John Deardorff, tried to get her to walk past the Capitol on her way to work for a campaign commercial she replied: "I do not walk past the Capitol on my way to work. I don't have time for these games." Deardorff had to make do with footage of her descending into a House office building parking garage.

And throughout any presentation she always returns to her own point of view whether it's with a little segue: "When I was first married..."

or "I don't know how such things can happen. . . ." We always feel she is talking to us, sharing her private thoughts, never that she's making a formal presentation as the representative of a position. She talks as though to a friend: "Let's face it, dear. . ." she'll often say, and it makes us want to see, understand and listen.

CHALLENGE #3: GETTING THE REAL STORY

Just before Gertrude Stein was wheeled off to her last—and as it happened, fatal—operation, her longtime companion, Alice B. Toklas, seized her hand and exclaimed: "Gertrude, what is the answer?" to which Stein is said to have replied: "What, my dear, is the question?"

"One of the key things in business is asking the right questions," asserts Paul Wilson, President, The Mader Group. "The people who ask pertinent, tough, meaningful questions that focus issues do well, and their companies do well."

Do you know how to ask the kinds of questions that keep subordinates, clients and/or experts on their toes? Questions that focus issues and are phrased in such a way as to get specific answers? Questions that pierce through evasions, distortions and generalities, uncover the real facts, divulge the whole story? Get at the problems beneath the apparent problem? How good a *detective* are you?

Can you create the kind of atmosphere (whether one-on-one or on a larger scale) that induces people to open up to you? Gets them communicating freely, honestly, directly? Gets them to reveal themselves? Do you, in other words, *facilitate* communication?

Do you know how to ask the kind of pungent, provocative questions that get people stimulated, enthusiastic, alive with ideas? Do you know how to foment productive interaction and turn a potential confrontation into a cooperative struggle for a win/win solution? In other words, are you a *catalyst*, an instigator?

Finally, can you shape the meetings over which you preside in such a way as to do more than simply "accomplish the business at hand"? Can you, by the way you define problems and goals, connect with larger values that you'd like to have disseminated throughout the organization or department you control: values like the pursuit of excellence, taking responsibility and individual initiative? Are you a *pathsetter?*

To truly excel in the world of business or politics, or any career, you must be able to get to the heart of an event or issue that affects you! Only then can you tackle problems effectively. Only then can you manage crises or make sound policy decisions.

To do all this is to be a communicator in the deepest sense of the word. As Roger K. Smith, Chairman of General Motors, put it: "The truly great executives . . . endeavor to free [their subordinates] and guide them toward developing their own conceptions."

Ted Koppel, host of ABC-TV's "Nightline," is this kind of communicator. True, he doesn't make policy decisions, nor is he responsible for solving the problems he examines. Nevertheless, the communication skills he deploys are so impressive that one reporter, after watching Koppel moderate the New Hampshire debate in the 1984 presidential campaign, said that "Ted Koppel should be running for President!"

Koppel's probing, no-nonsense dialogues with leading experts and notorious figures, statesmen and private citizens involved in some issue of social importance, have won him the ear and approval of intellectuals and policymakers, as well as of the average TV viewer. The media, among them *Time* magazine, the Associated Press, *The New York Times* and the *Los Angeles Times*, have called him "the best interviewer on TV." Comments Jody Powell: "He has the ability to hit pretty hard and get at the guts of something without coming across as offensive or badgering in his manner."

In essence, what Koppel does is to take a single topic on each broadcast of "Nightline" (e.g., IRA Guns: a Cash Controversy, or Herpes and Children: How Great a Danger?) and attempts to find out what's really going on: Why are we doing what we're doing? What are our underlying assumptions? What are the implications of our policy? What objections could be raised, alternatives offered?

Koppel is at once a detective, a facilitator, a catalyst and a pathsetter.

As a *detective,* Koppel manages to get the real story, even when the person to whom he's speaking does all he can to withhold it. The following excerpt from an interview with Pieter W. Botha, president of South Africa, is a study in "how to push in a proper way with a government official who is being deeply disingenuous."

KOPPEL: If you wanted to go to Johannesburg right now . . . you could
  get up and leave.
BOTHA: Yes, but it's my country.
KOPPEL: Most black men can't.
BOTHA: Most black men can.
KOPPEL: Cannot.
BOTHA: Can.
KOPPEL: Without permission from the government?
BOTHA: That's right.
KOPPEL: Just leave, go from one place to another.
BOTHA: Yes. Yes.
KOPPEL: Stay there, settle there.
BOTHA: No, not settle there . . .

Checkmate! No position is exempt from challenge in Koppel's eyes.
Consider the following interchange with Roy Cohn, who was appearing
on "Nightline" to defend the controversial McCarran-Walter Act au-
thorizing the administration to bar leftist artists and writers from speaking
or performing in the United States if their presence should be deemed
"dangerous to the public welfare."

KOPPEL: Mr. Cohn, if I wanted to talk to one of these Nobel Laureates,
  I suppose we could . . . book a satellite and they come into every
  American home that chooses to tune in "Nightline" at that particular
  hour of the evening. So if they can broadcast their ideas here in the
  United States, what is the additional danger of letting them come in
  and be here physically?
COHN: I suppose the danger is that it touches off—frequently it touches
  off riots and other things . . .
KOPPEL: When is the last time that the presence of an author or an artist
  or a poet or a composer has touched off a riot in the United States?

But Koppel is more than a crackshot D.A. He is a diplomat. A
facilitator. He knows how to create an atmosphere that makes his guests
feel safe, open up and speak out with amazing, eager candor. "He has,"
as Frank Snepp, former CIA analyst, says, "the grace and ability to
touch something in other people that ordinary reporters can't, and make

you feel that he's not merely a reporter but someone who can empathize."

Consider an interview with Christopher Boyce, the so-called Falcon of *The Falcon and the Snowman* fame, now serving forty years for spying for the KGB. At first, Boyce held back. He was reluctant and had difficulty talking. But as he began to sense Koppel's genuine interest in his feelings, Boyce opened up to him.

KOPPEL: Tell me about what it is [espionage] then? Why is it not glamorous? I mean, apart from the fact that if you get caught you end up in the slammer as you did, but what is unglamorous about it?

BOYCE: Well, it's just not what people think it is. It's like picking up a 60-pound stone that you're never going to be able to set down. The KGB is forever. . . .

KOPPEL: Well, give me a sense of—it's an interesting line, the KGB is forever. What do you mean by that? How did it become that for you?

Soon Boyce was revealing with vivid, pointed language what it was like to be a spy. "Espionage is something that grabs you by the stomach and just holds you down and doesn't ever go away. . . . It's like walking into a dark room and falling down a hole." Boyce went on to confess that "I went to them [the Russians] because I was 21 years old and I was so foolish."

And eventually he even drew a moral from his case. "And if the four million Americans with security clearances really knew what espionage was . . . there wouldn't be any espionage. And the government is derelict in its duty if it does not communicate to the four million . . . that fact. That should be done." He himself was communicating so much, so beautifully, that Koppel was moved to say: "Christopher Boyce, I think you've done it, and done it very eloquently tonight."

As a *catalyst* Koppel asks the kinds of questions that stimulate his guests to respond and give. In a group situation, he gets "an electricity going among the participants," as he puts it, while as a masterful orchestrator he keeps the discussion moving forward and focused on the meaningful issues.

An example is one segment of the five-part series on "Nightline" broadcast live from South Africa and anchored by Koppel himself: a discussion between Afrikaner Cabinet Minister Gerrit Viljoen, one of the most powerful whites in office today; Sheena Duncan, the president of Black Sash, a pro-black organization of white South Africans; and Dr. Nthato Motlana, a black physician/activist. Koppel immediately challenged Dr. Viljoen to justify apartheid, while warning him that: ". . . from overseas, it is hard to understand how [these policies] can be justified on moral or ethical grounds. Would you like to try?" To Mrs. Duncan, on the other hand, he suggested that Viljoen's remarks indicated "there is all kinds of willingness to be reasonable, all kinds of willingness to negotiate," thereby getting *her* going. She responded: ". . . negotiations for the destruction of a settled community seem to me one of the most irrational kind of things you could be negotiating about."

Revealing his deep anger toward a ruling class that has so debased his people, Dr. Motlana added: "I've . . . seen movement . . . all of it backwards . . . They're moving the few rights he [the black man] does enjoy . . . These people lost their fertile lands and are now settled in areas where they cannot produce anything."

Under combined pressure from both Duncan and Motlana meanwhile, Viljoen's careful facade of tolerant good will began to crack, laying bare a strong undercurrent of impatience and resentment toward black South Africa: ". . . where . . . a chief is appointed . . . in the traditional fashion and then confirmed by the government, he's considered to be a puppet because he was not elected. But in the case of the elections . . . people refuse to participate and then . . . consider themselves to be the authentic leaders . . ."

Resettlement, pass laws, issue after issue was explored in-depth by the three leaders, with the same level of intelligence and passion. For his part, Koppel remained primarily a catalyst, once he had gotten things truly under way. I was once told by a labor negotiator that "the secret of arbitration is to know when and how to get out of the way, and let the process happen." Koppel did that but from time to time, he stepped in playing devil's advocate, offering insights of his own, citing facts, scoring points first for one side then the other, so neither would be overwhelmed, and each had a fair chance to state his or her case clearly. Ultimately, however, he got them to express their grievances openly without putting words in their mouths. In this way, the real dynamics of the South African conflict began to make itself dramatically visible, including the serious lack of trust and perceptual distances between the Afrikaner government and the black leadership, as well as the emotional forces at play: the rage, frustration, bitterness and fear that are tearing that nation apart.

As David Halberstam put it: "Koppel unveiled South Africa's troubled soul."

What is so remarkable is that Koppel fosters the kind of dialogue that reveals much, without the dialogue itself breaking down. Equally striking is the way this pathsetter can open up a dialogue by leading his guests to consider the subject under discussion in terms of important questions or underlying issues they might not have broached on their own (or even been aware of).

Consider the following interchange with Atlanta Mayor and former U.S. Ambassador to the United Nations Andrew Young vis-à-vis Jesse Jackson's personal diplomacy in the Middle East. (Jackson had recently flown to Syria on his own initiative to "negotiate" the release of Navy Lieutenant Robert Goodman. Welcomed enthusiastically by President Assad of Syria, he returned victorious, but debate raged over whether the then presidential candidate had acted from humanitarianism or political self-interest.)

KOPPEL: Mayor Young, let's sharpen the focus a little bit. Humanitarianism, sure, why not; political motives, who doesn't [have them]; but what about the business of a private citizen engaging in foreign policy? . . .

YOUNG: . . . the decision-making process in the State Department requires about 17 different clearances before a diplomat can get his talking points. . . . I just ignored them, frankly, and I think any success I had was due to that. . . .

KOPPEL: Well, if I hear you correctly, what you're suggesting then is, as far as diplomacy is concerned, scrap the State Department and let's all go our own way and do the best we can.

What Koppel does here is to shift the focus away from the Jackson/ Goodman incident as an isolated event, and zero in on the general question it raises: Should a private citizen take it upon himself to engage in state business without official authorization? What kind of precedent is Jackson setting no matter how honorable his intention? And what sort of attitude toward legally sanctioned organs of power like the State Department do his actions suggest?

In the final analysis, Koppel is an educator. He educates himself, he educates his audience and he educates the people he interviews by challenging their assumptions (Roy Cohn), their values (Gerrit Viljoen and Andrew Young) and sometimes simply by making them feel that what they have to say matters (Christopher Boyce). Under the best circumstances, his guests leave with a more acute perspective and enhanced awareness of the problems with which they're involved.

Koppel's formidable expertise as a communicator enables him to cover any issue or event with equal finesse, even a story that has just broken one-half hour before he goes on the air. In fact, he is at his best when the going gets tough and he's called on to cover an on-going crisis as it unfolds day by day. Untangling complexities, separating rumor from fact, honing in on key issues—he does all within the context of a rapidly changing and enormously confusing situation. His coverage of the Iranian hostage crisis (1979–80) and the Americans held hostage in Beirut in 1985 prompted *Wall Street Journal* reporter George V. Higgins to write: "Ted Koppel is a most outstanding 'crisis manager'... he functions most effectively when things are at their worst."

In a world rife with surprise takeovers, terrorism, and catastrophes on the scale of Union Carbide's Bhopal disaster, what professional can afford not to be able to handle crises effectively?

Although the nature of Koppel's work is quite different from Fenwick's and Iacocca's (he asks questions, they answer them), his effectiveness can be traced back to the same basic attributes.

• Like them, *he is devoted to what he does.* "I love doing 'Nightline,'" he exclaims. "If someone said create for yourself a program that is the quintessence of what you would like to do... I would have a hard time coming up with anything more than I have. When other kids wanted to to be firemen, I wanted to be Ed Murrow. What could be more exciting than having a chance to talk every night for a half hour to the greatest experts in the world? 'Nightline'... is my dream job."

• *He has clarity of purpose and approach.* Although he doesn't write his questions out beforehand—because, as he explains, "If you come in with just your own questions in mind, you may find that the person you are interviewing says something interesting and you may ignore a very good follow-up question"—he does have a vivid sense of what he wants to get out of the interview. Just as a businessman attends a meeting with a clear agenda in mind, a sense of what he wants to get out of that meeting, Koppel comes to the anchor desk each night knowing what he wants to cover, what he's interested in finding out during this particular broadcast. That's what gives his discussions direction and focus.

In a program on DPT (the legally mandated anti–whooping cough injections to which an unknown number of infant deaths have been attributed) Koppel's purpose is to find out what a concerned parent would want to know: Why hasn't the AMA come up with an alternative? Are alternatives available elsewhere? What are the risks involved? With that sort of agenda in mind, Koppel keeps the discussion moving forward while staying free to dip into whatever happens at the moment or follow up as needed.

• *Koppel's knowledge is power.* It is a knowledge that comes from twenty-three years' experience as a top ABC reporter under his belt. And like Fenwick, he's voraciously inquisitive. In addition to reading at least six major newspapers a day and preparing for his program, Koppel keeps track of all the major news broadcasts. He is constantly probing, questioning the information he absorbs. (Hearing that General Motors just recalled half a million cars, he exclaimed: "It's the most extensive and expensive recall they've ever had. What goes on at GM when this happens?" and scribbled a note to himself.)

His broad knowledge gives Koppel the wherewithal to make his questions and objections specific and rigorous. Challenging Dr. Viljoen on the South African government's right to even consider resettling blacks, he asserts: "—why should people who had land deeded to them by Queen Victoria's government, who have been on that land with that kind of authorization for certainly the last 80-some years . . . why in heaven's name should they be moved at all?"

• *Verbal skills.* Koppel has the ability to formulate his questions and comments in plain, concise, clear English. William Lord, vice president of ABC News, credits this facility with enabling Koppel to "re-ask and

THREE OF THE BEST

rephrase his questions, and not let [his guests] go on a quick and simple answer."

In one of the segments on South Africa, Koppel interviewed journalists Percy Qoboza and Otto Krause, and Dr. Beyers Naude, a white leader in the anti-apartheid movement. Koppel asked Dr. Naude why he had suddenly converted from a strong racist position to a supporter of the black cause:

DR. NAUDE: I came to the conclusion . . . that . . . apartheid was unchristian, it was immoral, and it was unfeasible. . . ."

KOPPEL: Mr. Krause, is the policy of apartheid justifiable on moral and religious grounds, do you think?

MR. KRAUSE: I think that one cannot look at these things solely in moral or religious lights.

KOPPEL: I'm not asking you to do that. I'm just asking you whether it can be justified on those grounds.

MR. KRAUSE: I think it can very much be justified. . . . But the point is that what is necessary in this country . . . is growth. . . . And this is a matter of a country raising up all its people, uplifting them in standard of life . . . we are doing this job. . . .

KOPPEL: All right. Here we have Percy Qoboza, a man who was a Niemann fellow at Harvard—I suspect he doesn't need any more uplifting, at least intellectually. Your response, Mr. Qoboza, to the notion that the white man's burden in this country is to lift up the blacks.

Koppel used the most precise words to phrase his question, making it very difficult for Krause to avoid a direct answer.

Even his on-the-spot retorts come out in complete grammatical sentences, unmuddied by "uhm's" and "uh's." When at the outset of a discussion of cold-war politics William F. Buckley began criticizing television's journalistic integrity, protesting: ". . . how is it that American television feels that we can be informed . . . by listening to the paid propagandists of the Soviet Union?" Koppel suggests that if Mr. Buckley answers the questions put to him on television, the American people will be informed.

Not only are his questions and comments extremely clear, they're almost always phrased in such a way as to help the interviewee get right to the point. In a one-on-one discussion with former President Carter, Koppel did not generalize: "What do you think about present Mideastern policies?" but instead specified: ". . . you were . . . critical of the strategic relationship . . . between the U.S. and Israel . . . Why?" He didn't ask: "How do you feel about moving the American embassy in Israel to Jerusalem?" but "[A] Why is that such a Key issue and [B] . . . why do you disagree?"

Koppel's command of language includes a sense of humor that plays freely on well-worn sayings and phrases: "Gentlemen, you're in danger of talking over everybody's heads but your own." "On that minor note of agreement let us take a commercial break." It's a subtle but powerful tool which helps break down his guests' defenses and transform potentially unpleasant confrontations into constructive and honest exchanges.

• Probably the most important quality Koppel has as a communicator is his masterful way of *listening*. There's an extraordinary attentiveness about him, a highly developed capacity to focus completely on the person he is interviewing. "You have to keep the antennae out," he insists. "You have to try and sense how your guests are feeling. Are they in a humorous mood? Are they in a belligerent mood? Do they want to get involved in a fight, and if they do, and if that fight is going to be a useful means of exchanging ideas, then you encourage them. If it's just going to be a couple of people nose to nose yelling at each other . . . then you have to nip it in the bud."

Koppel's own antennae are excellent. He knows how to listen *actively*—asking himself all the while what the communication he's receiving implies, questioning, probing. This, more than anything else, is what permits him to get on a wavelength with his guests, and hear the hidden message beneath their words. The nine years Koppel spent as a diplomatic correspondent taught him how to read between the lines and understand the subtleties of what was being said, especially when the person speaking was trying not to say anything.

What is more, he listens not just to confirm what he already thinks, but to find out something new. He's open. Interested. Eager to learn. Willing to hear the truth even if it's different from what he would have expected. "As a journalist you have to listen. You are not imposing your own opinions, you are listening to opinions exchanged by others. What you have to do is be careful not to rush to judgment because there really are other points of view."

This attitude not only helps Koppel reveal the key issues behind the story. It helps him become part of a "team" with his guests. Although he is not an active participant imposing his own opinions, he is "in there with them," struggling to grasp what they are saying as they struggle to express themselves clearly. His listening galvanizes the interview into a dynamic give-and-take.

People tend to open up more easily to Koppel because his listening shows a respect and a desire to hear what they have to offer, whether it's the expertise of a former president of the United States or the simple experience of an auto mechanic. He is human and keenly sensitive to their positions.

This humaneness comes through most clearly when he's dealing with victims of social outrage or political oppression. We feel a real warmth in him, an enormous delicacy and tact, but one that is absolutely without pity or patronization. Unlike so many interviewers whose attitude of "I understand how much you've suffered" is a bit too easy and smacks of condescension, Koppel seems to know that he *can't* understand what these people have gone through, that all he can do is try to feel it. In this way, he grants them their integrity and their dignity. By openly admitting to the difficulty he has in addressing their pain—as he did with the Hiroshima survivor Mrs. Shibama to whom he said: "Was it painful for you to see that film [*The Day After*] or—I don't quite know how to ask the question." His vulnerability comes through. Then, too, he can ask terribly painful questions and not be offensive, because he does so with an acute awareness of the pain involved. To Mrs. Shibama, for example: "Then please tell us, what is in your heart, what is it that you want people to know about those days—"

"If you are listening to find out, then your mind is free, not committed to anything; it is very acute, sharp, alive, inquiring, curious and therefore capable of discovery," wrote Krishnamurti, the Indian philosopher.

It is this kind of listening which encourages, and gets responses for Ted Koppel.

• *Confidence.* "Ted is the most self-confident man I've ever met, and I've met a lot of people, including Henry Kissinger and Charles de

Gaulle!" says Barrie Dunsmore, colleague and friend of Koppel's for twenty-five years.

He is not afraid to intrude when necessary: to call someone on evasions or deliberate lies; to demand more precise definitions; to cut in when one participant in a discussion becomes overbearing or goes on and on, and to do so firmly and directly. At the same time he is sure enough of himself never to allow irritation to get the better of him. If someone insults him, he's able to let the provocation slide. If one guest proves impossible to reach, he goes on to the next. He doesn't need to prove anything about himself, or keep himself in the spotlight.

In his book *The Savage Mind*, French anthropologist Claude Lévi-Strauss describes two ways of approaching any situation. One way is that of the technician who has learned a formula for dealing with a finite set of situations. If he's confronted with an unforeseen situation or doesn't have the right tools on hand, the technician is at a loss.

The other way is that of the *bricoleur*. He is flexible, dealing with each problem as it arises on its own terms and using whatever tools are handy. If he doesn't have a hammer to nail two boards together, he'll pick up a stone and use that. Sustained by his confidence, Koppel is the *bricoleur par excellence*. He builds his questions out of what the other person gives him and uses the other person's language and behavior to tell him how to proceed. This is true interaction, communication in its highest form.

• Ted Koppel is *real*. In loving what he does, being truly interested in the issues he addresses and addressing those issues from his personal background and experience, he brings his unique self to bear in each segment of "Nightline." He reasons things out using his common sense and intuition, and he asks questions to which he is truly interested in having an answer.

I'll never forget how struck I was by Koppel asking a disabled athlete: ". . . is it ever an advantage to you just to have one leg?" The same question had been on the tip of my tongue, but I would never have asked it, feeling it to be crude or insensitive. Yet when Koppel asked it, it ' came out of a sequence of ideas and acceptable logic.

"If you are watching some guy hop up to a high jump, and here is a man with only one leg, and he is about to jump 6 feet 8 inches, which is something 99.9 percent of the public with two legs could not do, all of a sudden the thought comes to you: 'Well, wait a second, he's carrying less weight, right? He's got one less leg.' I don't think there's anything improper or rude or stupid about asking that question."

As the orchestrator of the action, his personality takes second place. Yet in the way Ted Koppel orchestrates that action, his own personality does come through. And that is what being real is all about: being true to the action you're involved in, true to yourself and true to your response to the world around you.

We have talked about how three excellent communicators use their skills to meet challenges and achieve success. Their styles are vastly different: Lee Iacocca, the bold businessman; Millicent Fenwick, the cultivated public servant; and Ted Koppel, the detective/facilitator. Yet they have much in common.

- They love to communicate, perhaps because it is their way of sharing their unique gifts.
- They have a purpose, and they believe in that purpose. Also, their reasons for speaking are generally larger than themselves.
- They know what they are talking about. And they've made the information they've gathered their own.
- They have good verbal skills. They use images, aphorisms and humor to give clarity, directness and earthiness to their language.
- They know how to connect with their listeners. They make the person they're talking to feel acknowledged. Their communication is two-way: it invites give-and-take. It elicits a response.
- They have confidence and control.
- They are real. They are comfortable with who they are. They don't try to play a role.

These are qualities you too can possess. They do however take time to develop. Success rarely hits you like a moonbeam and transforms you. You need to commit yourself to the challenge of taking one step at a time as these three communicators did. At the beginning of his career Iacocca recalls: "It wasn't easy. I was bashful and awkward . . . and I used to get the jitters every time I picked up the phone. Before each call I'd practice my speech again and again, always afraid of being

turned down." Ted Koppel had been working at his craft for seventeen
years when he became host of "America Held Hostage" in 1979. He
was not ABC's ideal choice of an anchorman, but his superb ability to
communicate turned the network management around in his favor and
convinced them to keep him on the air. Millicent Fenwick began her
career by communicating at informal meetings, school board meetings
and the New Jersey House of Representatives before tackling her biggest
challenge—Congress.

In my work as a coach, I've seen that once people begin to practice
the method set forth in these pages, they experience significant and
exciting changes. Even a few weeks of practice can make a dramatic
change.

The basis of everything you will learn in this book is what I call "being
real." When you are real, you are there, responding to your listener,
sharing your own thoughts and associations. *Becoming* real is a process.
It is a constant, a continuum, yet an ever-changing element of successful
communication. It's what makes you unique.

Chapter Two

THE KEY: BEING REAL

At every moment you choose yourself. But do you choose *your* self? Body and soul contain a thousand possibilities out of which you can build many I's. But in only one of them is there a congruence of the elector and the elected. Only one—which you will never find until you have excluded all those superficial and fleeting possibilities of being and doing with which you toy, out of curiosity or wonder or greed, and which hinder you from casting anchor in the experience of the mystery of life, and the consciousness of the talent entrusted to you which is your I.

—Dag Hammarskjöld
Markings, 1964

Your real self, with all your experience, insight and strength, is the most valuable resource at your disposal. If you use it wisely, after making a presentation, interviewing for a job or negotiating a raise, you will be left with a very special feeling. You won't feel as though you have only shared information with your listeners, you will feel that you have shared yourself with them. And if they believe in you, they will believe in what you have to say.

Success as a communicator, in fact, depends on how much self you allow your audience to see. You must present that self as authentic and important—what I refer to as "real."

"That man is absolutely for real! He got to me." At rock bottom, this is the sort of response every person in the public eye—be he or she lobbyist or diplomat, businessperson or politician—must go for. If achieved, true effectiveness, believability and impact—all will be won. But while many people, especially in this era of media consciousness, feel the need to "do something" about how they come across, most believe that this means hiring a public relations firm or an image consultant to create a persona for them. This is a mistake, just as misguided as delegating all responsibility for your text to a speechwriter.

The invent-an-image method does not work; witness any number of politicians who hire consultants to mastermind their campaigns. They are taught how to dress and how to sit, given cue cards to read from and little lectures about "smiles" and superficial "eye contact," external devices aimed at making them look "natural." All they end up looking like is stiff, detached robots. You can't create humanity from the outside in.

We live in the era of the "global village." Television has brought the starkest reality into our living rooms—the assassinations of John Kennedy and Anwar Sadat, war atrocities in Viet Nam, John Glenn launched into space, Neil Armstrong walking on the moon, and U.S. citizens held hostage in Iran and Lebanon. We have been witnesses to all these. As a result, lifeless or artificial presentations no longer make the grade. Whether on television or in front of a group, communicators today must project their real selves if they're going to have any impact on sophisticated TV-conditioned audiences.

To project your real self, you must do so from the inside out, in terms that mean something to you. Also, you must respond to how you uniquely experience thoughts and sensations. If you are really thinking, you can maintain that train of thought, say what you want to say in an organized fashion and at the same time be flexible enough to have your thought broken and return to it. People who know what they are saying can absorb an interruption very well. In other words, you must react honestly and flexibly to whatever happens to you while you talk (questions, harassment, laughter and so on) and be able to deal with these things while maintaining a previously arranged structure to your communications.

As one of my most brilliant and receptive students, the late Jessica Savitch, anchorwoman for NBC, put it: "I find the best way to be an effective communicator is to be what you are on the air as well as off the air. ... Viewers will respond positively if you are real. They don't know—there is no sign that comes up over your head saying 'this woman is real, this woman is not a fake,' but it is a *visceral* reaction. Somehow when you are yourself, you become three-dimensional instead of two-dimensional."

Three dimensionality, being in touch with real feelings, at one with your body, reacting honestly and humanly to the world—these qualities make the successful communicator stand out.

So what do you do? Where do you go for the persona that will draw people to you? How do you present your *self* to the public so as to win them over?

You trust that self. To get at what is involved in such trust, consider for a moment a notion I first came across in my acting career.

BEING PRIVATE IN PUBLIC

Lee Strasberg, the famous acting teacher whose students included Marilyn Monroe, Dustin Hoffman and Robert de Niro, pointed out that what people really want to see on stage is the actor being private in public. I think that is exactly what audiences are moved by, whether at a play, a speech or an event of world importance televised live. They want to experience real people.

When you read a book, listen to a piece of music, watch a sunset or think about something important to you in the privacy of your own home, you get in touch with your truest self. When you are moved, your thoughts, feelings and associations flow uncensored. You cry, smile, wince without even thinking of how you are coming across. In other words, you respond intimately and openly to whatever you are experiencing. Being private in public means tapping that sensitivity and intensity within.

In his book *Robert Kennedy and His Times*, Arthur Schlesinger, Jr.,
describes a speech Kennedy gave in an Indianapolis ghetto the night
Martin Luther King, Jr., was shot. I'd like to quote Schlesinger here
because he so effectively captured how stunningly and courageously real
that speech was.

> It was a cold and windy evening. People had been waiting in the
> street for an hour. . . . They had not heard about King. Kennedy climbed
> onto a flatbed truck in a parking lot under a stand of oak trees. The
> wind blew smoke and dust through the gleam of spotlights. "He was
> there," said Charles Quinn, a television correspondent, "hunched in
> his black overcoat, his face gaunt and distressed and full of anguish."
> He said: "I have bad news for you, for all of our fellow citizens and
> people who love peace all over the world, and that is that Martin Luther
> King was shot and killed tonight." There was a terrible gasp from the
> crowd. . . . "Martin Luther King dedicated his life to love and to justice
> for his fellow human beings, and he died because of that effort. . . .
> For those of you who are black, considering the evidence there evi-
> dently is that there were white people who were responsible, you can
> be filled with bitterness . . . or we can make an effort, as Martin Luther
> King did to understand and comprehend and to replace violence, that
> staining bloodshed that has spread across our land, with an effort to
> understand with compassion and love. For those of you who are black
> and are tempted to be filled with hatred and distrust . . . I can only
> say that I feel in my heart the same kind of feeling. I had a member
> of my family killed. . . . But we have to make an effort in these United
> States. . . . Let us . . . say a prayer for our country and our people."

Kennedy admired King. He felt his death personally, the more so
because it recalled the death of his own brother. His pain was unmitigated
and profound; yet instead of trying to hide this anguish he spoke from
it. He allowed himself to be private in public. In addition, however,
Kennedy cared deeply about the black underclass and this caring gave
him a sense of purpose. He allowed himself to be vulnerable, the more
dramatically so because he didn't know what their reaction to King's
death would be, and because the police refused to protect him in the
midst of the crowd.

Whether as a statesman grappling with the agony of a terrible tragedy or as an executive announcing the closing of a plant, allowing yourself to be private in public is the essence of being real.

You need not feel that Robert Kennedy's depth and achievement are out of your league. If you look to yourself to express your inner life, as Kennedy looked to himself, true communication can result.

There is a method you can use. It involves three processes:

Relieving Tension

"Being Alive"

Developing Sensory/Emotional Awareness

RELIEVING TENSION

Tension is the greatest barrier to becoming real. To understand this, try to move a piano or lift a two-hundred-pound weight, and in the midst of the effort ask yourself: "What is 702 times 4?" You'll find that you can't think because your whole being is locked up in trying to move the weight. The same holds true when you are tense. Tension impedes concentration and stops the natural flow of your senses, so you can't focus on speaking freely. Tension traps your energy.

How can you learn to relieve tension?

Clear your mind of distractions, particularly of urgent business back at the office, so that you're not bringing your desk with you to the speaking situation.

Concentrate on what you're going to say for ten or fifteen minutes beforehand, without anyone else's intrusion. This is particularly difficult in a luncheon or dinner situation, when the people at your table want to make conversation. Still, it's perfectly acceptable to either excuse yourself for a few minutes or politely state that you must review your notes during dessert and coffee. If you choose the latter, just sit quietly and let the conversation flow around you.

Let go. After you've reviewed your remarks, sit quietly and concentrate on releasing tension from your forehead, eyes, mouth, neck and shoulders. If you have any specific areas of tension, concentrate doubly hard on them. Say to yourself, "Let go, ease up." Once you've perfected this technique, you'll find that even your breathing will change, a sure sign that you're relaxed and ready to go to work.

"BEING ALIVE"

Oral communication takes place on many levels. Words are important, unquestionably, but to make those words provoke, excite, sting or comfort another person, you must be keenly aware of what the text means, both to you personally and to your listener.

Relate to What You're Saying

"I cannot sell a painting unless I think it has an artistic value," a New York art dealer told me recently. "Even if I know it will be a good investment for the buyer, I have to believe in it as art to make an honest case for it."

That kind of commitment to product or service creates conviction. When what you talk about is important to you, conviction and belief come automatically.

Recall Lee Iacocca's commercials. The company's survival was on the line, as well as his own. And when he said, "Chrysler's cars will be better than other cars because they *have* to be," he convinced us he would make them better, single-handedly if necessary.

Sometimes, though, you have to *work* at uncovering why the material is important to you. Here are two helpful rules:

1. Learn everything you can about your subject. The more you know about it, the more excited and passionate you'll become.

2. As you learn, ask yourself: "How does this relate to me?" "Do I care?" "What does this mean to me?" For example: "The disease of muscular dystrophy, which I am discussing with this group, could it strike my little girl?" Or, "The beautiful car I am presenting to this customer, would it make my own family happy?"

If you are handed a pre-designed presentation, complete with slides and text, you need to make it your own. Tell the story as you see it and experience it. If you're given slides, put them in a sequence you feel will get the message across.

IBM executive Jim Cassell tells this story about himself:

"Back in 1972 when I had to give a presentation to 4,000 people in Cobo Hall in Detroit, Michigan, I went to the arena to check it out beforehand. I even practiced the carefully written-out speech IBM wanted me to give with a tape recorder so that I could give it exactly as written. After it was over, I couldn't remember a word I had said, or how it went. I was paralyzed with fear during the whole thing.

"Eight years later I had to give a presentation in Cobo Hall again, but this time I did it my way. Instead of a speech that was written out word for word, I used an outline. I knew what I wanted to say, having thought it through and made it my own. I practiced, but I wasn't trying to please a boss, or anyone but myself. I was much more real and spontaneous. I even enjoyed giving the speech."

Relate to Your Audience

To communicate with your listeners, talk *with* them and not *at* them. When you recognize and absorb your listeners' reactions, an electrical circuit is sparked between you. There is an energizing give-and-take. Smile if the response pleases you. Show a touch of hurt or anger if necessary. If you see confusion in the eyes of the person you're talking to, clarify. *Acknowledge the reality of your relationship to your listeners.*

Much more will be said about give-and-take in chapter 5, "Practice and Delivery." For now, just be aware that these interactions create a vital bond between you and your audience.

During our school years, there was for many of us one teacher who made an indelible impression on us. That teacher cared, gave of herself, and helped shape our lives.

There is a "learning need" inside each one of us. If you can care about the people to whom you are speaking with the intensity and rapport of a teacher who cares, you will trigger that need. You'll establish a connection, as all successful communicators do.

Relate to Your Surroundings

You must also be sensitive to your physical environment. Be aware of the lighting, the temperature, the "atmosphere" of the room. Is it cozy and inviting or sterile and cold? The way you sit in a chair, lean across a podium or notice the flowers on a colleague's desk plays a part in defining who you are to the people around you.

Sometimes things go awry, but if you are tuned in to your surroundings, you can actually take advantage of the surprise factor.

Johnny Carson is a master at handling the unexpected. No matter what goes wrong he incorporates it into his show. One night, Carson had a guest on the "Tonight" show whose act included a singing parakeet. The bird simply would not sing and the trainer was in danger of falling flat on his face, bringing the show down with him. But Carson turned the bird's silence into a joke far more entertaining than the original act could have been. "Well, I think we might just have to eat this bird," he deadpanned at one point. The audience howled.

When you handle distractions and mishaps with grace or humor, you set your listeners at ease and create a more intimate relationship with them. You take the audience into your confidence. When you *fix* something that's gone wrong right there in front of the audience, your listeners feel they are, for an instant, transported "backstage." You are truly private in public, human.

Relate to Yourself

If you are aware and responsive to your words, your listeners and your surroundings, then you will be in touch with yourself.

Consider the great violinist Itzhak Perlman. Perlman seems overpoweringly physical. His face reflects his own reactions to the sounds he is making. Sensation, thought and emotion flow through him. During a TV performance I watched his face in close-up. His expression went from a twitch to a kind of snarl, from a heavenly smile to an impish grin, to pain, laughter, sadness, surprise. Throughout it all, sweat was pouring off his nose—and you could see him feel it.

Paradoxically, communication is achieved as a result of awareness of self. Being in touch with himself makes Perlman's music transport the listener to faraway worlds. So, in order to move people, you not only reach out to them, you stay in touch with yourself. Being there, being at one with yourself and your own physical, sensory reality is the essence of "being alive."

But you can't learn how to connect with your material, your listeners, your environment or yourself simply by reading this section. It takes time, practice, relaxation and use of your senses.

LEARNING SENSORY/EMOTIONAL AWARENESS

We experience the world around us through our five senses—sight, hearing, smell, taste, touch. It's one thing to know intellectually that people are listening, but only when you see their faces, and hear them laugh, grumble or applaud do you really connect with them.

Yet seeing and hearing are by no means the only senses. The remembered taste and smell of salt air can make you experience a day at the beach more immediately than any picture can. Helen Keller, who lived her entire life both blind and deaf, makes us realize how much we miss by ignoring the feel of things: "My body is alive to the conditions around me," she wrote. "The rumble and roar of the city smite the nerves of my face, and I feel the ceaseless tramp of an unseen multitude, and the dissonant tumult frets my spirit. . . ."

Developing the Senses

Just as muscles can be developed, all five senses can be developed.

When I was in acting class, we spent weeks and months honing the quality of our five senses. We would, for example, try to re-create a sensory experience like one of these:

Smell	Garlic
	Perfume
	Garbage
Sight	Sunset
	Dead Animal
	Ocean Waves
Sound	Church Choir
	Fire Engine
	Bird Singing

Touch   Block of Ice
             Baby's Skin
             Thorns
Taste   Chocolates
             Castor Oil
             Tobacco

After you have relaxed, and released your tension, imagine touching a block of ice. Try to re-create its temperature on the palm of your hand and fingers, its wetness, its texture. Or imagine a baby and run your hand over its face. Experience the delicate texture, its velvety quality, its warmth. Don't consciously try to show or indicate a reaction on your face. If you are practicing smelling garbage, for instance, don't try to grimace. Don't think about what your face is expressing at all. Concentrate on the sensation alone. The more patient and gentle you are with your senses, the more they will reflect what you are experiencing.

Sensory Recall

If your senses are sharpened, not dulled with tension, you will automatically connect to your material, your environment, your audience and yourself. But to make sure your presentation will "live" under any circumstances, structure your remarks so they are sensorially provocative to you. Make what you say appeal to your senses. This gives both you and your listener triggers with which to create aliveness.

For instance, we know a lot of money and technical expertise are involved in making a television commercial. The goal is to make the viewers' mouths water when a good orange juice commercial is presented. In a similar fashion, your words can stimulate your listeners' senses and your own. Hearing you, the listeners experience in a visceral way whatever you are talking about.

When she returned from the Sudan, Barbara Bush spoke of a child she had held in her arms who was seven years old. He weighed the same weight as her seven-month-old grandchild. The impact of that image left an indelible impression.

A remembered event lives in our ears, noses, fingertips, throats, eyes. You don't remember your child being sick with fever as an abstraction;

you remember stroking her damp hair with your fingertips, feeling her burning forehead on the back of your palm, hearing the sound of uneven breathing and of blankets swishing as she tossed about, smelling the vaporizer's fumes filling the room. The past comes flooding back in torrents of sensory impressions. Indeed, the more profoundly moving a past event is, the more vividly it will express itself through the senses.

Jacqueline Kennedy described the President's assassination less than a week after the event:

"There'd been the biggest motorcade from the airport. Hot. Wild. Like Mexico and Vienna. The sun was so strong in our faces. I couldn't put on sunglasses.... Then we saw this tunnel ahead, I thought if you were on the left the sun wouldn't get into your eyes.... They were gunning the motorcycles. There were these little backfires. There was one noise like that. I thought it was a backfire. Then next I saw Connally grabbing his arms saying no, no, no with his fist beating. Then Jack turned back so neatly, his last expression was so neat... you know that wonderful expression he had when they'd ask him a question about one of the ten million pieces they have in a rocket, just before he'd answer. He looked puzzled, then he slumped forward. He was holding out his hand... I could see a piece of his skull coming off. It was flesh colored, not white—he was holding out his hand—I can see this perfectly clean piece detaching itself from his head. Then he slumped in my lap, his blood and his brains were in my lap...."

Theodore White writes: "She remembered, as I sat paralyzed, the pink-rose ridges on the inside of the skull, and how from here on down (she made a gesture just above her forehead) 'his head was so beautiful. I tried to hold the top of his head down; maybe I could keep it on... but I knew he was dead.'"*

The almost clinical detail of this description is amazing. But Jacqueline Kennedy's emotions and their effect on us are far from clinical. Indeed, it is because Mrs. Kennedy's experience was so traumatic and the depth of her reaction so profound, that she could relive it through all her senses. And with this reliving, she makes us feel the full tragedy of her loss.

*Theodore White, In Search of History (New York: Harper and Row, 1978), pp. 521–22.

Use the Technique of Emotional Recall

The first time you speak on a subject that is deeply moving to you, your message will most likely come across powerfully. But if you have to make several appeals to Congress, say, or rehearse a TV public service announcement twenty times, you may find the emotional juice running dry. Then you may need to use an emotional recall exercise. This exercise was created and developed by Lee Strasberg of The Actors Studio.

Think of a traumatic experience you have lived through—the infidelity of a loved one, the death of a child, a stinging personal failure. It should be several years old so that it is deeply implanted in your psyche.

Once you've pinpointed an experience, try to re-create the sounds, smells, sights, tastes and touches associated with the event: the beep of a car horn in the street, the steady downpour of rain, the touch of a loved one's hands against yours. Experience these memories with your senses rather than intellectually. Search for them. Talk the exploration out loud. Don't rush. Let the recall of the senses take over. You are creating these sensations, so you are in control.

Here is an example of how I go about the exercise, step by step.

I sit in a chair, relax and let tensions flow out of me. I start recalling whichever sense comes to the surface first. In this instance, I begin with touch. (There's no need to speak in complete sentences.) "I'm wearing ... it's rough, alligator, brown little slits in them..."

When one sensory image has been thoroughly explored, I go to another: "The air is ... my throat is dry, nostrils ... the smell is old, musty, choking my throat ... the bottoms of my feet hit the soles of my shoes, I feel the slap, the rush, slap, go, sting, rush, body, chest hard, air stifling, hard to breathe, go, go, rush ... I see him ... soft, white hair, eyes bloodshot, thin, smooth cane, textured spring coat, beige hat, felt brim, gray, sharp, quick, lips on my face, eyes red, watery, expressionless..."

There is no need to create a story line or narrative. Your experience will be private in nature, so there's no need to reveal it. The sensory awareness is key. But to help you understand the process, I will tell you that the above emotional memory did concern a traumatic experience of mine. At the age of twelve, I was late getting to the train station, and barely made it in time to say good-bye to my father. It was the last time I saw him alive.

As you do the exercise and speak the words out loud, connecting to and experiencing your sensations, the incident you are re-creating takes on a life of its own, and you feel deep emotion.

The purpose of the exercise is to reawaken the senses, so that at the appropriate moment, in a speech, in a meeting or whenever you choose, you can be moving and *real*.

I found that I could use the emotional memory I experienced in several plays. I used it while playing Anne Sullivan in *The Miracle Worker*, in a scene that called for me to beg Helen Keller to keep trying and not be overcome by frustration. I had to keep spelling words into her "mute" hands, reaching for some sign that she understood. In another play, *Hogan's Goat*, I used the exercise at a key moment when I confronted my husband with my shame for not being legally married in the eyes of the Church. So far in my speaking career, I have not made an impassioned plea or been in a situation where I needed that emotional recall, but I'm ready for it should it occur.

This is how an effective actor can create reality while repeating the same text for eight performances a week. This is how, in a crucial speech, you can call on your own resources (in this case, your senses) to make the dramatic or poignant moment happen.

Your senses are the tools of your craft as a speaker. If you learn how to use them, then everything—your tone of voice, your choice of words, all facets of the way you speak—will be real, and moving.

Use Literature

If you find it hard to re-create sensory and emotional responses through such exercises, don't despair. The feelings within you are there. Every individual has a rich personal reservoir of sensory and emotional memories, but sometimes this treasury is difficult to tap. Here literature can be of great help, for there is practically no emotion or sensation that fine writing has not beautifully evoked.

Read a passage you find especially moving. Immerse yourself in the sensations and emotions it arouses. Then close the book and continue creating the sensations and the images evoked. You can even do this right before a speech, "warming up" just as an actor prepares off-stage before making an entrance.

If you are giving a speech, consider using a moving quote from literature. John F. Kennedy and Winston Churchill were famous for this. For example, Kennedy, addressing the joint session of the Dail and Deanad Eireann, Dublin, Ireland, June 28, 1963, said: "George Bernard Shaw, speaking as an Irishman, summed up an approach to life. 'Other people,' he said, 'see things and say 'Why?' But I dream things that never were, and I say, 'Why not?'"

Winston Churchill's sense of Old Testament retribution was evident in his judgment after the London blitz: "They have sown the wind; let them reap the whirlwind."

Use Real Objects

One Gulf & Western executive I know was giving a talk on the various applications of zinc, exhorting his listeners to buy the metal even though its price was high. At a crucial point early in his presentation, he asked his listeners to reach under their chairs. Mystified, the participants did so and found, taped to each chair, a small container of zinc vitamins. The executive spoke about the valuable properties of zinc, how it "improves your sense of smell and your sexual prowess, and removes white spots from your fingernails." They were a delighted and attentive audience from then on.

Real objects used skillfully in a presentation will engage the audience by appealing to their senses of sight, touch, smell, taste and/or sound.

VULNERABILITY

On a "Donahue" show several years ago, Eleanor Smeal, president of the National Organization for Women, felt she was losing the debate to her opponent, Phyllis Schlafly, whose language skills and smooth delivery techniques seemed more effective than hers. But at a critical moment Smeal turned the situation around. Schlafly kept refusing to answer a question put to her by Phil Donahue concerning the Right to

Life Movement's proposed amendment to prohibit the use of IUDs for birth control. When Smeal called her on that, Schlafly retorted by describing Smeal's face as that of a woman who wanted to kill and continue killing a million unborn babies a year. In a husky but calm and steady voice Eleanor Smeal replied: "You know, I was raised a Roman Catholic, and this issue is very important to me, very important, because I *had* to practice birth control. . . . I happen to have a disease called Mediterranean anemia. Mrs. Schlafly has six children. I probably wouldn't live if I had six children. . . . I don't like saying this on national television . . . but I think we should treat this situation seriously, because it is a serious issue."

Smeal's sensitivity to what she felt was an intimidating attack made her response meaningful and powerful for many women. At that moment the tide turned in the St. Louis auditorium. The audience supported her. Having been open and vulnerable, Smeal relaxed and grew stronger in the debate. She confronted Schlafly as she had never done before.

Being real means that at times you may have to be vulnerable. However, I don't think of that as a negative quality. It can be a positive thing in communication, as it was with Eleanor Smeal. When you are able to acknowledge a sense of vulnerability within yourself, you can win the hearts and respect of those around you. People will empathize with you because everyone has at one time or another been in a vulnerable position.

The following story shows how another person allowed his vulnerability to surface. Along with time, energy and commitment, it helped him develop into a "real" speaker.

John Sculley's reputation preceded him, and I was intrigued by the prospect of working with the forty-five-year-old dynamo who was then the chief executive officer of Pepsico and is now president of Apple Computer, Inc. A slightly built but powerful man, he had developed a considerable reputation among his colleagues as a charismatic speaker.

"Wait till you see him. He's dynamic, he's poised. He really knows what he's doing."

What I saw, in fact, was a man who reminded me of the way great orators of the past had spoken: he strode about the stage making dramatic pauses, and carefully timed his gestures to coincide with certain theatrical effects, such as an American flag dropping from the rafters during his conclusion. Impressive, yes. Personally compelling, not quite. Something was missing. Given his intelligence and his commitment to his company, I felt he could have done much better.

When we met in my office, we began by viewing a videotape that Sculley had brought along. He wanted me to help him look more at ease on camera.

"What do you think?" I asked him when it was over.

"It's forceful," he said confidently. He was right. There had been power in his voice, and energy in his body. I went to the next question.

"What would you like to improve upon?"

"I look a little stiff," he responded. "I could be more conversational."

"Did you make your point? Was your message clear?"

"Not specifically enough."

I suggested we look at the written script and mark it for clarity: underlining the key words, circling the key thoughts, enumerating the points leading to the climax, and so forth. After we did this, John spoke the text into the video camera and microphone. We played it back. The improvement was evident. He was more direct and his message came through more potently.

But still, something was missing. So I decided to give John the exercise I usually reserve for the third or fourth session with a client—Interpretation of Literature. He was to choose a literary passage which moved him. He opted for a passage from William Agee's *A Death in the Family*.

After reading it through silently, he spoke the passage out loud to me. About two sentences into the text, his voice broke and the words began to come out choked and haltingly. Finally he couldn't speak at all.

"I can't go on," he said quietly. Confronted as he was with a passage that moved him as deeply as this one did, his voice simply stopped working. The connection was intense.

I too was moved. It is always a poignant moment when I see someone connect with their deepest, innermost responses for the first time.

"What happened," I explained to John, "is that you touched a deep chord within yourself. In time you'll learn how to express a deep response verbally without choking. Still, what you let me see here involved more of your real self and grabbed me more than anything on those videotapes."

At the end of the hour, John Sculley knew, not just intellectually, but through personal experience, that there was much more of himself available for use as a real communicator.

After that first session, which Sculley called a "consciousness-raising experience," he decided to broaden his commitment to become a better communicator. We worked on several skills—relaxation techniques, vocal variety and body language—but we always came back to that seminal experience with *A Death in the Family*. We used it as a continuing "connection" to get all his presentations to matter the way that reading had mattered.

The first major test of our work came five months later. Pepsico was holding a national convention in Las Vegas to mobilize all its bottlers in a confrontation the company considered crucial. It was fighting a 1971 ruling of the Federal Trade Commission that declared that the seventy-five-year-old tradition of allowing soft drink companies to set up exclusive franchises resulted in a restraint of trade and was therefore illegal. If the decision stood, the bottlers would not only have to compete against bottlers of other soft drinks but against companies trying to bottle Pepsi as well. Many of the bottlers would have been driven out of business.

Rather than allow the traditional system to be disrupted, Pepsi decided to fight the government. John Sculley went around the country talking to bottlers, inspiring them to fight the ruling in Congress. It was a decisive moment for his company and he needed to communicate as effectively as possible. The Las Vegas convention would be the climax of the mobilization campaign, and John Sculley was to be the principal speaker.

It was a grandiose affair, replete with onstage elevators two stories high, a marching band and numerous special effects, including a trapeze artist. Two thousand people were in the audience. If there was ever an opportunity for all our preparation to pay off, this was it.

At the appointed moment, John Sculley strode out on the stage with confidence and poise. His gestures were in sync with his text and his voice was free to respond to what was going on inside him, and a *lot* was going on.

He knew what was at stake, what the battle meant to him and to his audience. And even though the lights were bright and he couldn't see the audience, he didn't talk *at* them. He talked *to* them, as individuals with the same stakes, the same hopes and fears. He dug deep down into himself as he had done with *A Death in the Family*. Only now he was able to control the choking.

John Sculley didn't try to be as "big," or theatrical, as the twenty-foot-tall, three-panel slide presentation projected behind him, or the fifty-piece band that played "America the Beautiful." But he was big; he held his audience spellbound because he spoke to them from within. He let them see how much he cared. He let them see who he was and what he stood for. The speech was a success. The convention was a success. The Pepsi Cola Bottlers Association worked hard and convinced Congress to kill the restrictive legislation.

You may be thinking: "I'm not John Sculley. I don't have his talent, commitment or expertise." Perhaps not, but you have reserves of emotion and energy that you too can learn to tap whenever you want to express yourself. Thousands of my clients who are not CEOs or public figures have followed the methods described in this book and made stunning progress. The changes take place gradually. Even the so-called "naturally gifted" communicators practice for years to hone their techniques and become real. As Margery Williams wrote in *The Velveteen Rabbit*:

> "What is REAL?" asked the Rabbit one day.
> "Real isn't how you are made," said the Skin Horse. "It's a thing that happens to you."
> "Does it hurt?" asked the Rabbit.
> "Sometimes," said the Skin Horse, for he was always truthful. "When you are real you don't mind being hurt."
> "Does it happen all at once, or bit by bit?"
> "It doesn't happen all at once," said the Skin Horse. "You become."

PART TWO

ALL YOU NEED TO KNOW TO GET YOUR MESSAGE ACROSS

The Lilyan Wilder Program
(Steps One–Three)

Chapter Three

ORGANIZING YOUR THOUGHTS

(Step One)

To profess to have an aim and then to neglect the means of its execution is self-delusion of the most dangerous sort.

—John Dewey
Reconstruction in Philosophy

Being real is your foundation as a speaker. Though a look of effortlessness is your goal, it takes hard work to achieve that look. Being real is not the same thing as being "natural." If, during a sales presentation, for instance, you showed your "natural" enthusiasm for your product only by gushing and exclaiming "It's stupendous!" you would not be very persuasive. To be effective, your enthusiasm must be backed up by a strong, well-worded argument.

A sportscaster who came to me for coaching had fallen into the "being natural" trap. He was upset because the producer of his show had asked him to use good grammar and organize his thoughts. "They want me to be natural," he complained, "but when I talk like myself, or use 'ain't,' they say, 'No!'"

His producers were right. The sportscaster started designing his presentations for clarity, taking into account the needs of his audience. The
self that began to come through was not his "natural" unprepared self,
but the self that was there for the purpose of communication. He now
uses good grammar, and can answer such questions as: "WHAT do I
have to say? WHY am I doing this piece? HOW am I going to present
it?"

In this chapter you too will learn how to design a presentation so that
it is both articulate and "the real you."

CHOOSE AN OBJECTIVE

Whether you are going to be making a thirty-second toast or a thirty-
minute speech, you begin by asking yourself what you intend to accomplish. All effective communication tries to influence other people, to
make them think differently, act differently, support a cause, buy a
product, laugh, get angry or find new hope.

What do you want your remarks to do?

What do you want from the people you are addressing?

The answers to these questions will give you a clear sense of purpose,
an objective.

Sample Objectives	*Desired Response*
To negotiate a book contract with a publisher that will win you, the author, the greatest support and exposure.	A great contract.
To sell your bank's C.D.s	Customers purchase them.
To raise money for cystic fibrosis research.	Contributions.

Choose an objective that is simple, clear and achievable. Formulate
this objective in a single sentence: "I want to. . . ."

Arouse Instinctive Drives

"The roast pigeon won't fly into your mouth!" advises an old proverb. To accomplish your objective, you have to move your audience. This means appealing to one of the four basic drives that motivate all human beings: survival, ego, pleasure, altruism.

The instinct for *survival* is the strongest instinct of all. We care about the arms race, the economy, jobs and taxes because any one of them can threaten our lives. Politicians routinely address themselves to the survival instincts of voters when they campaign, as do certain activists— Ralph Nader and Helen Caldicott, for example. But even a junior executive appeals to his boss's survival instinct when, in presenting a proposal, he makes it evident that his ideas will strengthen his boss's stake in the company. Self-preservation is a universal need.

The need to maintain one's *ego* is also extremely important. Tap this drive by appealing to your listener's ambition and pride.

What I'm about to describe is an unusual event, but it illustrates how people's sense of themselves, their egos, can be tapped for a worthwhile cause.

On July 13, 1985, upwards of 60 rock stars donated their talent to a "Live Aid" television concert to benefit Africa's starving masses. The response was overwhelming both in terms of dollars (approximately 70 million) and the human "fellow-feelings" it provided.

Those who saw the concert, 92,000 in the JFK stadium in Philadelphia, Pennsylvania, and about the same number in Wembley Stadium in London, England, plus over a billion television viewers, were proud to be part of an event of this stature and excitement. Our egos identified with and were inspired by the rock stars who performed. "If they could give of their time and talent, we could be there, and contribute money," we thought.

Though you and I need to motivate on a smaller scale, we too can use our listeners' desire for identity, status and recognition to accomplish our goals.

The drive for *pleasure* makes us crave sex, good food, vacations, Giorgio Armani suits. A superior hi-fi salesman won't just show potential customers his new quality equipment; he'll appeal to the pleasure principle and make their ears tingle!

Altruism provides us with a fourth motivational drive. If you ask a neighbor to contribute money to the Fidelco Guide Dog Foundation (and you're not a rock star with whom he wishes to identify), you're appealing to his sense of altruism: "These German shepherd dogs are well bred, trained on the blind person's premises, and given to blind people for a nominal fee. Certainly this is a worthy cause that needs your attention."

Try to find ways to motivate your listeners throughout your presentation. It will keep their responses flowing.

ANALYZE THE SITUATION

Look at the speaking situation from all angles and answer these four questions.

To Whom Are You Speaking?

How much do you know about your listeners? What do they know about your subject? If you are trying to sell someone a car, find out if he or she knows what fuel injection is before launching into a pitch on the marvels of the Bosch-J Tronic injectors.

According to Millicent Fenwick: "You've got to be responsive to the audience. If they seem puzzled by something, you've got to expand on that before going on to something else."

Robert Kennedy was keenly attuned to his audiences. But he did not defer to them. He didn't don the work clothes of a grape picker when addressing the United Farm Workers, or start using Chicano slang. Simply knowing their experiences, "he could see things," said Cesar Chávez, "through the eyes of the poor. It was like he was ours."

Who Else Will Be Speaking?

When possible, learn as much as you can about rival salesmen, co-negotiators, other speakers on a panel, etc. If you find out in advance who they are and where they stand, you'll be able to anticipate rebuttals, challenges and questions, and plan your remarks so they don't echo those of another speaker.

When the discussion follows a specific order (e.g., in a panel situation) find out what the order of presentation is. If you are first, it will be up to you to break the ice. If you aren't first, what kind of act will you have to follow? An excruciating bore? A rival with eighty researchers at his disposal? Or a brilliant wit whom you couldn't dream of topping? The secret in this third case is: Don't try! Vice President George Bush, following on the heels of Art Buchwald at a benefit banquet, knew he could never be as funny, but he could be charming and persuasive by simply being himself.

You can't always know everything about the people you're dealing with; I merely suggest that you try to get as much information as you can to enhance your presentation.

What Is the Occasion?

Find out all you can about the occasion. How formal is it? How much time do you have? Is this a once-a-year meeting where you'll be expected to make a twenty-minute presentation, or is it a weekly rap session with more flexibility and range?

If you are up for an interview, is it one-to-one or will you be facing a panel of four?

Where Will It Take Place?

As part of your planning, consider where you are speaking. When appropriate use humor, personal reminiscences and historical references about the place to add flavor to your presentation. For example, in the shadow of the Lincoln Memorial, Martin Luther King, Jr., said: "Five score years ago, a great American, in whose symbolic shadow we stand today, signed the Emancipation Proclamation. . . ."

Adjust the tenor of your remarks to the environment. In a church, make sure your language, images and references don't clash with the solemnity of the surroundings. In a bare, unadorned meeting room, use humor: "We didn't want you to be distracted by the scenery." Outdoors, refer to the weather, the landscape or even urban blight if this is what surrounds you!

Once you have determined your objective, your listeners' motivations, and analyzed the situation, you are ready to plan your thoughts.

PLAN YOUR THOUGHTS

While conducting a seminar for a group of managers at a private bank, I asked each participant what he wanted to achieve during our two and a half days of developing communication skills. Five out of eight wanted to learn how to "be in control." Fortunately for them, they had something to be in control of—content.

Concerning yourself with how you come across, with being "in control" or "conversational," are empty goals without first taking into account what you want to say, and how you're going to formulate your thoughts so that they connect to your listener. Without substance, style is superficial.

Finding Materials

Most people who are good at communicating work at it all the time. They are inveterate clippers of magazines and newspapers, keeping files of quotations, statistics, biographical data and transcripts.

To decide what materials will actually go into your presentation, ask yourself these three questions:

Does this clarify what I'm saying?
Can my listeners relate to it?
Does it excite me?

If you're dealing with current technology or financial statistics, it's essential that your information be current. Robert Metz, managing editor of the Financial News Network, works to keep ahead of the business news. At a presentation he made for the Food Marketing Institute, Metz was making changes and checking statistics even as he rode up the elevator to the meeting room.

Using Tools

Lay your thoughts out on paper by either talking them into a tape recorder and then transcribing them, or by writing them out, sketching them in outline or note form. There's no one right way; do whichever is best for you.

Complete your first draft as simply and quickly as possible. If you stop and fuss too much the first time through, you may lose the flow of your language and thought. This flow is vital. If you get stuck on a particular point, move on and come back to it later.

As you edit your presentation, cut and paste. Next to paper and pen, scissors and tape are the communicator's most valuable tools. If what you've put on paper doesn't seem to flow properly, cut each thought into a strip and try arranging these strips in different order, like a collage. Nine times out of ten you will see something visually you would never have hit upon by rearranging the same thoughts in your head.

As you approach a more final version, you might also paste your pages onto a wall or a board. That way, you can get a picture of your presentation as a whole, determining at a glance if you have given your points their proper weight.

Deciding on a Length

Find out what maximum time has been allotted to you, then settle on a length. Make your points quickly! Your boss is more likely to promote you if you save him time than if you weigh him down with an excess of detail. Even on more formal occasions, advises a top-notch political speechwriter: "Keep your introduction short, your conclusion short and leave as little as possible in between!"

Use the following table as a guide, keeping in mind that it is somewhat arbitrary because each situation is different.

Kind of Presentation	Length
Toast	1–2 minutes
Award acceptance speech	3–5 minutes

Serious, in-depth speech (makes about three major points)	15–20 minutes
Remarks and/or answers at an interview	15 seconds to 2 minutes
Sales talk	3–10 minutes
Presentation to the boss	1–10 minutes

Select One Main Point

Boil your thoughts down to *one central message.* If you bombard your listeners with too many ideas they won't absorb any of them. Give them one big, clear idea they can really sink their teeth into. Note: Within one central point you can make subsidiary ones, as we shall see, but you need that main theme or message, tailored to accomplish your objective, to pull your presentation together.

For example, a doctor running for mayor of a medium-sized city was preparing to deliver a major campaign address and simply could not decide on a central theme. As a result, the speech he showed me went all over the place and was bound to leave his audience confused. I asked him, "If you could leave your audience with only one thought, what would it be?" He immediately answered, "I'd tell them that as a doctor I am a healer; as a mayor, I want to heal the city." His message had been there all along; he just needed to pin it down. He returned to his speech and reorganized his points around that one theme.

Now you have a reservoir of back-up information, a length and a main point. You are ready to enter into the final stages of organization and give your presentation structure and style.

STRUCTURE

In its final form, your presentation should have an Introduction, Body, Climax and Conclusion.

The Introduction tells the audience what you're going to tell them.

The Body tells them.

The Climax clinches your main point.

The Conclusion tells them what you told them.

For practical reasons it is usually best to prepare your presentation in a different order.

Begin by structuring the *Body.* This is the heart of your presentation and will naturally lead you to the Climax, the Conclusion and, lastly, the Introduction.

Here is an example using the structure described above.

In negotiating a job transfer from Detroit, Michigan, to New York City, the manager of a beauty salon enters the boss's office (with this skeletal outline) and says:

[THE INTRODUCTION]

Good morning, George. You were terrific in the marathon yesterday,. Have you recovered? . . . Thanks for taking the time to see me today. I need to cover four important areas with you about managing the New York salon.

They are:

1. What I've done in the past.
2. What I can do in the future.
3. What my personal and professional needs have been in Detroit.
4. What my personal and professional needs will be in New York.

[THE BODY]

First, as you well know, in Detroit I've built a strong staff with the depth that will allow us to help strengthen the other North American units. The team is loyal, morale is high and the salon is profitable.

Second, I can build a caring, trusting rapport with the staff while at the same time evaluating them for proper positioning. I'm able to establish the sense of security necessary for the foundation of a well-run salon.

Third, my mobility rests upon the liquidation of my condominium in Detroit and I would appreciate any advice you may have. The approximate costs involved in moving me will be. . . .

Fourth, in order for me to move laterally and maintain my present standard of living, this is the financial package I need. . .

[THE CLIMAX]

Without sounding self-serving, let me tell you that I feel I'm the best person to manage the salon in New York. That salon's bottom line is the result of an insecure, unstable staff and I can turn it around.

[THE CONCLUSION]

So—now you have a better idea of:

What I've done in Detroit.
What I can do in New York.
What my needs are in Detroit, and
what I'll need in New York.

I am really looking forward to the challenge. I want to go all the way for our company, like you went all the way in the marathon. How does what I've outlined strike you?

The structure of this example can be repeated on any number of occasions. But what if you expect to be in a situation where there will be a lot of give-and-take? "How can I plan an introduction, body, climax and conclusion in advance when I don't know what will come up when?" you may ask.

I advocate what I call the *"minispeech"* to guide you when you need to present information in more flexible situations.

The minispeech is a structured approach to whatever your speaking situation may be. If you depend on another person's questions and contributions to determine the flow of your remarks, you are putting that person in the driver's seat. Go into every encounter prepared to be a one-man or one-woman show!

Oprah Winfrey, talk show hostess of WLS-TV's "AM Chicago," was invited to be on the "Tonight" show with hostess Joan Rivers. I suggested she prepare her remarks in the form of a minispeech: "Know your objective. Ask yourself why you're taking that long trip to California." Oprah prepared. When she got to the studio, she found that everything was scripted for both herself and Joan Rivers, but that Ms. Rivers did not follow a word of it. Oprah was stunned: "I was waiting for Joan Rivers to ask the questions. I saw that she had the script in front of her, but she ignored it. So, I started talking."

Oprah started by describing her upbringing ("little white girls were 'spanked,' I was 'whupped'"), the reason for her overweight ("I ate a lot") and her work as a talk show hostess ("I'm going to Ethiopia in three weeks"). It all came rolling off her tongue in a wonderfully funny, exuberant and moving way. Her presence enhanced the show tenfold, because she brought her minispeech with her and was fully prepared.

Familiarize yourself with your minispeech as completely as possible. If you're knocked off your course, or rattled by an unexpected question (or no question at all), recall its structure. Use it as a guide to get back on course and maintain control.

Now let's move on to the actual shaping of your speech, or remarks, by beginning with the Body.

Developing the Body: Tell Them

After determining your objective and central message, select two or three subsidiary points to support your central message. When possible, make a numbered list—the three-point program, the four reasons, etc. The mayoral candidate who wanted to present himself as a healer developed his theme by saying he planned to:

1. Rebuild the inner city, so his constituents would have decent homes in which to live
2. Shape up the city's health services, particularly the hospital emergency wards
3. Go at crime tooth and nail, so people could feel safe in and out of their homes

Organizing your material this way focuses your listeners' attention and helps them remember your message later on. If reporters are present, they will pick these points out of the speech for their own stories.

Next, choose one of the six following formats to link your points together:

The Topical Format presents two or more aspects of a program, phenomenon or theory. The mayoral candidate used the Topical Format.

The Chronological Format links your points together sequentially in time. The first event goes first, the second goes second, and so on. A recipe instructing you to (1) beat eggs, (2) heat a skillet and (3) pour the eggs into the skillet would be an example. So would the three steps of artificial resuscitation, the four stages of the French Revolution, or the six phases of a two-year program to salvage corporation X.

The Comparison or Analogy Format describes one program or phenomenon in terms of another. For example, this year's marketing plan in terms of last year's marketing plan (goals, strategies, costs);

> The goal we set for ourselves last year was to expand our sales and distribution apparatus, and we were successful. This year our target is to achieve greater sophistication in our sales approach. [goals]

> We plan to do this by setting up a series of regional sales conferences to plan a national campaign that will take into account the unique requirements of each different territory. This will replace the one national meeting and one campaign approach of last year. [strategies]

> We were limited in our sales strategy last year by strict cost eliminations, but this year we can spend more because of the gratifying increase in overall revenue. [costs]

The Mixed Time-Frame Format takes stock of the *present*, flashes back to the *past* to explain "how we got here," and then sweeps forward to a vision of "what lies in store," the *future*. Here is an example taken from a speech delivered to college graduates:

> President Reagan may have made optimism fashionable by clinging to it and articulating it at a time when Americans were in a receptive mood. But in our own city and state—where many of you will pursue your careers—the forces of a positive attitude are bearing remarkable fruit. [present]

> Lord knows Detroit and Michigan went through some truly profound economic miseries during the last recession. . . . Michigan has been an industrial giant through most of the century. [past]

Well we're on the road back . . . bringing business back to Michigan.
. . . Detroit is building again, growing, exploring new ideas and working
to regain its status as a premier convention city. [future]

> —"Information, Gateway to Success"
> Beverly A. Beltaire,
> President, PR Associates, Inc.
> Warren, Michigan, May 10, 1985

The Problem-Solving Format makes three points: (1) what you want
to do, (2) what the opposition wants to do, and (3) how your plan is
better than theirs. An example is President Reagan's address defending
his proposed budget for 1983:

[Point 1] Not only must those deficits be reduced, they must show a
decline over the next three years, not an increase. Our goal must be
a balanced budget.

[Point 2] Apparently, the philosophical difference between us is that
they want more and more spending and more and more taxes.

[Point 3] There hasn't been too much opportunity in the last 40 years
to see what our philosophy can do. But we know what theirs can do.

The Gestalt Format informs the listener with an overwhelming barrage
of facts, statistics and quotes. Instead of limiting the number of points
you make to strengthen your central message, in the gestalt speech you
multiply them to include as many as you can. The audience doesn't
come away from this sort of speech with one central point in mind, but
rather with a strong, visceral reaction.

An example is Dr. Helen Caldicott's speech against nuclear arms
buildup:

Today America has between 30,000 and 35,000 hydrogen bombs . . .
both countries have enough to overkill every person on earth about
sixteen times . . . every person would be vaporized, turned into gas . . .
concrete would burn . . . there would be decapitations, traumatic organ
injuries . . . millions of shards of flying glass and steel, objects hurled
against people, and people hurled against objects . . . a fire storm would

spontaneously ignite . . . there would be no people to come to help because they would all be dead.

Caldicott was unrelenting, bombarding us with fact after fact, image after image. At the end of the speech the audience may not have remembered a single specific image, but there had been an aggregate effect.

Developing the Climax

The climax, for both speaker and audience, is a moment of release, or catharsis—the moment when the audience experiences: "I get it! You've made your point!" Whether it is met with a hush of silence, gales of laughter or thunderous applause, your climax is the real clincher, the moment of payoff.

It generally comes at the end of the body or in the conclusion. Arrange your thoughts in increasing strength so that they move to a peak of intensity. You can do that by (1) setting the background or (2) stating the points which lead like stairs up to the climax. No better example exists than the brilliant conclusion of the Martin Luther King "I Have a Dream" speech.

Developing the Conclusion:
Tell Them What You Told Them

"This is the way the world ends," T. S. Eliot lamented in "The Hollow Men"—"not with a bang, but a whimper."

I try to get my clients' presentations to end not with a whimper but a bang! Your conclusion should be attention-getting and compelling, pulling everything said into sharp focus and driving your message home. Resist the temptation to keep talking.

The Summary Conclusion tells the listeners what you told them. For example, a Group Product Manager in charge of the Tylenol account could end his report on promotional strategy to an executive staff meeting as follows:

To sum up, we're initiating a two-pronged campaign to go after the Extra-Strength Tylenol business. One, we have a TV campaign aimed at the trade which will establish pressure there, and two, we have a promotion planned for the consumer involving coupons, rebates and discounts.

The Motivational Conclusion appeals to higher values, the ego drive or powerful emotions such as pity, fear or compassion.

Speaking to a group of AT&T salespeople on how to improve corporate efficiency, Michael Sherlock, executive vice president of NBC, ended with an appeal to the egos of the audience:

> So we end where we began, with you. With the individual performance. That's what excellence is all about. . . . The pay-off is financial, sure. But more than that, it's a personal sense of satisfaction at a job well done, a job that counts.

The Application Conclusion suggests concrete steps the audience can take to follow up on what you've told them. "Go home and write your congressman," you might say, or "Call this number and pledge $15 or more to help combat cerebral palsy," or "Go back to your desks and put the 'Blueprint for Action' kits to use."

The Dawn-of-a-New-Day Conclusion is meant to be inspirational. Grant Tinker, president of NBC, concluded a pep talk to the NBC affiliates:

> You've been promised a rose garden before, and you've gotten mostly weeds. I'm asking you to have faith in one more promise. We need each other, and together, we have nowhere to go but up. If you believe, we'll meet here at the Century Plaza a year from now, and . . . we will springboard that day from a different word. Gone will be "inertia." We will be dealing with "momentum." Look it up.

Developing the Introduction: Tell Them What You're Going to Tell Them

With your climax and conclusion all worked out, it's time to go back and work out an introduction. There are three requisites. You need to:

Seize attention. Use a provocative attention-getting tactic to attract your audience right off the bat. CBS Anchorman Charles Osgood told me he always tries to begin by playing off the meeting's "running gag":

> I went to Denver for a two-day seminar to speak before a group of money-managers. When I asked the Program Chairman how long he'd like me to speak, he said: "As long as you like, but I hope you won't speak as long as Louis Rukeyser did last year." It turned out he had talked for two and a half hours. "I have fourteen points and I want to make them all," he said. As he proceeded to deliver the talk, I was told, at table after table, people got up and left. There were only a few people left at the end. So when I got up to speak I said: "Good afternoon. I have ten points to make." They all knew what I was talking about.

This is but one of many attention-getting tactics. In a section called "Highlights" starting on page 97 of this chapter, you'll find others.

Establish rapport. You may use one or any number of the following suggested tactics. These are just guides. There are infinite ways to establish rapport, and you will no doubt discover tactics all your own. You might:
- Graciously acknowledge the introduction given you
- Refer in a generous way to something someone said
- Make a joke about yourself. Julian Gibbs, the late president of Amherst College, began one speech as follows:

> When I received the invitation to speak at your commencement, I asked Mr. Williams to give me some advice about my speech. He said: "There are three things to remember: keep it brilliant, keep it witty, and keep it short." I said: "You're asking an awful lot." He said: "Well in that case just forget the first two."
>
> I'll try to follow his advice.

- Express a sincere feeling of pleasure. You can comment on anything from your listeners' civic concern to their recent accomplishment as a work team. Just be sure to mean what you say; false compliments are easy to detect!

• Tell an anecdote inspired by the place or occasion. History doesn't move us as much as a current association: "Everytime I come to Cooperstown to talk to you, I feel a pang of regret for not having pursued a career in baseball."

• Work with the special interests of your listeners. One of my students knew that her boss loved chocolates. When she arrived to ask him for a raise, she presented him with a box of Godiva's. "But you must open it now," she said. When he did, he found a typed memo outlining what she intended to cover during their meeting. "The real chocolates come after you've heard me out!" This particular boss loved the humor and the chocolates. Caution: not every boss will.

• Refer to an idea of an event which is of dominant concern to your audience. On the day Robert Kennedy was shot, the daughter of a friend of mine was graduating from high school. No one knew if the senator was going to survive. Two or three fathers in the audience had worked personally with Kennedy, and were crying openly. Rising to speak, the headmistress paused for a moment, then began:

> We all mourn the tragic event that took place this morning in Los Angeles. I seriously considered cancelling today's ceremonies in view of what has happened. But finally I decided against this. Senator Kennedy would want us to proceed. He was a firm believer in the power of education to change the world, to curb violence, to spread compassion and understanding and so, in his spirit, let us continue here today.

In trying to establish rapport, a problem can arise if there is disagreement between you and your audience. Acknowledge it openly, but be sure to maintain a good-humored, sportsmanlike tone. James C. Miller III, then FTC chairman (currently Director of the Office of Management and Budget), once spoke about government regulation of health care before the aggressively anti-regulation Oral and Maxillofacial Surgery Political Action Committee: "It's a pleasure to be here to discuss with you the FTC's activities in the health care field," he began. "After hearing this, some of you may question my sanity, but surely you won't question my courage!"

Tell your audience what you're going to tell them. This is the third important element of introductions. Franklin Roosevelt began one of his Fireside Chats by saying: "I want to talk for a few minutes with the people of the United States about banking. . . . I want to talk to you about what has been done in the last few days, why it has been done and what the next steps are going to be."

Let's look at an example of how one speaker managed to accomplish all three goals within a single opener. The speaker: California Governor George Deukmejian (then state attorney general). The subject: crime in California in 1980.

> Today in California you are four times more likely to be the victim of a murder, four times more likely to be the victim of a robbery, and three times as likely to be victim of a rape, than you were in 1960.
>
> Facing as we are this criminal crisis in California we have to give some thought to how we can best reduce the crime on our streets and by reducing that crime, allow every citizen the freedom to live in safety and happiness.
>
> The best way to reduce crime is to prevent it before it happens. More resources need to be put toward this—the front end of the criminal justice spectrum.

(1) Deukmejian leads off with three eye-opening statistics to grab the audience's attention. (2) He establishes rapport by relating to the community. And (3) he talks about what he will talk about: the problem of escalating crime and how to solve it.

STYLE

Two words sum up the most important thing you need to know about style. *Be yourself.* If that sounds too easy (or too hard), keep in mind three specific ways to help you "be yourself."

First, *use your own language.* Many people have the notion that a presentation ought to sound formal or different from real talk. They tend to sound like the embodiment of a cause or an institution instead of like themselves. When I ask them: "Is this what you really want to say?" they invariably answer: "No, here's what I mean . . ." and in their own words, make their points beautifully.

Begin with those words.

Second, while you plan your remarks, *imagine yourself talking to a close friend*. This is the way FDR organized his fireside chats. He made millions of Americans feel as if they knew the President personally and could trust him as a friend. "I hate war, my wife Eleanor hates war, and even my little dog Fala hates war," he said once.

Third, *use your own personal kind of humor* to say what you mean. Humor doesn't mean planted jokes but an overall good-natured approach to life which leads one to chuckle, smile or even sigh at an ironic truth.

Try to follow these guidelines. If you do, your personality will reach and touch your audience.

Clarity

Before anyone can be affected by what you say, he must understand you. Clarity of expression is the essence of good communication.

First of all, *use good grammar*. If you don't know a particular rule, look it up. (A good reference is Strunk and White, *The Elements of Style*.) Thoughts grammatically expressed line up in the listener's mind with the order and neatness of pearls on a string. Bad grammar tangles the string so that your audience has trouble seeing just how the pearls align. Remember, though, you're writing for the ear and not the eye. Certain points of grammar can and should be relaxed in favor of more idiomatic usage. Recall how Winston Churchill made wry fun of a common taboo, not to end a sentence with a preposition: "It is the sort of nonsense up with which I will not put."

Second, *simplify your language*, especially if you're dealing with a highly technical subject. No thought is so complex that it can't be stated simply, but as Somerset Maugham put it: "To write simply is as difficult as to be good." Though it is tempting to use professional jargon to sound more "authoritative," you will usually sound pompous and dull instead. Don't hide behind complex language.

Simplicity has power. One prominent Philadelphia lawyer made himself a fortune by putting this axiom into practice. At the turn of the century, people were suing railroad companies for deaths and injuries incurred at railroad crossings. The Pennsylvania Railroad Company hired the lawyer to write a legal notice that would tell pedestrians what their responsibilities were in averting accidents. His fee was $10,000.00, a lot of money, especially in those days, but a small price to pay for stemming the tide of liability suits. The company may have had second thoughts when they received the lawyer's notice. It was four words long: "Stop, Look, and Listen."

Yet these four words branded themselves on the mind of every American as no erudite dissertation could have done. Pedestrians became aware of their responsibilities. The accident rate at crossings fell. The tide of suits evaporated overnight. As the architect Mies van der Rohe said: "Less is more."

Eliminate unnecessary adjectives and adverbs. Nouns and verbs are more powerful without a lot of window-dressing. Compare:

The industrious maid gently but deliberately applied a hot iron to the trousers of her employer, Mr. King.	The maid pressed Mr. King's trousers.
Henry had the good fortune to discover a one-dollar bill lying on the sprawling thoroughfare.	Henry found a dollar on the street.

Eliminate unnecessary qualifiers. Be direct. Words like "almost," "nearly," "quite" and "somewhat" weaken your points and plant doubts in your listeners' minds. Compare:

She was quite overjoyed to receive the rather costly jewelry.	She loved receiving expensive jewelry.

Put your statements in positive form. A lot of negatives weaken your remarks. Compare:

He did not think that the film was interesting in the least.	He found the film uninteresting.

Use active constructions. They sound simpler, more direct, more energetic. Compare:

(PASSIVE)	(ACTIVE)
The ball is watched by the batter.	The batter watches the ball.
My elders will always be respected by me.	I shall always respect my elders.

Flow

To make your presentation interesting, you need variety of language.

Vary the length of your sentences.

> Hitler said that as things develop he's going to wring England's neck like a chicken. Some chicken. Some neck.
>
> —Winston Churchill

> Grenada, we were told, is a friendly island paradise for tourism. Well it wasn't. It was a Soviet-Cuban colony being readied as a major military bastion to export terror and undermine democracy.
>
> We got there just in time.
>
> —President Reagan,
> October 28, 1983

To check for monotony of length, look at your sentence structure on the page and listen to yourself speaking your remarks on tape.

Move from the abstract to the concrete, from the general to the specific. An example:

> These are perilous times. Inflation is wreaking havoc with the economy, diplomacy remains ineffective in the face of international skirmishes, babies are starving and the common man is afraid to walk the streets at night.

Explain the unfamiliar in familiar terms:

> What is a trillion? Now we all know that a billion is a thousand million and a trillion is a thousand billion, that's easy. But . . . we couldn't

really envision a trillion [so] we did it in time. If somebody was born when Jesus Christ was born and had lived all this time and started counting seconds—"1 . . . 2 . . . 3 . . . 4" he'd be up to 62.5 billion right now, which is 6¼ percent of a trillion. It takes 31,700 years to count a trillion seconds. Now that's 317 centuries and we're in the 20th, so it's the same old 6 percent. It keeps coming back to you.

> —"The Problem of Big Government"
> J. Peter Grace
> Economic Club of Detroit
> March 18, 1985

Focus

Keep your listener focused on what you are saying and where you are going.

Make smooth transitions that lead him firmly from section to section. This means from introduction to body, between sections of the body, and from the body to the conclusion.

Your transitions should be like guideposts that remind the listener of where you have been, and point to where you're going.

> Coal may be our most immediately available alternative energy source, but solar holds the way to our energy future.

> But enough of the past. Let us take a look at the future.

Use a recurring phrase, question or set of images to give your speech a through-line. A through-line is the continuous connection that gives sensible progression to changing thoughts. In his Lincoln Memorial address, Martin Luther King, Jr., kept a through-line going with his repetition of the phrase "I have a dream."

Clarence Darrow, in a speech defending a young black man on trial for murder, asked repeatedly, "What has Harry Sweet done?" and varied that question linking Sweet's position to the larger issues of justice, racism and moral responsibility.

> What would you have done [in Henry Sweet's position]?

The law has made [the Negro] equal, but man has not. And, after all, the last analysis is—what has man done?—not what has the law done?

Use repetition and rhyme to keep your listener's ear focused. Examples of each:

We shall fight on the beaches, we shall fight on the landing grounds, we shall fight in the fields and streets, we shall fight in the hills, we shall never surrender...

—Winston Churchill

Ulster will fight, and Ulster will be right!

—Lord Randolph Churchill

Highlights

Use the following attention-getting tactics to get and keep the audience involved throughout the course of your talk.

Tell a personal, moving story.

In the early 1900's I was brought to this country by my parents to escape the tortuous "pogroms" waged against the Jews in Russia. My brother, I and the other immigrant youngsters were eager to share in the freedom of the land of opportunity—and there was opportunity! We would go to school, to the neighborhood houses, to libraries. We burned with the desire to learn.

One day, when I was about eight or nine, I made my usual journey to the 10th Street Library, on the Lower East Side. But this time the librarian stopped me at the front door. She asked to see my hands. "They're not clean enough," she said. So I ran home, ran up our five flights of stairs, washed them and ran back to the library. Again the librarian asked to see my hands, and again she said they weren't clean enough! Again I ran home, up the stairs, washed them, down the stairs and back to the library. Again I was refused admittance. After the third try I quit. Years later it dawned on me that the librarian was sending kids home because the library was overcrowded with all the children who loved to go there.

Is the love of learning as strong today as it was then? Obviously it is in the young man I am here to honor...

—Irving J. Katz,
Humanities Award
Address,
Midwood High School
Brooklyn, New York, 1955

Create curiosity with a controversial statement:

The state of California spends more than $4 billion every year on MediCal... and [Dr. Edward Rubin has been] building an empire on these dollars... his medical financial practice has been under scrutiny for years. Nonetheless, he continues to operate...

—"60 Minutes," on
Edward Rubin, M.D.

Ask a controversial question:

Would you like the government to stop supporting college education [meaning that only certain people could attend institutions of higher learning]?

State a striking fact or statistic:

Do you know there are more rats than people in New York City?

—Robert Kennedy at a
business luncheon in
Vincennes, Indiana

Just remember that the statistics you use must be geared to your audience. A presentation filled with highly technical figures on the gold market might be a piece of cake for an audience of financiers, but utterly incomprehensible to the general public. You should also make sure that you use the same units (denominations) for both terms in any comparison. Don't, for instance, try to compare fractions and percentages, bushels and tons, yards and miles.

Refer to famous quotations, or even turn them around for effect:

I've never seen more of less.

> —An architect describing
> what he considered to be
> a particularly boring
> monument, in reference to
> Mies van der Rohe's
> proverbial "Less is more"

If we cannot now end our differences, at least we can help make the world safe for diversity.

> —President Kennedy's deliberate
> reversal of Woodrow Wilson's
> stated ambition to make the
> world "safe for democracy"

Sum up a point with a pithy epigram:

Nothing lasts like temporary.

> —Diplomatic saying

In finance, everything that is agreeable is unsound and everything that is sound is disagreeable.

> —Winston Churchill

Look for and use memorable labels:

Iron curtain

> —Winston Churchill

MBWA: Management by Walking Around

> —Peters and Waterman

Give a definition that does more than define, that appeals to the imagination. Walter Heller, chairman, Council of Economic Advisors, defined economic growth as "the pot of gold and the rainbow."

Use a striking metaphor, an analogy or an image that appeals to the senses:

> The rest of mankind is the carving knife while we are the fish and the meat.
>
> —Sun Yat-sen to an audience
> of Chinese followers

> It is easy enough to say that man is mortal simply because he will endure, that when the last ding-dong of doom has clanged and faded from the last worthless rock hanging tideless in the last red and dying evening, that even then there will be one more sound—that of his puny inexhaustible voice, still talking.
>
> —William Faulkner,
> Nobel Prize acceptance speech

Ask a series of questions:

> What do you prefer: that we keep Social Security the way it is now? Or we change it to a totally different system? Would you rather pay a higher Social Security Tax now so that in forty or fifty years you'll be taken care of? Or would you like to know that the retirement age will be sixty-seven instead of sixty-five?
>
> —Senator Bill Bradley,
> Leadership Seminar
> for High School Seniors,
> Paterson, New Jersey

Humor

"I'll start with a joke and warm up the audience" is a phrase I hear often. Certainly, healthy laughter is a way of bringing people together. But unless there is an organic connection between your joke, your subject and you, it will be recognized for what it is, a contrivance.

You are not a stand-up comic, nor are you expected to be. Good comics agonize over the quality of their material. It is very difficult to be funny. So why should you expect satire, surprise, exaggeration and other elements of humor to come rolling off your tongue without a lot of hard work and research?

The definition of humor is not narrowly confined to just the telling of jokes. Humor includes irony, understatement, appreciation of life's foibles, the simple, "awful" truth and a clever use of self-deprecation.

I am reminded of the time the late Jessica Savitch took advantage of a moment to turn self-deprecation into humor. She was David Letterman's guest on his late-night show. In fine fettle, mixing good cheer with information, she described how she chose her wardrobe for the "NBC Nightly News." Then abruptly her mood changed, and she admitted she felt ill at ease. When Letterman asked her why, she pulled out a typed lineup for the show, which stated the order of guest appearances, time allotments, and so on. "I found this format," she said, and proceeded to read it out loud: "'First segment, interview with Jessica Savitch, second segment, interview with Jessica Savitch,' then down a little further it says, 'third segment, Jessica continued or Bob the dog.'" Turning to the audience, Jessica said, "So this means, folks, if I do well I'll be back for segment three, and you'll know if I don't do well because Bob the dog will be here instead." The audience burst into laughter and applause.

The annoyances we experience when we travel are made a bit more bearable when we realize others share our feelings. In an essay entitled "Chicago," Charles Kuralt, CBS Anchorman, describes the typical hotel room with thin walls. He can hear the fellow in the next room taking a shower, having a fight with his wife over the telephone, and so on. Kuralt begins to dream:

"In the perfect hotel room, the laundry bags would accommodate more than one shirt and one pair of socks before tearing. The maids would not congregate outside my door at 6:30 A.M. to laugh and chat, and they would not knock at 7:00 A.M. to see if the DO NOT DISTURB sign is on there by accident. There would not be a picture of Montmartre on the wall of the ideal hotel room, or, indeed, a picture of any other place in France. Once, in a string of Holiday Inns across four states in the Middle West, I got the same picture of Montmartre five nights in a row.

"In the hotel room of my dreams, I could turn down the heat, and—I hesitate even to mention it—I could actually open the window. Probably that's going too far.

"Well the guy in the next room has finished his shower. Now I can hear him putting on his socks."*

Smiles of recognition are more desirable than humor that is squeezed out. My advice is to look to yourself for humor. You may not lead an audience to uproarious laughter, but you can give them a glimpse of how you look at life and experience its foibles as well as its joys. That in itself is pleasurable. Leave the joke books to the writers of them. Granted, a wonderful, appropriate story that matches your intelligence and taste is delectable. I'm all for humor, but not the contrived kind.

You—with your perceptions, beliefs, values, and knowledge—are your most valuable resource as a speaker. Learning how to connect to yourself, the circumstances surrounding the occasion, and your audience is the first step to becoming real.

You owe it to your listeners to take that step. As Lew Sarett, one of my professors at Northwestern University, said: "If you give a speech that's 20 minutes long to an audience of 100 people, that's 2,000 minutes (33½ hours) of time you are taking out of the lives of your listeners—time that could be spent thinking, working, creating, experiencing. Time that is never going to come again. You'd better make it worthwhile!"

I would like to add this thought to Sarett's insight: even when you are speaking to a single colleague, you are using up time that could be spent in a dozen other valuable ways. *Design* your remarks and you'll prove yourself worth listening to. You'll prove yourself of value.

But your homework isn't done yet. Whether you read your speech from a text or deliver it extemporaneously, you will need to create a visual guide, something to give you confidence and keep you on track. Let's see how it's done.

*Charles Kuralt, *Dateline America* (Harcourt Brace Jovanovich, 1979), p. 122

Chapter Four

YOUR VISUAL GUIDE

(Step Two)

Behind making your own stuff there's another level: making your own tools to make your own stuff.

—Stewart Brand
The Last Whole Earth Catalogue

"An oral agreement is not worth the paper it's written on!" said Sam Goldwyn of Metro-Goldwyn-Mayer in a classic malapropism. Well, I believe that oral *communication* is worth more, and is much more effective, when backed up by something written on paper.

Whenever you speak for professional purposes—giving a presentation at a meeting, or even speaking on the phone—it's a good idea to have a visual guide in front of you. It can be anything from a note with three key points jotted down to a full outline, from a memo to a completely written-out text. Something thought out and written down before you speak will be of great help to you.

Your visual guide becomes a road map that reminds you where you want to go and how to get there. It keeps you from getting lost or sidetracked along the way. With a good visual guide you don't have to struggle to remember the key phrases you want to use, because the phrases are there and your meaning stands out. Within the structure of your guide, you have the freedom to be real and to think your remarks through as you give them. You'll be clearer, more in touch with your audience and more alive.

OUTLINES

It is almost always preferable to use an outline rather than a written-out word-for-word text. The exceptions are scientific papers, financial statements or complicated material that has the listener weighing your every word. But for most occasions, a well-constructed, well-conceived outline is a better tool. Your eye sweeps down the page, and you can see where you're supposed to go. You can direct the flow of your thoughts. You can pay more attention to your listeners because you don't have your nose stuck to the page, and because you are not bound by a completely fixed text, *you are forced to think*, rather than read perfunctorily. In other words, you can speak *extemporaneously*. (Most people use the word "extemporaneous" to mean spontaneous or impromptu speaking; however, like other speech specialists, I use the term to mean *prepared* speaking and I use it quite broadly to include not only formal speeches but any speaking occasion in business or elsewhere in which you want to present a body of information.)

Include whatever facts and phrases you personally need in your outline, such as key thoughts and transitional sentences that will help you achieve a smooth, clean delivery. You shouldn't have to struggle to remember anything while speaking. A number of my clients write out all their transitional sentences since these tend to slip the mind; for others this might be unnecessary. Remember: These notes are for you. Let your needs and habits be your only criteria in formulating your visual guide.

At an informal meeting, discussion or interview you may find that 3×5 or 5×8 note cards are more convenient than an awkward sheaf of papers. You can also use note cards to refresh your memory before and during the meeting for statistics and facts, when absolute accuracy is important.

There are three kinds of outlines: the sentence outline, the phrase outline, and the thought-by-thought outline. To show you how they compare, here is part of a speech I delivered to the Toastmasters Club. First I present it word for word and then in the three different outlines.

Neolithic Man Started It

INTRODUCTION

After attending the November 29th Toastmasters meeting, I decided you are very good speakers. You're developing your voices, your diction, vitality, organization, and good language. What could I add? I asked myself. I thought of one principle of good speech which was not talked about at the meeting I attended.

I believe the most vital element in communication—the *most* vital—is man's nature. I'll explain.

(PAUSE)

BODY

A lot of communication takes place without words. If your stomach is churning, Mr. Luxemburg, because you ate the fruit salad too rapidly, it's affecting the way you hear me. And if just before I came here today I landed a big contract from Ford Instrument Company, it will make a difference in the way I communicate. This may seem like an incongruous thing to say to people who are endeavoring to improve their speech, but think of the thousands of feelings and thoughts that are absorbed without the aid of words, a child's smile, the mushroom following an atom bomb explosion, the touch of a woman's hand.

Eight thousand years ago, Paleolithic man didn't use words—just sounds, such as "haa" when he was happy, "ugh" when he was sad. Today language is much more complicated.

Listen to this:

In the case of individuals other than farmers, if 80% of the tax exceeds the estimated tax, and in the case of farmers, if 66⅔% of the tax exceeds the estimated tax, there shall be added to the tax an amount equal to such excess or equal to 69% of the amount by which the tax so determined exceeds the estimated tax so increased, whichever is the lesser.

Translated, it means:

If you guess your tax too low, you pay a fine, but they can't fine more than 6% of your error.

Sentence Outline

The sentence outline includes every word of your text in a point-by-point format. Because all is laid out for you it is like a safety net, but it is also very confining.

Neolithic Man Started It

INTRODUCTION
   A. After attending the November 29th Toastmasters meeting, I decided you are very good speakers.
       1. You're developing your voices, your diction, vitality, organization and good language.
       2. What could I add? I asked myself.
       3. I thought of one principle of good speech, which was not talked about at the meeting I attended.
   B. I believe the most vital element in communication—the *most* vital—is man's nature. I'll explain.

BODY
   A. A lot of communication takes place without words.
       1. If your stomach is churning, Mr. Luxemburg, because you ate the fruit salad too rapidly, it's affecting the way you hear me.
       2. And if just because I came here today I landed a big contract from Ford Instrument Company, it will make a difference in the way I communicate.
       3. This may seem like an incongruous thing to say to people who are endeavoring to improve their speech, but think of the thousands of feelings and thoughts that are absorbed without the aid of words—
          a. a child's smile
          b. the mushroom following an atom bomb explosion
          c. the touch of a woman's hand

    B.   Eight thousand years ago, Paleolithic man didn't even use words, just sounds
        1. Such as "haa" when he was happy
        2. "ugh" when he was sad
    C.   Today language is much more complicated. Listen to this.

etc.

Phrase Outline

The phrase outline, as you might assume, contains key phrases only. This means you really have to think about what you're saying and use spontaneous language. It's a good tool that keeps you on target and alert.

Neolithic Man Started It

INTRODUCTION
    A.   November 29th meeting
        1. Good speakers
        2. Developing voice, diction, vitality, organization, language
        3. Add?
        4. One principle of good speech
    B.   Most vital element—man's nature

BODY
    A.   Without words
        1. Mr. L's stomach
        2. I landed a contract
        3. Thousands of feelings and thoughts unspoken
            a. a child's smile
            b. mushroom—atom explosion
            c. touch of a woman's hand
    B.   Paleolithic man 8,000 years ago
        1. No words
        2. Grunts
    C.   Complicated language

etc.

Thought-by-Thought Outline

The thought-by-thought outline gives you the most freedom and the least support. It is therefore for seasoned speakers only, or for quick notes before an unexpected meeting.

Neolithic Man

INTRODUCTION
- A.   You are good speakers
- B.   Man's nature is the most vital element

BODY
- A.   Communication takes place without words
- B.   Paleolithic man communicated
- C.   Complicated language doesn't communicate, etc.

It's up to you to determine which of the three types of outline best suits your needs. If the material is fairly simple, very clear to you, and easy to express, a thought-by-thought outline will suffice. A sales presentation of a new line of fabrics might be a case in point. A phrase outline might be more appropriate for a somewhat longer and more complex situation, for example a consumer advocate presentation on "The harmful effects of re-circulated air in 'sick' buildings."

On the other hand, a twenty-minute presentation on a difficult subject such as: "Are donations of art to charitable institutions acceptable tax deductions?" requires a fuller and more precise outline. In this case, use the sentence outline

Type or Print Your Guide

Your outline must be tidy and uncluttered so that you can glance down and refer to it with ease. If you have to search for your place, you may lose your audience. You should leave wide margins and double or triple space the lines. Use whatever size type is best and clearest for you depending on the circumstances, the light, your eyesight, and so on.

This is large, heavy type.

SOME PEOPLE LIKE ALL CAPS.

Some people prefer upper and lower case of regular type.

If you print your presentation on cards, do so very neatly in large block letters.

SO BETWEEN THE SHARKS IN THE WATER, THE EXOCETS IN THE AIR, AND THE CUSTOMS OFFICIALS ON LAND, THE WAR IN THE PERSIAN GULF IS A VERY DIFFICULT THING TO COVER.

Here is an example of heavy type, all caps.

SOME SAD NEWS FOR CHRYSLER CORPORATION TODAY FROM HOLLYWOOD: THE DUKES OF HAZZARD HAVE WRECKED THEIR LAST CAR.

Senator Edward Kennedy uses this large-size print (handwritten) on 8½ × 11 paper in a loose-leaf notebook.

GOOD EVENING FRIENDS OF BEN GURION UNIVERSITY

Marking Your Outline or Presentation

Marking should be used for three purposes:

1. To highlight key words or thoughts,
2. To indicate rhythm and pace—where to pause, where to slow down, and where to speed up,
3. To remind you where you want the listener to laugh or applaud so that you can start building ahead of time to make the desired response happen.

Only 5 percent of most forms of communication delivers the essential message. The remaining 95 percent embellishes, ramifies, enlarges upon the 5 percent nub. Of course both parts are necessary. The 5 percent expresses what must be said and the 95 percent serves to increase the listener's interest and attention. Marking pinpoints this 5 percent so that you need only glance at your guide to grasp the core of your remarks, and then give it to your audience.

When it is mandatory that you use a written-out text, marking becomes crucial to highlight key words and indicate rhythm. Otherwise your key words and thoughts will be hidden by a lot of filler. You also run the risk of lapsing into a monotonous drone.

Your basic marking tools are:

1. The single or double underline
2. The circle or asterisk
3. The slash
4. The verbal cues PAUSE, LAUGH, APPLAUSE
5. The arrow
6. Marginal notes

How should you go about choosing your markings? Begin by talking your thoughts and/or your text out loud. You can also tape-record what you say. *You need to think* about what your words represent—their sense, their import and their significance.

You need to experience what you are saying. Marking is a good tool to use, but it springs from a dynamic which is an "interfeeding" process involving your thoughts, your language and practicing out loud.

Use the tape recorder as your ear and play back what you've practiced. You will hear whether you've stressed what you want to stress, swung through a section in order to get to your key thoughts and built momentum to your climax. You will also hear whether you're believable or not.

The following suggestions are offered as guidelines. But remember, without thought, sensitivity and the ability to keep the communication alive (all of which you'll learn how to do in chapter 5, "Practice and

112   **TALK YOUR WAY TO SUCCESS**

Delivery"), you might be better off handing the audience your notes, outline or text rather than putting them through a dull, lifeless recital of words.

Step 1: Underline all key words, such as nouns, active verbs, numbers and comparisons or parallelisms.

Step 2: Circle your central message and put an asterisk next to it in the margin. Then double underline key points supporting the central message.

Step 3: Use a slash to mark the places where you will stop to breathe, often just before a key word which you wish to emphasize.

Step 4: Write "PAUSE" between sections of the presentation—between the introduction and body, the body and conclusion, and between the subsections of the body itself. Write "APPLAUSE" and "LAUGH" where you want these reactions.

Step 5: Where the speech is punctuated with a period or comma, but you don't want to stop, indicate this with an arrow. (See pages 114–15 for examples.) Arrows remind you to drive your points forward and keep up the momentum.

Step 6 (optional): Make marginal notes that sum up each key point in one or two words. They constitute a kind of outline of your talk, reminding you of its overall thrust.

Here is a marked sample of the introduction of a speech to illustrate the six steps in action.

How Pension Plan Sponsors Can Manage the Impact of Portfolio Technology

Most companies have paid more attention to pension fund matters since <u>ERISA</u> was passed in 1974. But where <u>managerial</u> <u>resources</u> are concerned, pension funds are still getting dangerously <u>little</u> <u>attention</u>.

In fact, internal pension fund management, as it is usually practiced today, violates just about everything we all learned in Management 101.

(PAUSE)

I'm going to divide my remarks into three parts. First, I'm going to tell you exactly how pension funds get the short end of the stick. Second, I'm going to tell you why this is dangerous. And third, I'm going to offer a solution. Specifically, I'm going to discuss the role and responsibilities of a hypothetical Vice President of Pension Assets. . . .

Now let's look at an overdone, confusingly marked version of the same speech.

How Pension Plan Sponsors Can Manage the Impact of Portfolio Technology

Most companies have paid more attention to pension fund matters since ERISA was passed in 1974. But where managerial resources are concerned,/pension funds are still getting/dangerously little attention.//In fact, internal pension fund management, as it is usually practiced today,/violates/just about everything we all learned in Management 101.//

I'm going to divide my remarks into three parts. First, I'm going to tell you exactly/HOW pension funds get the short end of the stick. Second, I'm going to tell you/why this is dangerous.//And third, I'm going to/offer a solution.//Specifically, I'm going to discuss/the role and responsibilities/of a hypothetical Vice President of Pension Assets. . . .

You can't see the words for the markings! So much double underlining and double slashing is overkill.

Note: When marking an outline, use the same tools and technique:

How Pension Plan Sponsors Can Manage
the Impact of Portfolio Technology

INTRODUCTION
    A. More attention paid since ERISA
       1. still getting little attention
       2. internal pension fund management violates Management 101

BODY
    A. How pension funds get short end
    B. Why this is dangerous
    C. Solution

The most thrilling delivery I ever heard was Dr. Martin Luther King, Jr.'s "I Have a Dream" speech. The emphasis, phrasing and rhythm arose out of his passion and deep commitment to justice. Since it's possible to hear recordings of him giving this speech, and since many people still remember its stunning sounds, I thought it would be valuable to find out if he used any markings to deliver it. His daughter, Yolanda King, told me that he did not ever write out his speeches, let alone mark them. King would establish the basic theme and then bounce off that. Judging by the way it was delivered, I give you my idea of what a marked version of "I Have a Dream" would look like. (Just remember, if you don't have divine inspiration like Martin Luther King, Jr., had, you'd better learn how to mark your script yourself.)

This will be the day/when all of God's children will be able to sing with new meaning, "My country 'tis of thee, sweet land of liberty, of thee I sing. Land where my fathers died, land of the pilgrims' pride, from every mountainside, let freedom ring." And if America is to be a great nation, this must become true.
    So let freedom ring/from the prodigious hilltops of New Hampshire./ Let freedom ring/from the mighty mountains of New York./Let freedom ring from the heightening Alleghenies of Pennsylvania./Let freedom ring from the snow-capped Rockies of Colorado./Let freedom ring from

the slopes of California./But not only there!/Let freedom <u>ring</u> from <u>Lookout</u> <u>Mountain</u> of Tennessee./Let freedom ring from every <u>hill</u> and <u>molehill</u> of <u>Mississippi</u>. From every mountainside,/let freedom ring.⤴

And when this happens;/when we <u>allow</u> freedom to ring,/when we let it <u>ring</u> from every <u>village</u> and every <u>hamlet</u>,/from every <u>state</u> and every city,/we will be able to speed up that day when ALL of God's children, <u>black</u> men and <u>white</u> men, <u>Jews</u> and <u>Gentiles</u>, <u>Protestants</u> and <u>Catholics</u>, will be able to <u>join</u> <u>hands</u> and sing, in the words of the old Negro spiritual, "<u>Free</u> <u>at</u> <u>last</u>, <u>free</u> <u>at</u> <u>last</u>, THANK GOD ALMIGHTY, FREE AT LAST!"

All the markings should be familiar to you by now except the wavy underline, which indicates that a word is almost sung.

King begins the conclusion with a verse from "My Country 'Tis of Thee," spoken with its original rhythms intact. Then he drives back to his own text (arrow) without pause or separation. And the rest of the oration, up to the climax, is a series of variations on the anthem's last line: "Let freedom ring." The repetition doesn't become tedious because King keeps varying his phrasing, rhythm and pacing. Also, he shifts his emphasis from "ring" to various objects and places.

The arrows show where he thrills us by topping himself: rushing from one sentence into the next without stopping and with even more volume, energy and power. With the last phrase, "And when this happens," we know the climax is near because the sweep doesn't stop. The rhythm becomes grander and smoother and everything ends with the final climactic "Thank God Almighty, free at last!"

The next excerpt is from a speech by William B. Reed, president, Southern Company & Services, Inc. Reed's speech is very different from King's, yet he also skillfully manages phrasing, rhythm and pacing to build momentum and grip his audience.

Three Key Words for Vocational Education: Rigor, Relevance and Profit

Everyone who hires entry-level workers can tell you <u>sad</u> <u>stories</u> of young men and young women who walk in with diplomas and certificates—but <u>cannot</u> <u>read</u> and fill in the application form. We can also tell you <u>infuriating</u> <u>stories</u> about young people who don't understand why we make a fuss about coming to work <u>daily</u> and coming <u>on</u> <u>time</u>./ <u>How</u> <u>could</u> <u>they</u> <u>understand</u>—when they are allowed as many as <u>20</u> absences <u>without</u> <u>penalty</u> during a school term?

Ladies and gentlemen, there's more to vocational training than learn- ing to work a drill press, a weaving machine, or even a computer. (Attitude <u>counts</u>.) And I suggest that greater rigor in the schools will ✳ help build the right attitudes. . . .

(PAUSE)

It's true that most large businesses—like the one I represent—do offer <u>training</u> <u>programs</u> for our employees after we hire them. <u>We</u> <u>accept</u> the need to train <u>new</u> people in <u>our</u> <u>ways</u>—on <u>our</u> <u>equipment</u>.

What we do <u>not</u> <u>accept</u>—what we find <u>deplorable</u>—is that often we have to begin this training by <u>going back</u> almost to <u>step one</u>. Often we have to <u>retrace</u> the educational path and teach new employees the <u>basics</u> they should have learned in the schools.

This takes <u>time</u>. It takes <u>money</u>. And—very frankly—it does <u>not</u> make us feel that we're engaged in a <u>satisfactory</u> <u>partnership</u>.

In his first three sentences, Reed communicates his frustration with a series of images: "sad stories," "cannot read," "infuriating stories," "on time." He also builds momentum with three phrases contrasted in length (long-short-long). This creates a mini-climax: "Attitude counts."

As Reed describes what he is prepared to do, the rhythm becomes calmer and more measured: "We accept the need to train new peo- ple. . . ." When he begins to discuss what he is not prepared to do, there is a shift to choppy, abrupt phrases and a staccato rhythm. "This takes time. It takes money. And—very frankly—it does not make us feel that we're engaged in a satisfactory partnership." We feel his impatience in his pauses.

If you are prepared to bring out the key thoughts and words of your presentation, your communication will have a life of its own—even if you don't feel particularly "on" or energized at the moment that you face your audience. As you think through your meaning, the phrasing and rhythm fall into place. You get invigorated, and your listeners do, too.

• • •

Remember that the visual guide is a means, not an end, to help you speak your mind more effectively. You mark your copy to bring out key words and thoughts because they are *your* words and thoughts, and to capture a phrasing, rhythm and pacing that will project your meaning to your listeners.

Like a pianist, you have a score—your outline, text or notes—to guide you. A musician can look at a score and say, "Here the theme is established, here it moves into a series of variations, and here it returns to the original melody line." You too can learn to express each nuance of your "score." The visual guide is one more tool to help you deliver your real self to your listeners.

Chapter Five

PRACTICE AND DELIVERY

(Step Three)

You cannot acquire experience by making experiments. You cannot create experience. You must undergo it.

—Albert Camus
Notebooks, 1935–42

It is a great temptation to people who have mind and imagination to substitute the *idea* of the thing for the *experience* of the thing itself.

—Katherine Butler Hathaway
*The Journals and Letters
of the Little Locksmith*

The communication skills that make for effective delivery are the same, whether you are speaking to a few colleagues or a packed auditorium. Let's look at the small-scale encounter first.

The time: 10:00 A.M.
The place: A conference room
The occasion: A book publisher's editorial meeting

An editor is presenting a first novel she would like to put under contract. First, she frames her presentation by noting that the novel, though unique in itself, bears comparison with the work of other successful writers in the same genre and would attract the same readership. Briefly but tantalizingly she describes the novel's plot, main characters and themes, and cites a couple of amusing twists to the story that help bring the book alive. Finally, she tells why she thinks it would gain strong advance interest, possibly a book club adoption, and sell well. As she speaks, other editors offer their own observations. Most are supportive, but a few question the project: is this genre wearing thin? Aren't some of the plot devices overly clichéd? The comments spur the editor to explain certain points in greater detail. If you were to study the session on videotape, you would note that the following elements came into play:

- *Clarity*: The editor clearly described and explained her vision of the book, and went about "selling" her colleagues on it in an orderly, coherent and colorful way.
- *Response*: The editor and her colleagues were tuned in to one another. It was a meeting of minds. They responded to each other's statements not only vocally but visibly, with gestures, smiles and eyes lit up.
- *Aliveness*: The editor was personally involved in the business at hand. Her admiration for the book and her interest in her colleagues' views stirred her own thoughts and associations, bringing life to everything she said.

Now let's turn to a more formal occasion. Same editor, same novel, but this time she is presenting the book at her publisher's sales conference. In the audience are sales reps, marketing executives, her fellow editors—about one hundred people in all. Her preparation for this event is different from what she had done for the editorial meeting. Her visual guide is more structured and detailed. She has expanded the content to fit the time allotted her. Yet she will not let the fact that she has "scripted" her presentation stultify her delivery. Though there are more people in the audience, she speaks to them as she did to the editors—to one hundred *individuals*, each of whom she wants to fire up about the book. She may not get the audible response she had received from the smaller group in the editorial meeting; their questions may come after rather than during her presentation, or she may anticipate their questions and answer them in the text of her presentation. Yet in essence, she is going to work with the same elements that helped her communicate well back at the office: she is going to speak with *clarity*, tune in to her listeners' *response*, and turn on her own *aliveness*.

In this chapter you will learn how to practice and deliver your message to one person, to a small group of two or three people, or to larger groups of 15, 150, or 1500.

PRACTICE

To be good at anything—whether it's ice skating, driving a car, or communicating effectively—takes time and practice. I can't emphasize enough the importance of practicing out loud *before* the event. Many people feel awkward speaking words out loud in an empty room, so they wait until the actual moment of delivery to verbalize their speech. Yet only by practicing out loud can you hope to speak with maximum effectiveness. This crucial step can be difficult at first, but if you stay with it you'll find that the initial awkwardness passes. With each rehearsal of your speech you'll make heartening improvements. You will be convinced that a simple "reading over" of your speech in your head is as unrewarding as practicing a concerto on a cardboard piano!

Practicing for Clarity

First, go to your visual guide. Read over the main sequence of your ideas, and then say them out loud. At this point, don't dwell on details but only on the key thoughts, concentrating on how your presentation moves from point to point and builds to a climax and conclusion. This is a very important step. To take your road map and say it out loud is to make it a part of your life experience. On the day of delivery, you won't stray off course because the signposts will be ingrained in your mind and your goal will be clear.

Second, note where you have underlined and circled the key words and thoughts, and work to make them stand out vocally. Here's how:

Pause before and/or after the key word.

Say the key words in a higher or lower pitch than the rest of the sentence, or give it an inflection. Then say all the words in between the key words quickly and lightly. This will emphasize the key words and subordinate the less important ones. Such emphasis and subordination are the speaker's punctuation; they provide clarity for the listener.

You also want to make your key thoughts stand out. To do that, you precede a pivotal remark with a meaningful pause, and then you speak it with greater intensity. Intensity doesn't mean loudness or unbridled dramatics; it means you convey a greater depth of feeling. In this way, you make your key thoughts memorable. I may not remember all the words of a TV commercial done by John Houseman, but thanks to his intensity, I do remember the name of the corporation and what they do: "Smith Barney. They make money the old-fashioned way. They earn it."

Warning: Don't let this technique become mechanical! You emphasize key words and thoughts because the meaning requires it, not just because you drew a line under them. You subordinate, or skip quickly and lightly over, the rest of the text, because that helps the key words and thoughts to stand out. *Pay attention to what the text means to you.* That's what keeps your message alive.

Third, do an actual run-through by talking your presentation into a tape recorder and then playing it back. Did you emphasize key words and thoughts? Did you move with momentum to the climax and make your points clear along the way? Was it fun to listen to? Compelling? Repeat the practice sessions until you can answer each of these questions with a yes!

As you practice, make adjustments. Your text isn't sacrosanct, it's not the Bible or Shakespeare; it's perfectly okay to make changes. As you rehearse, look for ways to improve your language and phrasing.

When you are pressed for time, it may be impossible to manage a practice session with a tape recorder. (Some high-powered executives and politicos are handed their text on the plane or train hours or even minutes before they are scheduled to speak. They truly hit the ground running!) But no matter what the demands on you may be, take time out to mark your text and silently "speak" it, using the *"mute out loud"* *technique.* Move your lips as if you were speaking out loud and imagine the sound of your words and the changing emphasis. Marking and the "mute out loud" technique are godsends for the seasoned speaker whose schedule is frantic. It is a way not only of rehearsing but of making a speechwriter's speech your own on short notice.

Practicing for Response

If you are going to be speaking one-on-one, or with an audience made up of people you know, *try to imagine how they look and how they might react.* Will they understand? Will they object? Will they appreciate the joke? Imagine the questions and objections they will raise as you go along. Plan and practice your comebacks. This is also a good way to ease stage fright. The more prepared you are to cover any circumstance, the less nervous you'll be.

Don't rehearse in front of a mirror—after all, you won't be watching yourself when you speak—but if you are going to be speaking to a large group, do create an imaginary audience for yourself. Turn a lamp, a TV set or a chair into your listeners. Deliver one thought to the chair, another to the lamp. Look at the objects as if they were people and imagine their reactions. Silently ask: "Did I make that clear?" "Are you with me?" Use your imagination to envision the space as well. If you are speaking to a very large audience, say one thousand, imagine your reactors in the street outside your office window. The more real you can make the environment while you practice, the more freely and richly you'll be able to use the actual environment at your presentation. After you've practiced by yourself with imaginary people, practice with real people if you can—your spouse, colleague, friend. It's good to bounce off their real responses.

You should also use your practice sessions to work at building to peaks of enthusiasm that will lead your audience to bursts of applause. *Applause not only gives you great confirmation as a speaker, it gives the audience a chance to participate.*

Applause also follows naturally after introductions. Once I was helping an emcee go over her introductory remarks for a corporate symposium. There were eight people to introduce and I noticed that she'd marked "APPLAUSE" after each person's name. "Won't that slow things down?" I asked. "Absolutely not," she countered. "It's very important because each district head will receive a different kind of applause. This gives the audience a chance to express how they feel about their bosses." She was right.

When, because of its complexity or its newness to you, you need to read your speech, you'll have to take special measures to keep your audience with you. Make certain you *know the first thought or sentence by heart.* By giving your audience your first thought and not burying your head in your notes, you give them a hospitable welcome. They won't mind if you then go to your notes as long as you make renewed efforts to connect with them throughout your speech.

However, these efforts must be tuned in to your audience's ongoing responses. The biggest mistake made by people who read from a text is looking up at the listeners in a perfunctory way. Believing that all they need to do is "make eye contact," they shoot glassy-eyed stares at the group en masse or glance up at a listener's eyes while hardly waiting to get back to the text. To speak effectively, to make an impact, you must give your listeners 95 percent of your attention.

It is because he understands how to use delivery techniques with extraordinary skill that President Reagan has become America's number-one TV communicator. In press conferences, or prepared speeches, he uses the TelePrompTer as an aid, not a crutch. The way he emphasizes and subordinates words, uses pauses, builds to applause and focuses 95 percent of his attention on the listener is superb.

Communication always involves an exchange. You can give and give, but if you don't stop to take, to actively look for the effect of your words, you'll lose your audience.

The time to connect with your listener is at the end of a thought; that is when communication takes place. As you approach the end of a thought, you should look up from your text and seek a response. Your eyes ask, Are you with me . . . was that clear? When you've given your listeners a reasonable amount of time to absorb what you have said, give them the beginning of the next thought as well. Then, once again, you can return to your text. Remember, too, that the very last thought or sentence of your presentation should also be memorized so that you end by making a final connection with your audience.

When I teach this technique I am reminded of the late Jessica Savitch. Like most anchorpeople, Jessica read her news copy from a Tele-PrompTer. The device, intended to keep an announcer's eyes on the camera rather than a page of text, is difficult to master. Like many anchors, Jessica's eyes had a glazed look when she first started to read the news. I adapted the technique described above and showed her a way of grasping the information on the TelePrompTer and giving it to the viewer in digestible portions. The main thing she had to do was imagine the camera as a real person and actually look into that person's eyes, not read across his face. Jessica, a quick study, mastered this technique in only one week. The immediacy and live-eyed intimacy with which she read the news is still considered a model for young broad-casters.

Practicing for Aliveness

When you're excited about what you're saying, when it sparks your interest, when you're truly enjoying the give-and-take, thoughts and associations come to you automatically. That gives you "aliveness." But if you are reading a text because you have to, or saying words that you aren't thinking about, you'll be there in body but not in soul, and your delivery will be lifeless.

As you practice your presentation, continually ask yourself, "Does this move me? Amuse me? Why am I saying this?" Those questions will stir your personal thoughts and associations. Thinking fresh thoughts each time you practice keeps you fresh. When it's time to deliver your remarks, continue to think spontaneously, and that will keep the electricity flowing between you and your listeners.

Plan Ahead

Determine certain details in advance. The size of the space, the seating arrangement, whether the setting is indoors or outdoors—all have an impact on your presentation. The circumstances can work for or against you, depending on how you handle them.

First of all, *know your logistics*. Know where you are going (down to the floor and room number) and exactly how to get there, including how long it will take. If you are giving a speech or a training seminar, or if you are in charge of setting up a meeting, make sure you check the following:

Lighting	—Is it adequate?
Ventilation	—Will the air be fresh enough, even if some people smoke?
Equipment	—Are mikes, slide projectors, etc., in place and in good working order?
Lectern	—If there is one, it shouldn't be too high.
Seating	—Is it comfortable? Can everyone see? In a seminar, would you rather seat everyone in the round? In a negotiating session, would you seat everyone around a table, rather than line them up on opposite sides?
Refreshments	—Will coffee or soft drinks be available? For a morning meeting, do you want to offer participants a breakfast snack to help establish rapport?

If, for some reason, you cannot visit the office, restaurant or meeting place beforehand, call ahead and find out what you can about the place.

When you arrive on the scene, make sure the circumstances are comfortable. If your chair is broken, ask for another. If the light is shining in your eyes, ask to move. If the room is overheated, find some way of making the place more comfortable. Just mentioning how stuffy it is can help you connect with your audience.

Always have a glass of water handy, and not only for those times when your mouth goes dry. A catch in the throat can be frightening. Having the option of swallowing is a comfort. Similarly, if there is some aspect of public speaking that unsettles you, do something that will help you cope. If, for example, you hate walking across the length of an auditorium stage as the audience silently waits, start early and acknowledge someone in the first row as you approach the lectern to break up the walk.

• • •

You are well rehearsed and have thought of every detail right down to the backup glass of water. It's time to deliver.

DELIVERY

What you've just learned about clarity, response, and aliveness must now be employed during your delivery. Whether there are two, two hundred or two thousand people in your audience, *actively seek a response*. Place your ideas consciously. Direct one thought to one person, give him a second to respond, and move on. Talk to a person front and center, then to someone in the back on the right. Shift your focus, making sure to cover the entire room during the course of your speech.

Don't be discouraged by stony-faced "nonreactors." Within the first few minutes you should find two to four pairs of willing and reacting eyes. Use these, then look for others. Work with the audience.

Try breaking the audience down into manageable portions. If, for example, there are two hundred in the audience, break the number down visually into quarters (fifty each) and focus on one quarter at a time. Locate two to three reactors in the first quarter, talk to them for a few minutes, then do the same for the second, third, fourth and back to the first.

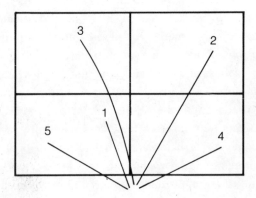

The accompanying diagram shows how you might direct your thoughts to a large audience. First, zero in on a person in the quadrant front and left, then move to someone in the rear right, and so on. The idea is to "work" the room in a way that seems unforced, not to just "look up" as if reading from left to right.

This is a good technique to use as a general rule. Your objective is always to stimulate response. It's particularly useful for people who get panicky addressing large groups.

Stage Fright

One of the most dreaded fears is having to speak in public. In a survey taken of one thousand middle managers, the Hawver Group found that more than 70 percent said they felt *most* uncomfortable speaking in front of large groups of people.

"Why is it that I'm perfectly fine speaking one-on-one, or in a small group, but I fall apart when I get up to speak to fifty or five hundred people?" How often I've heard these words, and worked through this anguish with students!

First of all, if you are addressing an authority figure (a boss or superior), you feel you're going to be judged by that authority figure. You consider him to have power over you. Therefore, you get anxious about presenting an idea for fear that your abilities will be diminished in front of "the boss." In a group of five hundred you are facing a thousand eyes instead of two, and many more judges. This increases the anxiety. That's why you get stage fright. The fear you experience comes from your projection that you are being judged as a speaker by many people.

The ironic truth is that *most audiences expect and want a good speaker.* With the exception of political gatherings, the audience is very receptive to what the speaker has to say.

Secondly, the speaker fears he will fail himself. The audience is one thing, but what is worse is the image that you have failed yourself. The audience isn't going to remember your faults unless you were just awful, but you will carry the least little defeat with you as an enormous blow to your ego.

You are under two pressures: (1) what you experience as audience criticism, and (2) your own idealization of what you want to produce.

A third factor involved is what is known in psychiatry as the pride system—the feeling that you *should* be able to deliver a speech that will <u>wow</u> the audience. In reality, very few speeches will be as good as Lincoln's Gettysburg Address, or Brutus's speech in Shakespeare's *Julius Caesar*. There are very few outstanding speeches and/or speakers. But striving for perfection puts you under such anxiety, you may not perform as well as you can.

Be clear. Your aim should be to *know your material thoroughly* and to realize that the material comes through you. Try to diminish the ego idealizations that you're struggling with. Be real, be humble and be human. At the same time, as you admit to your humanity, do what skillful speakers do, which is to take the attitude that the audience is going to ride with you.

Get a response soon, and *keep getting responses* throughout. And immerse yourself in your material, so that regardless of how anxious you get, the material will come out. "Out of me comes what I have learned. It isn't me delivering the speech. It is what has been studied that I am trying to give others."

Energy

Successful delivery always involves more—more intensity, more energy, more awareness, more concentration and more sensitivity than is normally required of you in everyday life. If you are genuinely excited about what you have to say, there is no need to pump yourself up artificially in order to perform. Believe that what you have to say is important and trust your audience to get involved. They are there for that purpose.

Develop a physical image of what energy means to you. Think of the way you feel while riding a bicycle or swimming across a pool. It's an exhilarating feeling, powerful yet calm. Even more important, it makes you aware in an instinctive, visceral way that it is your body, your physical being, that turns the wheels and pedals or makes the water stream by in currents. Projecting positive energy while communicating should give you the same kind of sensation: smooth and controlled. Energy should flow from deep inside you. John Naisbitt describes it as "constantly being on tiptoes."

Give-and-Take

When your audience bursts with laughter or applause, go with it! One politician had the annoying habit of bringing his audience to applause, then starting his next sentence while they were still clapping. In acting school, we were taught to "top" the applause, to start the next sentence just as the applause is dying down. That not only keeps your words from being drowned out, it keeps the give-and-take between you and your audience moving forward. If expected laughter or applause doesn't happen, be ready to move on swiftly.

The dynamic between a speaker and his or her audience is like a charged electrical circuit. If both are "on the same wave length," and "in tune," a power flows back and forth between them. Even when there's disagreement, the energy from a responsive audience flows out to you and keeps you charged up, stimulated, bubbling with fresh thoughts. And you send the energy flowing back to your listeners as you speak with new and inspired life. To keep this current running smoothly, turn your "listener sensitivity" up full volume.

A vice president of a banking institution turned his listener sensitivity up when he gave an address at a Philadelphia high school. The auditorium was filled with exuberant, noisy, restless teenagers, and he wondered how he could possibly win their attention. So shortly after he began, he said, pointing: "You know, when I attended this school, I was assigned to that seat." Then he actually walked off the platform and sat down in the seat. The teenagers roared their approval. After he returned to the stage, they listened attentively. Later he said: "I gave a little reach. It worked."

Fresh Thoughts and Associations

If you have followed the guidelines in chapter 3, "Organizing Your Thoughts," you will have planned "little reaches" of your own—a striking fact, an attention-getting opening statement, a gripping story. Remember, though, that just telling a story isn't enough. *You need to relish the telling.* The actor Kirk Douglas told the following story on a talk show, explaining how he had acquired the name of *Bryna* for his production company.

Douglas said it was his mother's first name. She had come to America as an immigrant and would often say: "America is a wonderful country!" Douglas taught his mother how to write her name, "Bryna." And one night (after Douglas had worked very hard for many years and had become a big star) he took her to Broadway in a limousine to show her her name in lights on a marquee above the title of his newest show. He said: "Mama, look! Your name is in lights." To which she replied: "Yes, America is a wonderful country!"

Douglas did not rely solely on the content of his story to make an impact. He allowed his emotions to come through. His face lit up with a big smile, his voice was warm and loving, and he drew close to his wife who sat next to him as he told it. He spoke the "punch line" directly to the camera lens (his audience) with the hint of a tear in his eye.

But, you may ask, what if my presentation involves dry facts or a ho-hum topic? How do I ignite sparks then? You do it by staying alert, by being alive to the moment with all your thoughts and senses buzzing.

For example, consider this somewhat colorless opening line:

> Thanks to all of you and your colleagues around the country, contri-butions to our pension fund have doubled this year.

Now try to imagine how a speaker who is spontaneously making the following associations would deliver it:

Spoken Line	Association
Thanks to all of you. . . .	(You, John, sitting in the front row—you're so tan, and your hair is so curly! What happened?)
and your colleagues around the country . . .	(I remember having a beer with you and Joe, back in Minnesota the day of the snowstorm . . .)
contributions to our pension fund have doubled this year . . .	(Mary will be so much calmer knowing we are well provided for in our later years.)

My corporate clients sometimes find it hard to give their thoughts free rein during a formal presentation. CEOs who overflow with brilliant wit and dynamism in their everyday lives cut themselves off from all associations because they're terrified of "going off the track" or abandoning the text of a written speech. Actually, they are slaves to that text—and by putting their minds in bondage they give lifeless, mechanical speeches.

I remember being very moved by two short sentences Charles Osgood delivered on the CBS TV News. He said: "For 75 years, the Cosmopolitan had been a leading hotel in Denver, Colorado. It was demolished in 8 seconds." When I asked him what he was thinking, what was going on inside of him as he spoke those words, he replied: "Construction is a long, tedious process. Destruction is instantaneous. I wasn't just talking about buildings. I was talking about reputations; how somebody can work all his life constructing what he believes is a work of art, or a lifetime of political activity, or whatever a person does. I thought, it's so much easier to be destructive than constructive."

Those thoughts and images juxtaposed against the instantaneous puff of smoke and the sound of the rubble as it hit the ground are what gave Charles's words "life."

Experiencing what you're talking about while you're talking about it is the essence of "aliveness." It's what draws people to you, moves them and makes them want to hear more.

Every time you communicate professionally, you are attempting to move your listeners, but to do so they must first understand you, then respond to you. For that to happen you have to understand what you're saying on much more than a surface level, respond to your listeners, and be moved yourself.

Body Language

How you hold yourself and use your body has a lot to do with how commanding and charismatic your presence will be, and hence how powerfully your message comes across. To see this, sit slouched and hunched up in a chair with your arms curled in and try to speak your introduction. It won't work.

No speaker would assume such an exaggerated posture, yet some do sprawl back in their chairs (during panel discussions), hunch forward on the lectern or sink into their hips, meanwhile peppering their remarks with "offhand" gestures in an effort to look casual, cool and "conversational." No matter what the intention, such a speaker comes across only as weak, directionless and dull! If you stand and gesture at the podium as you would at a cocktail party, you'll only get on your audience's nerves.

Don't, on the other hand, go to the formal extreme by standing or sitting ramrod stiff or using elaborate rhetorical gestures. Instead, stand so that you feel suspended by an invisible string extending from the ceiling to the top of your head. Next, imagine a line that passes from your ear to your shoulder, on down through your hip and knee, to the arch of your foot so that they are all aligned one above the other. It's an authoritative bearing, erect but relaxed.

Your movements should reinforce what you are saying, and seem spontaneous. It is usually counterproductive to plan what gesture to use with what word. If you stay tuned in to your presentation's inner momentum, the appropriate gestures will come naturally. Remember that *it's better to use fewer gestures than a lot of false ones*, and don't be tempted to point for emphasis. Pointing seems like "scolding" and your listeners will resent it.

Imagine the air as a thick medium which you are to disturb as little as possible. Make your motions clean and precise. If possible, use videotape equipment during rehearsal to pinpoint awkward mannerisms and distracting gestures.

Making inappropriate gestures is only one pitfall to avoid when you make a presentation. If you are excessively nervous, your body language may betray you. As you speak, take a mental inventory of your "symptoms."

Are you talking too fast or too slow?

Mumbling?

Biting your nails?

Are your hands trembling?

Is your throat dry?

Is your mouth twitching, your brow wrinkling, your foot jiggling?

Some people "freeze" into a stiff posture and stare blankly ahead, their faces expressionless. Others fall into nervous habits; they rattle money in their pockets, fiddle with a pencil, crack their knuckles or tap their fingers. They may sway from one foot to another as they stand, or rock back and forth in their seats.

If you recognize yourself here, don't castigate yourself but do admit that your tensions are getting the better of you, and then take steps to release those tensions. *Locate the tense area and say to yourself, "Let go."* Taking slow, deep breaths can also help steady your nerves. And if you can hide the tension, do so. As a young man, Robert Kennedy shook so noticeably he kept his hands under the table when he spoke. You can also use a legitimate prop. A trial lawyer found strength at the moment his hands touched the partition behind which the jurors sat. As he leaned on it, the trembling stopped. Holding on to a real object will calm you.

Mastering Props and Equipment

A picture really can be worth a thousand words. When used well, visuals add to the clarity of your presentation and get your listeners more actively involved. Yet, according to the Hawver Group survey, we found that most speakers feel they are weak in the use of audio-visual materials. Are you one of those? If so, here are some tips on what to do.

First, select the best visuals for the occasion. Slides are vivid and concise, and charts have a special immediacy if you generate them as you speak. You can even involve the audience by asking questions and incorporating their responses onto the charts. You can also write on projected transparencies, overlaying them in order to build up a visual explanation of a complex idea.

For one-on-one meetings, Dr. Linda C. Jones, an industrial psychologist in outplacement work, uses a flip chart which folds out of her attaché case. She sets it on the potential client's desk for him to follow as she speaks, giving the call an automatic structure. The client sees that Dr. Jones is leading up to the value of utilizing her service. One chart follows another, clearly and effectively to accomplish the goal of the presentation.

Whatever option you select, make sure that all your equipment is in working order. Don't assume this will be the case just because last night's presentation went without a hitch. Rehearsing is especially important when you plan to use visuals. Most people assume that the audio-visual material will fit into their presentation, but they don't practice out loud with their props. They may be defective. You may feel awkward operating the machinery or become a slave to a temperamental projector. When that happens, your presentation fizzles.

Here are some pointers for using visuals effectively:

- Remember to keep your body facing your audience. A half-turn is sufficient if you want to refer to your pictures.
- Make sure your listeners can see and understand the material. Ask them: "Is this clear?" "Can you see the diagram?" A cartoon won't be funny if the punch line is not legible.
- Put on a slide only when you start talking about the subject and turn it off when you're finished. Otherwise it will compete with you for audience attention.
- Don't show slides in darkness unless your voice is especially strong. The audience should be able to see you so that you can keep their attention.
- Avoid repetition from visual to visual. Your slides or charts should add to what you are saying, not duplicate it.
- Make sure that each visual is simple and expresses a single idea. A cluttered slide or diagram has diminished impact.
- Always know where you're going with your visuals, why you're using them, what's coming next. If you use a standard set of visuals provided by your company, don't do so mechanically. Make sure each one aids your particular presentation.

One note of caution: Many speakers feel their presentation becomes riveting the moment a visual goes up on the screen—"I've got my slides, so I've got my speech." Yet haven't you ever fallen asleep during a presentation when the lights were off, the slides were on and the projector was purring a lullaby? Only if visual aids are carefully coordinated with what you have to say, and the rest of your presentation is shipshape, will your audience stay interested and alert.

Using a Microphone

Keep three points in mind when you speak into a microphone: (1) make sure you can be heard, (2) stay on the mike; don't turn your head away from it, (3) use vocal energy.

If you are the first or only speaker to use a microphone at a meeting, you have no way of judging the quality of sound until you try it out yourself. (If you're second or third to speak, you can gauge the distance your mouth should be from the microphone by observing what the results are for others.) Ask: "Can you hear me in the back of the room, John?" "Let me know if the sound fades away." You can even insert humor if it seems appropriate. "I don't want you to miss a word of my carefully wrought remarks!"

If the microphone neck is flexible, bend it toward your mouth. Though there's magic in mikes, a five-foot person won't be heard on a microphone adjusted for a six-foot person. In general, try to be three to eight inches away from it.

It's very disconcerting to be in an audience and hear only part of the spoken sentences. This happens when a speaker turns his head toward someone on the dais or points to a screen to his right or left. The microphone does not turn with you. It's your listener's ear; don't forget about it.

Very few people need to back away from the microphone because their voices are too powerful. Just the opposite is the case. Most people feel the microphone will pick up their sound, no matter how low-keyed. My advice is use your full tone, make it as resonant as possible, project! In large groups, your listeners' attention is easily lost in hubbub, distractions, even daydreams. Your voice needs to command, invite and comfort. The microphone is there to help you. Use it well.

Taking Command

Ah, the "ideal" audience! When you want their rapt attention, they sit quietly in their seats, transfixed by your message. When you want audible responses, they laugh appreciatively and applaud with mighty thunder. Afterward, they give you a standing ovation.

In real life, you'll find that audiences are sometimes inattentive or that certain individuals in a political gathering try to give you a hard time. Under such circumstances, it's important to *let your audience know that you are in charge.* Here are some examples of difficult situations that might arise, and suggestions about how you can deal with them to take command.

A Restless Audience: Don't begin your talk to a noisy, inattentive group. If your audience can't settle down, say: "May we begin?" and then wait for silence. If some members begin to talk among themselves later on, ask them if something you've said needs clarification. That usually quiets them.

Hecklers: Address a heckler directly. Tell him he can have his turn when you're through. If that doesn't work, show him the door. One notable speaker told me he dealt with a heckler who shouted a four-letter word by replying: "Now that you've identified yourself, what is the question."

Once, presidential candidate John Anderson was disrupted by a heckler who threw an egg at him. The atmosphere was charged, but Anderson defused it wonderfully. "Well," he said, "now that we've had breakfast..." and proceeded as captain of the ship, in command of all that was happening.

A Skeptical Audience: If you are convinced you are right, you will be convincing.

H. L. Culbreath, President of Tampa Electric Company, is a charismatic and winning speaker. He cares deeply for the Performing Arts Center he spearheaded in Tampa, Florida. When he speaks about it, he is so persuasive, he turns people around to favor what they first opposed. "Why do we need such an extravagant cultural palace?" he was asked. "People don't attend concerts that are here in Tampa now."

"That's what was said before the stadium was built," H. L. responded, "and in 1984 it was the site of the Super Bowl. When you make a place for people to grow and develop in, growth and development will take place." Tampa's Performing Arts Center is due to open in 1986.

Questions and Answers

"It annoyed me as a student when a teacher said: 'I'll come back to that question later,'" mused Geraldine Dowd, a top-notch trainer of nurses. "Usually there wasn't enough time and he never came back to it. So when I lecture I tell my students up front, 'Stop me when you want to.'"

Unless it is a very formal presentation, get your listeners actively involved by inviting them to ask questions. Questions provide an opportunity to clear up confusion instantly so that every individual stays with you. They will stimulate, not ruffle, you if you pay attention to the Three A's:

Anticipate questions. If you know you're going to be under fire from a hostile audience while presenting a new product line, know your facts—all the facts, not just the ones that you use in your presentation. Write down every tough, challenging, embarrassing query you can conceive of and practice answering each out loud until you feel absolutely secure. If possible, have a friend or an associate grill you.

Answer questions succinctly and then bridge back to your main line of thought. If you don't know the answer, say so. Don't guess! No one expects you to be omniscient.

Ask questions yourself, and make them direct: "Did you read the proposal?" "Do your results agree with mine?" "Am I making myself clear?" If you ask a direct question, make sure you get a direct answer. If no one volunteers, zero in on a particular individual. For example: "How many of you know what your pension funds will amount to this year? What about you, Mr. Vance?" (He may have told you the amount during the cocktail hour, or you may feel pretty sure he's one who will know the answer.) Then, use his answer to illustrate your point: "Okay, given that amount of money, here are three ways you can safely invest it...." Asking a direct question is also like a "wake-up call" to everyone in the audience. Each person will be thinking, "Oh, Vance was asked a question. Maybe I'll be next."

A separate question-and-answer period can be tricky. Remember that awkward moment after a speech when the speaker asks the audience if they have any questions and nobody does? How do you avoid this?

Some speakers actually plant friends in the audience armed with spirited questions for which they've prepared pithy responses, but usually the effect is artificial. If questions are not forthcoming, make a statement and expound on it. If questions are forthcoming but are lackluster or controversial, you can still use them to say something interesting and important.

Bridging is a technique of moving from a question you are asked to a point you would like to make. It can help you react to an embarrassing or irrelevant question with a thoughtful and intelligent response by making a transition into a discussion of the points you want to make.

Here is an example.

Senator Howard Baker appeared on "Meet the Press" shortly before President Reagan's 1982 State of the Union address. Mr. Baker's objectives were to build up confidence in the administration and to stir up excitement for the President's speech. Charles Monroe asked: "Are you suggesting the President will make a talk in which he is not advancing any kind of tax increases or any new revenues to ease the deficits?" Senator Baker replied: "I can't say. The President can only say that. I talked with the President this morning and I simply don't know what he will say on Tuesday night about taxes. [Answer] But I do feel, however, that he is clearly in control of the situation. He has a clear idea of what he wants to do and he's going to do it, regardless of any advice from me or his staff or anybody else. He is a strong President, and he's going to make that decision. [Bridge] But what I am saying is that I think the speech—regardless of its tax consequences—is going to be an extraordinary or perhaps even an historic speech charting the future destiny of the government of this country." [Point Made]

If you end with a question-and-answer session, your answer to the final question becomes your closing remark. Make it memorable! John Naisbitt usually ends his Q & A sessions by bridging to a line that has become his sign-off: "And that's why I say, 'My God, what a fantastic time to be alive!'"

If there's a single image I'd like you to remember as you speak in public or one-on-one, it is this: Be a detective. Never put your spyglass down! Continually search the audience (or your listener) for clues to tell you:

Am I being clear?

Am I getting a response?

Am I speaking with aliveness?

PART THREE

HOW TO
SOUND
YOUR BEST

The Lilyan Wilder Program
(Step Four)

Chapter Six

IMPROVING YOUR VOICE

Voices—I think they must go deeper into us than other things. I have often fancied heaven might be made of voices.

—George Eliot

Your voice is a musical instrument of incredible power. The sheer quality of its sound can move an audience deeply. Masterfully used, your voice can be as rich and beautiful as an organ filling space with a hundred different sounds. Poorly used, it can be abrasive. A voice can convey an irresistible magnetism. Consider John F. Kennedy's upward, hopeful inflections. Or Winston Churchill's deep and crackling tones. Or Barbara Jordan's rich, rolling sound.

There are as many different voices as there are people on the earth. Each person's voice has fingerprint distinction. In fact, voice graphs are sometimes used by police departments in place of, or in addition to, fingerprint identification. There may be familial and regional similarities of sound, but not even identical twins have the same voice.

You may be thinking, "If my voice is like a fingerprint, then how can I hope to change it?" Or perhaps you suppose that serious voice work is only for professionals—singers, actors, orators. It certainly cannot be said that success requires a polished voice; plenty of harsh-sounding corporate tyros and political officeholders prove otherwise. The important thing is not whether the listener likes your voice but whether *you* do. Does it please you to hear yourself live or on tape? Does your voice express the real you? Do you wish it sounded softer or more commanding or less nasal?

You *can* change the sound of your voice. The vocal cords are muscles that grow stronger with use. They can be trained, relaxed and developed through practice and exercise. And just as the bodybuilder learns about his musculo-skeletal system before going into training, the speaker must understand the mechanisms of vocal sound. Or, to use another metaphor, before you can tune your instrument, you must know how it works.

YOUR VOCAL INSTRUMENT

The diaphragm is a large muscle attached to the bottom of the rib cage on its periphery (see figure 1). If you place your hand on your midriff

─────────────── FIGURE 1 ───────────────

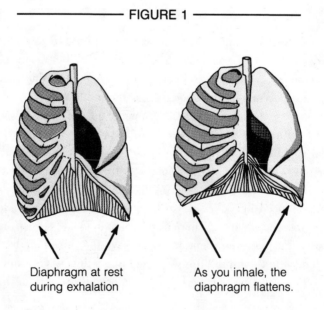

Diaphragm at rest
during exhalation

As you inhale, the
diaphragm flattens.

and breathe deeply, you can feel it operating like a bellows. During exhalation, the diaphragm relaxes into a half-moon shape, its natural position of rest. Through the combined movement of the diaphragm and the abdominal muscles, the air moves up from the lungs and through the trachea (see figure 2) into the bony cartilage where the vocal cords (also known as the vocal folds) are located (see figure 3). As it moves past them, the air causes the vocal cords to vibrate. These vibrations or sound waves are propelled through the chest, throat, mouth and nose, the four resonating chambers, where they become fuller, richer and more resonant (see figure 3). Finally, the tongue and jaw shape the sound waves into words.

Breathing from the diaphragm comes naturally. A baby has faith in his diaphragm. All he need do is breathe out and he will automatically breathe in. The mouth and nose are coordinated with the diaphragm, and that coordination is all that is needed for steady, peaceful breathing. We adults need to reacquaint ourselves with diaphragmatic breathing. It is the foundation of good sound.

——————————— FIGURE 2 ———————————

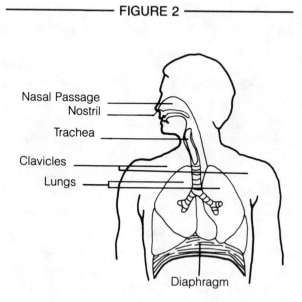

Nasal Passage
Nostril
Trachea
Clavicles
Lungs
Diaphragm

FIGURE 3

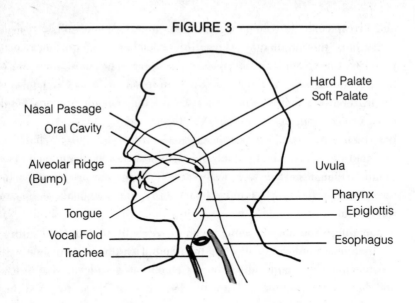

IDENTIFYING VOCAL PROBLEMS

It's difficult to hear yourself as others hear you. That's why a tape recorder is such a valuable tool. Yet people are sometimes shocked when they first hear themselves on tape. A doctor's assistant told me she won't even leave a message on her family's answering machine for fear of hearing herself later on. Of course, her chances of improving her voice aren't good.

Try taping yourself at various intervals during the day—while you talk on the telephone, give instructions or converse with a colleague. Then play it back. Try not to be subjective about the way you sound and listen for positive as well as negative qualities. Listen actively. Do you hear warmth, music, cleanness, energy, strength, variety, liveliness? Or do you hear strident highs, booming lows, whining tones or words dropping off at the end of sentences? Which, if any, of the following characteristics do you hear in your voice?

Excessive loudness: Some people speak too loudly because they grew up shouting to be heard over loud, aggressive parents and siblings, or deafening traffic. They overcompensate in their adult lives for problems they had in earlier days. Others speak too loudly because they just don't objectively hear the volume of their own voices. Whatever the reason, if you have this problem, you need to remember that in ordinary conversation the person to whom you're speaking is not more than two or three feet away; try to envelop that person in sound, not obliterate him. Remember, too, that true projection comes from breath support. Loudness, or shouting, emanates from the throat.

Excessive Softness: Do people often interrupt you with "What?" or "Excuse me"? If so, you probably speak too softly, a much more common problem than speaking too loudly. Insecurity or shyness may be the underlying problem, or you might be trying to project an image of cultural refinement. Unfortunately, you may only be hurting your credibility. No matter where you are—a living room, an office or an auditorium—your listener must not have to strain to hear you. The best remedy is to work at prolonging and controlling the air stream as you voice your vowels and consonants (see pages 154–56).

Excessive speed: If you talk too fast, people either won't understand you or will find it exhausting to listen to you. Remember, your mind works much faster than your mouth. If you try to speak as quickly as you think, you may end up sounding like a tobacco auctioneer. Slow down, linger on your vowels, concentrate on really reaching your listener or listeners.

Excessive slowness: If your audience is nodding, you may be plodding. Yet most people who plod actually worry that they are speaking too fast. They slow down to a snail's pace. The listener then has a hard time maintaining attention because the speaker's rate of speech is too slow for the listener's thought processes.

If you suspect that you may be a plodder, ask people you trust what they think. Speeding up may be uncomfortable at first, but the discomfort will go away and you will be a far more effective speaker.

Fading: You're fading if your voice peters out at the end of sentences. By not supporting your tone with breath control right up to the end of your thoughts, you lessen the authority you want to establish. If you fade, practice the breathing exercises on pages 154–56.

Breathiness: A breathy sound is overlaid with too much air. Breathy speakers, like those with soft voices, sometimes believe incorrectly that they sound more feminine. Marilyn Monroe had this vocal quality and it worked for her in the roles she portrayed, but for most people breathiness limits the music and richness of tone and robs the voice of authority. To overcome this problem, you must use diaphragmatic and abdominal control so that you really sound and linger on your vowels (see page 156).

Gasping: Taking too many little breaths between words and breathing from the upper chest (the clavicles) can lead to gasping speech. Remember Peter Lorre in the old Boris Karloff horror films? His little gasps were fine for the characters he played, but not for you. If you have this problem, try to trigger the breath from the abdomen-diaphragm area so that it moves in a controlled stream through the lungs, trachea and mouth. Aim it forward, always forward.

Hoarseness: Hoarseness, usually caused by the failure of the vocal folds to meet along their full length, may be a medical problem stemming from swelling, inflammation or nodes on your vocal cords. Consult a doctor if the problem persists. Hoarseness can also come from smoking, or the strenuous overuse of your voice at sports contests or other public events. If you have this type of hoarseness, give your voice a rest for a while, then practice your exercises in a relaxed, easy manner.

Glottal attack: To identify a glottal attack, say the following sentence, "I am at ease," and listen for a small explosive sound, like the beginning of a grunt, before words starting with a vowel. This "grunt," known as a glottal attack, comes from shutting the opening of the larynx just as the word is being initiated, rather than letting the breath initiate the word. If you feel the closure as you say the vowels, your sound has a harsh quality. To get rid of it, practice saying sentences like the following and work for a smooth connection between the words. Connect the final consonant to the beginning vowel and the final vowel to the beginning vowel.

I am awfully eager to eat the oatmeal.

Alligators and ocelots attack when excited.

Are we alone under the awning?

(Note: "to eat" and "we alone" are actually pronounced "to-w-eat" and "we y-alone." The "y" and "w" sounds here smooth out the passage between vowels, helping to eliminate glottal attack.)

Whining inflections: Whining is a sort of crying sound that makes you seem cranky and gets on your listener's nerves. It was aptly satirized on "Saturday Night Live" with the Whiner family. If you whine, and a lot of people do, you really have to make a conscious effort to speak directly and forcefully.

Nasality: A nasal sound is one that comes out through the nose rather than the mouth. Only "m," "n" and "ng" should have nasal resonance. All other sounds should come from the mouth. Place your fingertips on your nose and say the following sentences:

"The man went downtown."

"I am going to be home at nine."

If you feel vibrations on any sounds other than "m," "n" or "ng," you may have a problem with nasality.

Howard Cosell has built a career on his nasal voice, and he has been the source of much amusement to both critics and admirers. But there's really only one Howard Cosell, so don't count on a nasal voice working for you.

Denasality: The problem here is the reverse of nasality: you do not sound the "m," "n" and "ng" through your nose, as you should. People with head colds are denasal, so that words like "man" come out sounding like "bad." The cartoon character Elmer Fudd has a denasal sound. Hum a song. Practice poetry like Edgar Allan Poe's "Annabelle Lee." Listen for the "m," "n" and "ng."

Thinness: If your voice sounds thin and flat, you aren't using resonance and variety. A number of comediennes have turned their thin little voices into assets (the late Judy Holliday and "Georgette" on "The Mary Tyler Moore Show," to name two). But unless comedy is your metier, a thin voice will work against you. Most people have one special sound that comes out more resonantly than others. It could be "ah" or "aw," for example. Find that sound and practice it over and over. It will help to open your throat and round out your tone.

A clipped sound: A clipped sound occurs when you don't give your vowels their due, so make a concerted effort to linger on them. A clipped sound can be too hard and sharp to understand. New York's Senator Patrick Moynihan is a chronic clipper, and yet it's his style.

Hesitation: Listen for two many ur's and um's; they can disturb the flow of thoughts and begin to outweigh your actual words. Make an effort to dispense with these fillers, be quiet when you're not saying anything, and gradually your thoughts will connect more smoothly.

Don't despair if you found yourself checking off several of these flaws as yours. Remember that the actor Richard Burton had to rid his speech of peculiarities. The natural lilt and pitch of his native Wales were incomprehensible to other than Welsh people, but he learned a more standard English and developed his vocal qualities with the help of his foster father, Philip Burton, and his coaches at Oxford. Laurence Olivier made vocal re-education a way of life. To play Othello, for instance, he spent six weeks learning to lower the pitch of his voice. You too can have the voice you want if you commit yourself to the Lilyan Wilder program and take it step by step.

GETTING YOUR VOICE READY TO USE EVERY DAY

You need to warm up physically before you proceed to vocal exercises. Your body and mind must be relaxed for your sound to have richness, resonance and variety.
Let's look at some simple yet effective vocal relaxation techniques.

First Warm-up Exercise

Since the main areas that tense up are your neck, head and shoulders, the following exercises are especially helpful:

1. Shrug your shoulders, raising them up as high as you can, then letting them drop down so that you aren't exerting a single muscle to keep them in place. Repeat ten times.

2. Let your head drop forward. Just let it go. Then let it roll as deadweight to the right, then back, then to the left, then forward. Make sure you keep your shoulders down. Repeat slowly, reversing direction.

3. Put your hands on your shoulders, elbows by your side. Rotate your elbows forward so that they almost touch. To the side, back, around and then down. Repeat ten times, then reverse direction. See figure 4.

FIGURE 4

Second Warm-up Exercise

The following exercises will help you to really experience the connection of voice and body. Do them in an easy, relaxed manner. Do not do them vigorously à la Jane Fonda's workout.

1. *Flop your torso forward from your hips*, knees slightly bent, letting your head, neck, arms and shoulders hang like dead weights. See figure 5. Now let your torso swing back like an elephant's trunk. Move up and down slowly. Let your mouth hang open loosely. Now while you're swaying up and down, sing the words of a simple song, such as "Happy Birthday" or "Mary Had a Little Lamb." Don't try to articulate or formulate sounds. Let them burst out as a result of your movement. These won't be pretty sounds but they will be organic groans, grunts, whatever, similar to the sounds the microphone picks up when Jimmy Connors serves his aces. The important thing to remember is that these sounds are triggered by the movement of your torso.

Be aware of the kind of sound that is coming from your body, but don't try to manipulate it. Let it happen. Once you've established one rhythm (singing two or three lines of the song with one movement to one sound), change to another rhythm, such as a jiggle.

2. *Jiggle.* Shake all over, like a dog shedding water. Shake. Shimmy. Up and down, side to side, letting your head rotate or hang limply. Your mouth is open, no tension around the lips. Sing the next few lines of the song while doing this movement. (Note: This is not an easy exercise to do, but it can give you a sense of how the body and the voice connect, and experiencing this connection even slightly is a valuable discovery.) Change the rhythm again.

——— FIGURE 5 ———

UP

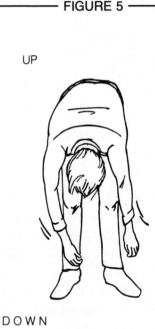

DOWN

3. Standing with your knees bent and flexible, *fling your torso* to one side, then the other. See figure 6. Do this rather gently at first. If you jerk, or twist violently, you may hurt yourself. Don't place your arms or hold them up. Your arms must be relaxed like a rag-doll, and following whatever motion they are thrown into by the trunk.

─────────────── FIGURE 6 ───────────────

4. *Jump up and down.* Imagine you are a ballet dancer. Imagine you are a bouncing ball. Don't strain, but do try to achieve some height. Listen to your sound now, catapulting out of your body, as you sing "Happy Birthday to You!" It should be different from any other sounds you've made thus far. Each time you change the rhythm of the jumps or the position of the torso and make the connection between body and voice, you will be experiencing your sound organically.

By this time, you should notice that as your body changes rhythms and positions, the sounds that come out of you change rhythmically, dynamically. There is no one right way to sound as you do these exercises. The results will be different each time. The exercises are designed to "wake you up" vocally and enable you to connect your body to your voice.

DEALING WITH PSYCHOLOGICAL STRESS

Sometimes we must go beyond physical exercise to free the voice. Physical tension, especially vocal tension, is often the external manifestation of deeper, on-going psychic stress. We know this instinctively when we use phrases such as "Her voice broke," "He was all choked up," "He began to stutter and stammer." We understand that these are descriptions of emotional stress or anxiety. Conversely, in a situation without stress, notice how mellow the voice can sound. For example, after lovemaking, when all physical and mental tensions have been released, the voice is at its most peaceful and most beautiful.

A good deal of stress-induced tension can be alleviated by the warm-up exercises in this chapter and the process of clearing your mind of distractions described in chapter 2, "The Key: Being Real." Other tensions are much harder to release. Consider the case of the world-famous novelist Jerzy Kosinski. As a child, at the beginning of World War II, he was separated from his parents. Kosinski grew up as a Polish Jew during the Nazi occupation, hiding in forests, roaming from village to village, and constantly suffering the cruelty of ignorant, frightened peasants who mistook him for an evil gypsy. At one point the child was sunk into a pit of excrement and left to drown. The experience left him literally mute and it was not until after the war, safe again with his parents, that he became psychologically free enough to speak.

If there is deep unrest in your life, you need to come to terms with it, to change what you can, and to accept what you can't. "You've done wonders for Peter," a friend of mine said to me about a client she knew. "His voice has improved amazingly." I told her I couldn't accept all the credit. After being embroiled in a difficult marriage for years, Peter had finally obtained a divorce. This one action did more for his voice than anything I could have taught him.

Occasionally, a voice tension can be traced back to a trauma that happened some time ago but lives on in the present. Such traumas must be faced if the voice is to be freed. One of my clients, a bright and cheerful woman, spoke with a choked quality that seemed curiously at odds with her personality. "I feel as though you want to scream," I said to her one day. In one of our exercises (when she had to make up lyrics to a song spontaneously) she suddenly volunteered that she had been raped eight years before.

We continued to work together. Often she read aloud emotionally charged passages from literature, including the scene from Tennessee Williams's *The Rose Tattoo*, where Serafina loses control while defending herself for locking up her daughter naked to prevent her from going out and meeting young men. Working with this soul-searing material was a catharsis for this woman. Anger, frustration and hurt came flooding out until finally her voice acquired a "calm" it hadn't had for years. The choked quality disappeared.

If your past holds a traumatic event that is limiting you vocally, investigate it and try to achieve a vocal release. Painting or writing, for example, might help you work through your conflict, but neither will erase the imprint on your voice. Dig into your psyche yourself, or with the help of a psychologist perhaps. Different people will use different methods, but whatever the vocal release your instincts lead you to, it must be achieved organically. You can't just start screaming. The scream, if it comes, has to occur because your feelings have been aroused by a poem, or a scene from a play or a short story that you are experiencing aloud in front of another human being. Oral interpretation of literature can help to make the connection between inner life and vocal expression. One word of warning: If this way of working proves too overwhelming for you, don't push it. Pick it up again at a later date, when you may be better able to handle it.

THE SIX BASIC PRINCIPLES OF VOICE WORK

The six principles that follow are basic to your work in every voice exercise in this chapter. To produce a superior sound, all six must be functioning at once. Practice them separately, but as the first principle becomes easier to do, add the second, then the third, and so forth. Eventually, you will be using all six principles at the same time. This takes concentration. The objective is that as time goes on, voice exercises should become as much a part of your daily routine as your physical exercise. It's important to keep your voice, as well as your body, in good shape.

1. Use Diaphragmatic and Abdominal Control

When you use the group of muscles extending from the abdomen to the chest to support your voice, the sounds you produce are characterized by power, consistency and ease.

Place your hand on your diaphragm and pant like a puppy. You will feel that area move in and out. Check it in a mirror. Nothing else should move. Shoulders and chest should not move up and down. If they do, you are using high clavicular, or chest, breathing and losing the benefit of abdominal support. That support is essential for good sound. Moreover, breathing that starts high in the chest can create tension in the throat.

If you have difficulty feeling the diaphragm move, lie on the floor and place a book flat on the area between your stomach and the point where your rib cage separates. Now try to bounce the book off. Expand as you inhale. Pull in as you exhale. Also, note that while you lie on your back in a relaxed manner just before dozing off to sleep, you will automatically start to breathe this way. Observe how it feels.

The objective is to use this abdominal breathing in an upright position. With the flow of your breath, your sound will go forward evenly and forcefully to surround your listener. Picture such a process as a clothesline extending out of your mouth. Your abdominal and chest muscles are like a spool that holds its line in place and allows it to be wound out. If the spool is too stiff and tight, the line will not pull out smoothly; if the spool is too loose, the line will come out too freely and hang limp. Similarly, your muscles should be held firmly but not tensely.

Once you have established a regular breathing pattern, try to extend your exhalation over a longer period of time. Your abdominal muscles will help you speak on this supported tone for longer and longer periods of time.

2. Focus

You begin this principle by using what I call the count-up exercise. This is a simple, easy-to-remember way of getting your voice revved up. Stand

erect, but not stiffly (you should be free of tension—yawning helps) and
focus your attention on a specific spot far away, a tree down the block,
a window across the street, whatever. Now try to get your voice to reach
that spot as you pull your abdomen in. Fully project one word on one
breath. Don't force the sound. Linger on the vowel.

ONE!	(breathe)
TWO!	(breathe)
THREE!	(breathe)
FOUR!	(breathe)
FIVE!	(breathe)

Now use one breath for five words, keeping the air flowing smoothly
as you pull in your abdominal muscles gradually.

ONE, TWO, THREE, FOUR, FIVE

Now utilize the flow of air the same way but speak a little faster,
saying ten words on one breath.

ONE, TWO, THREE, FOUR, FIVE, SIX, SEVEN, EIGHT,
NINE, TEN

And now just increase the rate you speak to include the numbers one
through fifteen, and then one through twenty. Don't rush. Relax.

As you move up to the longer and longer count-ups you must be sure
that your voice continues to reach forward to your focus—that it doesn't
die, that the clothesline doesn't slacken. Continually remind yourself to
use your abdominal muscles, make sure your breath supports your tone,
use your lower range, and linger on the vowels. The only sound you
make should be your vocalization. Your breathing should be noiseless.

When you do these exercises correctly you are projecting, not shouting. Shouting is a harsh sound emanating from the throat. Projection is
a clear, strong sound triggered by the diaphragmatic area. Many of my
students think they sound too loud, but in reality, they are hearing their
voices for the first time. Though this sound should be exaggerated for
practice, in real life the sound is adjusted for your particular purpose.

In addition to achieving better tone, your listeners will be grateful for not having to strain to hear you.

When you do the count-ups, you may hear an expulsion of air after each number: ONE! (air) TWO! (air) THREE! (air) and so on. Chant the vowels for at least four beats until all excess air is used up. Exaggerate. This helps do away with two things: excessive breathiness and gasping for air.

After a few count-ups your sound may be focused and effectively reaching toward that spot. But you want it to do more than that—you want it to surround the spot, just as, ultimately, you want your voice to surround your listener. Principles three through six are geared toward improving the quality of your sound so that in addition to reaching the target, it enfolds it lovingly.

3. Linger on the Vowels

Vowels contain everything that is liquid, musical and beautiful about the voice. They are like a river that carries the voice forward and keeps it flowing. The consonants are like rocks or stones in the river, which interrupt the smooth flow of the water, giving the sound dimension and outline as they channel its movement. Though some consonants—"m," "n," "ng," "l" and "v"—are also musical and flowing, all the others, such as "b," "t," "sh," etc., should be crisp and precise. Don't linger on them. The more you balance the vowels and consonants according to their spoken value, the more effective your voice will be as a pleasing instrument of communication.

As you practice the numbers in the count-up, linger on the vowel part of the word.

w – uh – n
t – oo
thr – ee
f – aw – r
f – i – v

The sounds underlined once are short, taking up about 5 to 10 percent of the time. The sounds underlined twice are longer, taking up about 90 to 95 percent of the time.

4. Keep Your Pitch Low

Don't confuse pitch with volume. Pitch is the position of your tone on the musical scale. Your voice can go up and down, high or low. (Volume is loudness or softness.) Generally speaking, the lower pitches are stronger and warmer. You may have to make a conscious effort to stay at a lower pitch, both because you hear your sound pitched lower than your listeners do and you usually raise your pitch when you think you're having trouble being heard or understood. Use the diaphragmatic area to support your lower tones.

To find and use your lower pitch, start counting from one to ten. Make each number lower in pitch until you can't go any lower. After you've done this, you can begin using some of the pitches you reached at numbers five and six, or wherever you are comfortable. That is the lower range to use while practicing. Try to carry it over to everyday life.

5. Keep Your Cheeks Up—Mouth Widened a Bit

Your cheek muscles should be raised as you vocalize and your mouth extended in the shape of a moderate smile. Yes, a smile! Every time I suggest to a client that he raise his cheeks in the shape of a moderate smile, nine out of ten say to me, "Do you mean you really want me to smile?" And I say, "Yes, I do." By doing this, not only do you have a look of self-confidence on your face, but the sound of your voice becomes stronger, and you become much more articulate. Try it. Say this sentence both ways—with your cheek muscles up and energized (see figure 7), and with your cheek muscles down and lax (see figure 8). "My country 'tis of thee, Sweet land of liberty." Raising the cheek muscles raises the soft palate inside your mouth so that your sound is less constricted, and this in turn makes your tongue work harder to articulate. Your sound becomes clearer and more crisp.

Keeping your mouth open in a smiling position further amplifies your oral cavity, and helps keep your jaw relaxed. Also, it's attractive to the eye.

———————— FIGURE 7 ————————
THESE CHEEKS ARE UP!

6. Keep the Larynx Low, the Soft Palate Raised

Tightness in the throat and soft palate will choke your sound before it even reaches your mouth. To see what it feels like to really lower your larynx and raise your soft palate, begin a yawn and say "ah" (see figure 9). This "begin-a-yawn" feeling should precede each vocalization. (When the doctor asks you to say "ah" it is so that he can more readily examine your throat.) So in addition to having an opening like a "yawn" in your throat, practice going from an "ah" to an "aw" sound. This automatically lowers and relaxes the larynx. A thin voice can become fuller doing these exercises, a strident voice more pleasing.

──── FIGURE 8 ────
THESE CHEEKS ARE DOWN!

──── FIGURE 9 ────
CROSS SECTION OF THE MOUTH

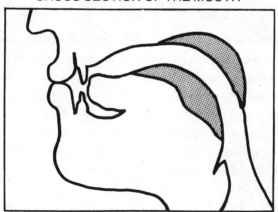

Voice is sound, and sound is made up of vibrating waves that travel through the air. A rich, resonant sound sets off sympathetic vibrations in all the resonating chambers in your vocal apparatus: in your chest, your throat, your mouth and your nose. To feel these in your lips and nose, hum; to feel vibrations in your chest, say "aaah" and pound it gently with the palm of your hand. The sound should break up into "ah-ah-ah-ah."

A truly resonant voice, however, will vibrate through the trunk of your body. It will even resonate off objects in the room; through the wood in your desk, in your chair. This is why Ella Fitzgerald's voice can break glass. It starts vibrations going into the glass which then actually split it into fragments. Or why a masterful Shakespearean actor will feel the stage vibrating beneath his feet.

To maximize the resonant quality of your voice, several things have to be working for you at the same time. *You must be relaxed*, for a tense body does not vibrate easily. *You must linger on the vowels*, and *you must keep your cheek muscles up and throat open* or the sound will be constricted. The resonance of your sound will build over time as you tune your instrument.

Eventually, all these principles will become more automatic and more reflexive. At first, however, you must consciously concentrate on all six principles as you practice. This sounds hard to do, but if you work at it, it becomes more and more habitual.

VOICE EXERCISES

The voice exercises I've developed, some of which I've already touched on in explaining the Six Basic Principles, are intended to help your projection, breathing and resonance. For teaching purposes I must arbitrarily separate these three qualities to show how each one is mastered. But during practice, and in your daily life, projection, breathing and resonance all work together. They are connected. You can't project without proper breathing. Breathing and projection are essential for resonance. Concentrate on one of the qualities more than the others as you practice, then try to combine them as you go along.

The exercises you are about to do here are demanding, and at times you may find your voice getting louder than you're used to hearing. Don't let these sounds distress you, and don't be self-conscious about the volume. This is all for practice. Don't try this at work, on the phone or in daily conversation yet. Modulation will come in time. If you have a speech teacher to practice with, fine. But in lieu of a teacher, use a tape recorder.

You'll be hearing your true sound for the first time.

"I practically got arrested in Central Park for doing my voice exercises," Sonny Jurgensen, the former Redskin football star, exclaimed in my office one day. We'd been working together about two weeks. CBS had asked me to help smooth his transition from the football field to the broadcasting booth. His high-pitched voice was getting in his way. I put him on a steady diet of the Six Principles.

At first Sonny felt uncomfortable doing the exercises. They can be somewhat bigger than life, often startling. But the results are startling too. Three or four weeks after we began work, Sonny confided in me with pride: "I called my wife on the phone and at first she didn't recognize my voice."

Plunge in and see what happens.

These voice exercises are designed to develop projection, breathing and resonance.

These commands should be done exactly as the count-ups, except that instead of saying ONE! TWO! THREE! you'll be saying SHIP! AHOY! HALT! and so on. There is no hard-and-fast rule as to when to breathe on these exercises. You can take a new breath, pull the abdomen in with each word, or take one whole line, or two, on a single breath. In fact, it's best to vary your breathing pattern; try different things. Each sound, however, should be uttered as if it were the most important sound in all the world; when you deliver "ALL ABOARD!" for example, "all" should be delivered with as great a force as "aboard."

Projection Exercise

1. Read through the following phrases.
2. The slash marks are indications of where to breathe, but they are not mandatory.

3. The underlining is suggested for extension of vowels.
4. Turn on your tape recorder. Say the words out loud.
5. Play back. Listen.

Ship!/Ahoy!/ Stand ho!/All aboard!/
Be gone!/Halt!/Who's there?/

A horse! A horse! My kingdom for a horse./
Charge, Chester, charge!/On, Stanley, on./
The sea, the sea, the open sea!/
Sail on, sail on,/sail on and on./
Boomlay, boomlay, boomlay, boom!/

The king is dead;/long live the king./

Wherefore rejoice?/ What conquest brings he
home?/What tributaries follow him to Rome?/

You blocks, you stones,/you worse than
senseless things./

Breathing Exercise

Learning to breathe effectively gives you control over your voice. Instead of "running out of air," fading or gasping, you can support and shape your sound into phrases and sentences of your choice. After you practice the count-ups, ONE! TWO! etc., ONE through FIVE, ONE through TEN, etc., and the "Ship Ahoy" exercise, this kind of exercise is the next step.

1. Read through the passage until you are familiar with it.
2. Use one breath per line.
3. At the end of each line breathe as unobtrusively as possible. To do this, as you say the last word of each line, relax the rib cage quickly for a moment. Use the diaphragm to take a quick breath.
4. Turn on your tape recorder. Say the words, and breathe at the end of each line.
5. Play back. Listen.

I am the very model of a modern Major-General;
I've information vegetable, animal and mineral,
I know the Kings of England, and I quote the fights historical,
From Marathon to Waterloo in order categorical;
I'm very well acquainted too with matters mathematical,
I understand equations, both the simple and quadratical,
About binomial* theorem I'm teeming with a lot of news—
With many cheerful facts about the square of the hypotenuse.†
I'm very good at integral and differential calculus
I know the scientific names of beings animalculous;‡
In short, in matters vegetable, animal and mineral,
I am the very model of the modern Major-General.

—W. S. Gilbert
The Pirates of Penzance

Resonance Exercise

Try to say this passage with the most mellow, most pleasant sounds you
can. Let your ear be your guide. Keep your body relaxed and keep your
throat open.

1. Read through the passage silently until you are familiar with it.
2. Turn on your tape recorder.
3. Read aloud:
    Linger on the vowels indicated by accent marks in the words.
    Linger on the consonants "m," "n" and "ng."
4. Play back the tape. Listen for the musicality of the sound.
5. Repeat steps two through four.

The luńatic, the lóver and the póet
Are of imágination áll compáct:
One sees more dévils than vást héll can hóld.
That is, the mádman. The lóver, all as frántic,
See Hélen's beauty in a brów of Égypt:

---

* binomial (bi – no′ – mi – al)
† hypotenuse (hy – po′ – te – nuse)
‡ animalculous (an – i –mal′ – cu – lus)

The poet's éye, in a fíne frenzy rólling,
Doth glance from héaven to éarth, from eárth to héaven
And as imágination bodies fórth
The fórms of things unknówn, the póet's pén
Turns them to shápes and gives to áiry nóthing
A lócal hábitation and a náme.

—Shakespeare
A Midsummer Night's Dream

Projection, Breathing and Resonance

Shakespeare is great for practicing all three techniques at once.

1. Turn on your tape recorder.
2. Read the passage that follows aloud. The syllables that are underlined should be stressed. "Be gone!" which is underlined twice,
   should be stressed more strongly.
3. Breathe where you see the slash marks: "Wherefore rejoice?"
   (breathe) "What conquest brings he home?" (breathe)
4. Say the words within the brackets on one breath. "Many a time
   and oft," through "yea, to chimney-tops," on one breath. "Your
   infants in your arms," to "pass the streets of Rome," on one
   breath.
5. Then slower over the images that follow.
6. Play back. Listen.
7. Repeat.

Wherefore rejoice?/What conquest brings he home?/
What tributaries follow him to Rome,/
To grace in captive bonds his chariot-wheels?/
You blocks,/you stones,/you worse than senseless things!/
O you hard hearts, you cruel men of Rome,/
Knew you not Pompey?/[Many a time and oft
Have you climb'd up to walls and battlements,
To towers and windows, yea, to chimney-tops,]
[Your infants in your arms, and there have sat
The live-long day with patient expectation
To see great Pompey pass the streets of Rome:]

And when you <u>saw</u> his chariot but appear,
Have you not made an universal <u>shout</u>,
That Tiber <u>trembled</u> underneath her banks
To hear the replication of your sounds
Made in her concave <u>shores</u>?
And do you <u>now</u> put on your best att<u>ire</u>?/
And do you <u>now</u> cull out a <u>holiday</u>?/
And do you <u>now</u> strew flowers in his way
That comes in <u>tri</u>umph over Pompey's <u>blood</u>?/
<u>Be gone</u>!//
<u>Run</u> to your houses,/<u>fall</u> upon your knees,/
<u>Pray</u> to the gods to intermit the <u>plague</u>
That needs must <u>light</u> on this ingratitude./

Shakespeare
Julius Ceasar

Vary your exercises from time to time with selections of your own. Go to your bookshelves and choose passages that appeal to you.

As you develop your communication skills, the desire and the need to be heard will be the most motivating ingredient in achieving an effective sound. Now with the tools of voice production in your hand and with what you are going to learn about articulation and fine-tuning, your message will be even more successfully delivered.

Chapter Seven

SPEAKING CLEARLY

They spake winged words to one another.

—Homer
The Odyssey

YOU HAVE NO RIGHT TO BE BORING

While I was searching around for a title for this book, Jim Snyder, Vice President of News for Post Newsweek TV Stations, suggested: "Lilyan, you ought to call your book 'You Have No Right to Be Boring.'" I didn't take his advice, but I thoroughly agree with the concept.

At a recent stockholders meeting at a brokerage firm, the president glanced apologetically at his audience, cleared his throat, and began: "I will be brief." Grateful smiles crossed the faces of some in the audience. The speaker had a reputation for being boring, not because what he was saying was dull but because he mumbled, swallowed and slurred his words to the point where even a one-minute comment was difficult to take—and nearly impossible to understand.

Yet all of us in the audience were there to get information that was very important to us. Our money, our investments were involved! Why the company did not have a more articulate spokesperson remains a mystery. This kind of thing happens every day. Capable, intelligent experts do not necessarily speak clearly. Some lisp, don't pronounce their "r's" or "l's" or speak with a general sloppiness which keeps the listener from hearing what is essential. Yet these are not major speech impediments. With coaching, they can be corrected. If you speak in public and have such problems, you owe it to yourself and your listeners to take active measures to improve.

Why is poor articulation such a common problem? We in America do not have a tradition of studying and valuing oral expression, as for instance the British do. Most Americans have never had a speech lesson, let alone speech training. Voice and articulation classes are not a priority in our educational system. Only when there is a glaring problem—a stammer, a sibilant "s," or a foreign accent—is attention paid to the student's speech.

In our culture, too, women are often taught that it is immodest to speak forcefully lest they sound domineering or masculine. On the other hand, some men may assume that good enunciation is precious or effeminate. As a result, we are for the most part a nation of well-mannered, educated mumblers!

DEFINITIONS

Before proceeding, let's pin down some definitions. *Enunciation* is the act of pronouncing or articulating words clearly. Good enunciation does not mean that you adopt an overly precise, affected type of speech. Affectation does not engage an audience. Clear enunciation does! A speaker's primary goal should be clarity, and good enunciation is a means to that end.

It is also important to note here that when I speak of the sounds we make when we enunciate I am referring to sound alone, not spelling. For example, long "a" (ā) can be spelled in eight different ways—as in age, aid, gauge, say, break, vein, weigh, and they.

Accents are determined by the way a speaker's native language is carried over into another language. A French person might pronounce "Thank you, Henrietta" as "Zank you, Ahnriette," and a Spanish person might say "Tank joo, Enrijetta" and both would also carry over into English speech the rhythms and melodies characteristic of their languages.

Dialects are varieties of pronunciation, grammar and/or vocabulary within a particular language. They differ from the standard speech pattern of the culture in which they exist. In America, we have many dialects: southern, New England, hillbilly, and so forth. Dialects are also associated with particular cities and states such as New York City, Boston, Oklahoma. "General American" as it is spoken in the Middle West is considered the standard. Another barometer of good American speech is that used by certain actors, broadcasters and political figures. There is no one way to speak English well.

If you have a slight foreign accent or dialect, your speech may well have character, style or pizazz. The Reverend Dr. Martin Luther King, Jr.'s regionalisms actually enhanced the beauty of his voice. President Franklin Delano Roosevelt dropped his "r's" but spoke with a sound that captivated the whole nation. If, however, your speech patterns interfere with your being understood, or fight the spirit and meaning of your words, then they are a handicap and you should try to change them.

Many a misguided speaker has tried to defend such ugly, abrasive vocal habits as "regionalism." If a Bostonian says "cah" (as if father) that's lovely, but if he says "ca" (as in cat), he's producing a harsh, offensive sound. Similarly, if a Pennsylvanian who drops his "ng's" and says "go-een" instead of "going" reacts to criticism by protesting, "I do it because I'm from Pennsylvania and it's part of my heritage," he's just plain wrong. Dropping one's "ng's" is a symptom of sloppy speech, nothing more. Don't use your native habitat as an excuse for laziness.

You don't have to feel that you are rejecting your roots when you exchange your regionalism for clarity. Gilroye A. Griffin, Jr., Vice President, Employee Relations for Bristol-Myers, put it this way: "I'm from Columbia, South Carolina. I didn't get out of the South until I went off to college. I don't feel that speaking the way I speak now is any sort of disenfranchisement of my own natural speech heritage. The way I talk now is an amalgam of the various experiences I've had, which does not mean that I can't converse with friends in South Carolina in ways that are comfortable to them and to me. If I felt a sense of 'conscience pain' every time I spoke to my boss, I wouldn't be working.

"People who are working in the corporate world have made a choice. One of the things I tell the black kids I speak to in the schools is that to succeed in the corporate world they must rid themselves of the jargon or the particular speech patterns that are typical of either a southern heritage or a ghetto heritage—things that might be considered 'cool' on the street but are exactly the opposite in the business world.

"Did you see the movie *Airplane*? It features a parody which is closer to the truth than fiction. There is an emergency on the plane. Two black men try to get help, but they speak in a language foreign to the ears of those around them. An elderly white woman says, 'I can translate for you because I speak jive.' She converses with the men in their lingo, then clarifies it for the other passengers. It's a meaningful joke. There's no point in carrying on a conversation for which your listener needs subtitles."

For a speaker to make an effort to be understood is just plain hospitable. When you entertain in your home, you make sure that the food is palatable, the meal pleasant and attractive in every way. Why not do the same with your speech? Don't your listeners deserve the same courtesy your guests do?

In order to enunciate clearly, you must understand how the articulating mechanism works. The lips, palate, cheek muscles, jaw and tongue coordinate to form each sound. The lips act as gates to let sound out, keep it in, or send it through the nasal passage. The jaw acts like a well-oiled hinge, not too tight and not too loose, to prevent muffling of sound. But it is the tongue, a unique, marvelous muscle, that does the most work. Attached only at the back of the mouth to the hyoid bone near the larynx, it tips, pushes, curls, raises and lowers and so transforms raw sound into speech. The rapidity with which the tongue moves in fluent speech is so great it can be monitored by only the fastest camera.

To perform at its peak, the tongue needs all the space it can get inside the mouth. The tip of the tongue can hit the hard palate, the back of the tongue can press against the soft palate, the tongue can be raised or lowered with agility. To see how much space you can create, widen your lips so that the upper teeth show. At the same time, elevate your cheeks so that the facial muscles are kept from sagging. Now the tip of the tongue has enough room to move with the accuracy of a sewing machine needle embroidering an initial. Note: this is the "cheeks-up, mouth-wide" principle of chapter 6, "Improving Your Voice," where we learned that raised cheeks help to raise the soft palate. When your face is semi-smiling, you not only look more confident, you give your tongue more space in the mouth so it has to work harder. This makes for crisper articulation.

Your speech mechanism operates unconsciously. You started making sounds as a child and you refined them into language without self-consciousness. Now, if you want to correct a particular sound, you need to do so consciously. By practicing the drills in this chapter, you can improve your enunciation dramatically. Anne Bancroft, the actress, had lived with sounds associated with "New York" speech all her life. Then she was cast in the title role of Brecht's *Mother Courage*, a part that demanded that she rid her speech of regionalism. She came to me for help, and we reduced the problem to teaching her how to correctly place her tongue in forming her "t's," "d's" and the "a" sound of "act." Six weeks later, after a good deal of disciplined hard work, all trace of New Yorkese was gone.

Now let's give your tongue a workout, exercising it so that in the future you can depend on its precision and agility to get your message across. You may have to break some comfortable old habits but your efforts will be rewarded. Most people have a healthy, strong and flexible articulating mechanism, but they don't necessarily make use of it. *The tongue is a muscle and it can be trained.*

CONSONANTS

A consonant is a speech sound produced by a partial or complete obstruction of the air stream.

The tongue is required to do a lot of work on the "l," "r" and "s" sounds, and that is why they are the most commonly mispronounced consonants.

FIGURE 10

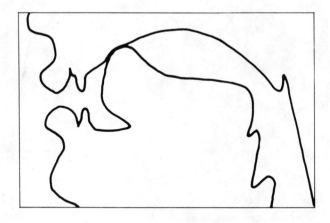

L

To make a clear "l" sound, the tip of the tongue touches a bony ridge which is about one-fourth of an inch behind the upper front teeth. The tongue tip does not touch the front teeth. We will call this area where the tongue tip touches, the "bump," instead of the more technical "alveolar ridge." It is the beginning of the arch that forms the hard palate. As a further check, note that if your tongue is positioned correctly to form the "l" sound, you should be able to see the veins on its underside in the mirror.

You may have no difficulty with "l" when it occurs at the beginning of a word, as in "lamp." But a word like "million" may give you trouble if your tongue tip is not pressing against the alveolar ridge. The "l" at the end of a word requires that you hold your tongue on the ridge as the sound is being produced, as in "bell" or "ball." The "l" before a final consonant such as in "cold," "milk," "film," and "bulb" is also held with the tip of the tongue on the ridge.

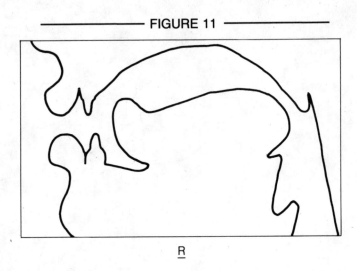

R

To produce a clear "r" sound, raise the tip of the tongue toward the roof of the mouth (but do not touch it). Curl the sides of the tongue to touch the inside of the upper molars.

In some areas of the country, mainly in Boston and other parts of New England, many people do not pronounce the "r" when it occurs at the end of a word, or before a final consonant. Words like "are" and "art" become "ah" and "aht." In this regional pronunciation, the tip of the tongue does not curl up. It stays down touching the lower gum ridge behind the lower front teeth. If you're not from New England or don't

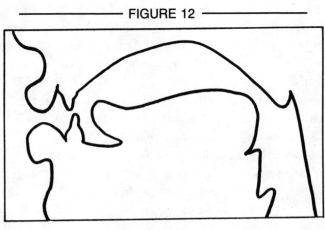

S

want to sound as if you are, curl the tip of the tongue up. Practice: "Are Art and Charlie taking the car?"

For those of you who want to conquer the hardest of all sounds to make properly and pleasantly, read on. The "s" sound is referred to as the "snake sound" by those who teach children because "sss" is supposedly the sound a snake makes. It can be whistley, slushy or lispy— but it can also be easy on the ears if you sound it with care.

Close your front teeth gently as you spread your lips to a slight smile. Allow the tip of the tongue to reach up toward the bump, or the bony alveolar ridge, without touching it. Now say "sss." The air stream will be felt passing over the center of the tongue and out between the closed teeth, the tongue not touching the teeth. If air is sent over the sides of the tongue, the sound will be slushy. This is called a lateral "s." If the tongue touches the upper front teeth, the sound will be wet and "whistley." If the tongue protrudes, producing a "th" sound, you are lisping. A good "s" should sound like steam escaping from a radiator.

Voiced and Unvoiced Sounds

A voiced sound is made when the vocal cords vibrate. An unvoiced sound is made when air passes through the vocal cords and no vibration takes place.

Place your fingertips on your throat. Say "s." You should feel no vibrations. Say "z." You should feel a vibration.

All vowels are voiced. Say "ah." Feel the vibration.

There are *only ten unvoiced consonant* sounds: p, t, k, s, ch, sh, th, f, hw and h. All the rest are voiced. It's important to understand this distinction. You can waste a lot of valuable air on unvoiced consonants if you explode them needlessly. This is what makes for popping "p" sounds on a microphone. The effective speaker balances the voiced and unvoiced sounds, holding some voiced sounds—i.e., the voiced consonants and all vowels—longer than the unvoiced ones. For example:

I went downtown.*

* ___ long
• short

The underlined sounds are sustained. The dotted sounds are spoken lightly and quickly.

Now stay with me; we have more interesting information. Did you know that "s" is pronounced "z" when a plural, possessive or active verb is formed?:

apples (z)
oranges (z)
valves (z)
his (z)
hers (z)
washes (z)
finds (z)

This occurs because the sound that precedes the final "s" in the words above is voiced. For instance, "l" is voiced, "eh" is voiced, etc.

apples (lz)
oranges (ehz)
valves (vz)
his (ihz)
hers (rz)
washes (ehz)
finds (dz)

When the final "s" in a plural or possessive noun is preceded by an unvoiced consonant, the "s" is pronounced "s."

fists (ts)	cat's
breaks (ks)	desk's
baths (ths)	earth's
whiffs (fs)	calf's

Cognates

Two sounds made in exactly the same position in your mouth are called "cognates." One is made without vibration (unvoiced), and one is made with vibration (voiced).

The "s" sound is not vibrated, but the "z" sound is. Just as you did to test for voiced and unvoiced consonants, put your fingertips on your Adam's apple (the throat) and feel the vibration in "z." "S" comes only from the mouth, no vibration takes place.

Here is a list of cognate words.

Unvoiced	Voiced
pin	bin
ten	den
fine	vine
cab	gab
think	that
sip	zip
ship	azure
champ	jam
whether	weather

Every sound vibrates except p, t, f, k, th, s, sh, ch, wh, and h.

VOWELS

A vowel is made by breath passing freely through the larynx and mouth without obstruction. Its sound is usually the most central part of a syllable.

Your voice is most readily identified by the way you sound vowels. They are like a river, carrying the music of your sound in a smooth, flowing stream. It is the vowels that resonate, enveloping the listener in a continuous, liquid current of sound. Revel in them, for they can be sensuously beautiful.

Good singers move from vowel to vowel, enunciating their consonants in between but not staying with them very long (except in the case of the pleasant, liquid consonants "m," "n" and "ng"). An accomplished speaker follows the singer's example and tries to achieve a level of articulation which gives a musical effect. The major difference is that in speech you don't sustain a vowel as long as you do in singing.

The principle of projection as described in chapter 6, "Improving

Your Voice," applies here as well. In articulating vowels, just as in producing your voice, you must have focus and aim. When practicing, aim your vowels and voice to a spot ten or twenty feet away. The sound goes forward, rather than back toward your throat, making it more flowing and pleasant.

Except for "m," "n" and "ng," "l" and "v," consonants are not particularly musical. To see this, compare the "ch" and the "oo" in the word "choose," the "g" in "gone." The "oo" and "aw" sounds are more lyrical than the "ch" and "g" sounds.

Vowels are tremendous assets, yet they can be used poorly. Watch out for:

1. Clipping: Many people clip their vowel sounds and produce a frenetic, jerky, staccato sound.
2. Stridency: Vowels sound strident when your tongue, lips and jaw are tense and unyielding.
3. Nasality: When sounds other than "m," "n" and "ng" are sounded through the nose, undesirable nasality results.

If you say a word with two nasal sounds in it, such as "man" or "nine," the tendency is to make the "a" and the "i" nasal as well as the "m" and "n." Only the "m" and "n" are supposed to be resonated through the nose. The "a" and "i" should be resonated through the mouth. The best way to avoid nasality on vowels is to keep the back of the tongue relaxed and the tip behind the lower front teeth.

THE HARMONY OF ARTICULATION

In chapter 6, I spoke of the general beauty of sound. There is also a *particular* beauty of sound—the melodious tones that emanate from a properly pronounced "m," "n" or "ng," for example, or the exquisite juxtapositioning of sounds that make our language beautiful to hear. By sensitizing your ear to how sounds interact, you'll be able to create moods and sensations that strengthen your message.

Think of spoken language as a feast for the ear and try to sharpen your auditory awareness. Three rhetorical devices are especially useful:

Alliteration occurs when several closely connected words begin with the same sound as in:

"Around the rugged rock the rakish rascal ran."

Alliteration often makes for catchy, memorable turns of phrase such as "the winds of war" or "democracy's dilemma."

Assonance is the repetition of similar vowel sounds within a phrase. Here's an example:

"The squaw wore a big shawl."

Onomatopoeia: Anthony Burgess, a master of language and sound, has written: "There was once a linguistic theory—put out by the German philologist Max Muller, and sometimes called the 'Bow-wow' concept—which stated that words originally all tried to imitate the things they described. If a child calls a dog a 'Bow-wow' he is fulfilling this theory, just as when he calls a railway train a 'Puff-puff' or a 'Choo-choo.'"

Onomatopoeia is the forming of words from sounds resembling those associated with the objects or actions that are being named. The words "buzz," "sizzle," "crackle," "zip," "gargle" are all examples. Yet you needn't confine onomatopoeia to individual words. Any piece of prose or poetry that replicates in its sounds or cadences the thing being described makes use of this device:

He sprang to the stirrup and Joris and he
He galloped, Dirk galloped, we galloped all three.

Spoken aloud, these lines reproduce the sound of a galloping horse. Onomatopoeia is a powerful poetic and rhetorical tool.

Quite a few of the articulation exercises that follow use alliteration, assonance and onomatopoeia. Read them out loud and let yourself enjoy the beauty the words evoke as they slide off your tongue.

PRACTICE MATERIALS

I asked two corporate vice presidents—coincidentally, both were Irish-Americans—to what they attributed their success in communication. One replied, "When I was growing up in the New York City area, my aunt said, 'Richard, if you're ever going to be successful, you're going to have to speak grammatically and without difficulty.' She used to harass me to make sure I didn't adopt the colloquial New York expressions." The other man told me, "I learned good speech from the Jesuit priests in high school." I found it fascinating that their ease and accomplishment as excellent communicators stemmed from an early emphasis on good articulation.

Yet it is never too late to set up a program of practice for yourself. Donna Lanahan, a manager in sales promotion, told me, "Now that I'm convinced that I have something of substance to say, articulating it clearly is important to me. It's not ridiculous to stand in the bathroom and do my voice exercises."

Following are consonant and vowel drills, each of which includes an explanation of the sound and words and sentences to practice out loud. If you can get coaching from an expert, do so. If not, at least find out more about your sound by hearing it yourself, not only with a tape recorder but by actively listening to yourself, and by being attentive to how your tongue moves as you do the drills. The objective is to be clear. Clarity gives your sound power.

Many of my students want quick results from the exercises I give them. But I think of Willie Mays, who said to me: "Well, I'm a rookie at this. It'll take me a season to get these sounds down, but I'll do it."

As you continue to practice articulation, you will find that your ear is becoming far more sensitive to the spoken words around you. The good speakers you hear on television or in the theater will please you more than ever because you'll be able to define what it is that makes their sounds so compelling. As for *your* sound, it is there! These exercises are meant to help you find it and develop it.

CONSONANT DRILL

1. Say the *sound* of the letter. Be aware of the contact. When you say "m," for example, feel your lips touch. On "f" and "v," feel your upper teeth touch your lower lip.
2. Turn on your tape recorder.
3. Say the sentences out loud slowly.
4. Play the tape back. Identify those sounds that are most troublesome.
5. Repeat the exercise, concentrating on the problem sounds.

r

Voiced; sides of the tongue touching inner borders of the upper teeth; tongue tip pointing toward but not touching the hard palate. Breath passes over the tip of the tongue.

Practice material for "r":

| | | | Before Final |
Beginning	Middle	End	Consonant
rice	carrot	car	art
royal	very	ear	girl
raid	grow	fire	cheered
written	tree	air	carve

1. A regal drumroll greeted King Harry's royal procession.
2. Ron merrily ran up the tree, hurrying after his brother.

<u>l</u>

Voiced; tip of tongue lightly touches the bump (the alveolar ridge); mouth opened wide, not long.

Practice material for "l":

Beginning	Middle	End	Before Final Consonant
lass	elect	call	film
lend	truly	isle	milk
light	Alice	pull	cold
low	follow	tale	salt

1. School was puzzling to Elaine and the other little girls.
2. Let's frolic through the lilies of the valley.

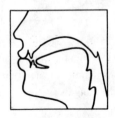

<u>m</u>

Voiced; keep the lips closed; emit the air through the nose.

Practice material for "m":

Beginning	Middle	End
may	drama	am
merry	human	him
mile	memo	some
modern	women	time

1. Mrs. Markham is a woman with no time to dream.
2. Simple, mundane events may make up the human drama.

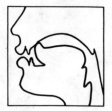

n

Voiced; mouth open slightly, press tip of tongue against the alveolar ridge; emit the air through the nose.

Practice material for "n":

Beginning	*Middle*	*End*
net	any	born
night	honest	fun
name	amount	John
know	snow	pain

1. Ned knows the pain of listening to an out-of-tune cornet.
2. The final snow of Indiana's winter numbed the ungrown corn.

ng

Voiced; raise back of tongue high, hold it to soft palate; emit the air through the nose.

Practice material for "ng":

Middle		*End*	
anger	along	saying
hunger	hang	going
longer	king	being
singer	strong	wanting

1. The king's anger was stronger than anything.
2. Inga sang a song about rolling along.

y

Voiced; front of the tongue is raised high toward hard palate; the tip of the tongue moves quickly behind the lower front teeth as sound is voiced.

Practice material for "y":

Beginning	Middle
usual	lawyer
yes	behavior
your	joyous
Yale	mayonnaise

1. The young lawyer from Yale usually yawned as "oyez" was yelled.
2. The union of youthful humans exhibits royal behavior.

w

Voiced; back of the tongue is raised; as the lips move from a rounded to a wider position, the jaw drops.*

Practice material for "w":

Beginning	Middle
we	away
will	someone

*"W" and "wh" are made with the same tongue position (as are each set of cognates). "W" is voiced, "wh" is unvoiced. See pages 174–75.

Beginning	*Middle*
wave	between
weary	pueblo

1. Willie would wave as he swiftly went away down the highway.
2. My wife Gwendolyn has a pet penguin named Wally.

wh

Unvoiced; force breath out through round lips; release air toward the position of the sound that follows. It should sound like "wh."*

Practice material for "wh":

Beginning	*Middle*
whale	anywhere
wheat	bobwhite
when	overwhelm
why	somewhere

1. Whitey's voice was nowhere near a whisper; it whined.
2. The bewhiskered man in the wheelchair whittled whimsical figurines on the wharf.

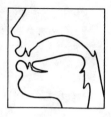

h

Unvoiced; throat open; force breath out into the position for the following vowel.

Practice material for "h":

Beginning	Middle
hair	behave
head	cowhide
high	Mohammed
who	Ohio

1. A hundred hippos behaved as if they were happy.
2. The best mohair and cowhide come from Ohioans who have the know-how.

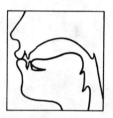

p

Unvoiced; press the lips together, stopping the sound, then explode it.

Practice material for "p":

Beginning	Middle	End
pack	depth	escape
pause	explain	sleep
pair	except	stop
penny	spread	type

1. Paul packed a couple of pairs of pants.
2. Penny paused to peer at the sleeping panthers.

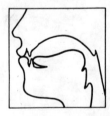

b

Voiced; press the lips together, then explode the sound through the closed lips.

Practice material for "b":

Beginning	Middle	End
bad	libel	cube
ball	prohibit	superb
bet	rebel	transcribe
book	debate	ad lib

1. Don't libel the rebel for the bad ad-lib bet.
2. The book transcribes superb debates.

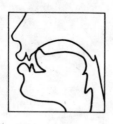

t

Unvoiced; tip of tongue presses alveolar ridge; quickly pull tip away as breath is expelled.

Practice material for "t":

Beginning	Middle	End
ten	fatal	at
too	mighty	foot
tunnel	Manhattan	right
town	poetic	start

1. The short tutu and the pointed left foot made the ballerina seem prettier.
2. Lester stood mightily and strong, but, a mortal, he fell to the fatal thrust.

d

Voiced; tip of tongue presses alveolar ridge; quickly pull tongue away as breath is expelled.

Practice material for "d":

Beginning	Middle	End
day	lady	bird
dime	shadow	good
do	laundry	head
dozen	fiddler	read

1. The doctor didn't diagnose my steady nasal drip.
2. Dinah dines on bird food and drinks only water.

<u>k</u>

Unvoiced; back of tongue touches soft palate, quickly releases, letting air escape in an explosive sound.

Practice material for "k":

Beginning	Middle	End
candy	lucky	book
code	Michael	like
cup	pocket	pick
key	frequent	thank

1. Michael frequently bakes chocolate cookies.
2. The workers took a break from cleaning the chicken coop.

<u>g</u>

Voiced; back of tongue touches soft palate; quickly release.

Practice material for "g":

Beginning	Middle	End
give	bigot	big
good	tiger	league
goal	Chicago	vague
guess	angry	fog

1. The Tigers were given the game by Chicago; the good guys always win in the big league.
2. Gilbert agreed with Olga that the ugly ragpicker was a great beggar.

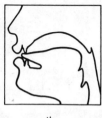

th

Unvoiced; blow breath out between tongue tip and upper teeth.

Practice material for "th" (unvoiced):

Beginning	Middle	End
thank	author	bath
thigh	Matthew	forth
thought	method	oath
third	pithy	teeth

1. I thought I'd read through Matthew and Luther before taking the oath.
2. My mythical fencing method is three fourths parry, one third thrust.

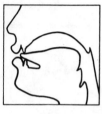

th

Voiced; vibrate breath between tongue tip and upper teeth.

Practice material for "th" (voiced):

Beginning	*Middle*	*End*
that	either	bathe
then	rather	breathe
these	rhythm	loathe
this	southern	smooth

1. They are bathed, then clothed, and lead a blithe existence.
2. Neither my father nor my mother could fathom such a loathsome heathen.

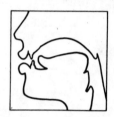

s

Unvoiced; teeth close together, tongue flat, tip pointing toward alveolar ridge or "the bump"; sides of tongue are inside upper molars; direct air stream to the alveolar ridge.

Practice material for "s":

Beginning	*Middle*	*End*
sad	acid	less
see	gossip	pass
say	person	race
soon	basic	nice

1. The straight-laced ladies gossip incessantly.
2. The speedy horse set the pace for the race.

z

Voiced; teeth close together, tongue tip pointing toward "the bump"; sides of tongue are inside upper molars; direct air stream to the alveolar ridge.

Practice material for "z":

Beginning	Middle	End
zest	easy	cause
zone	lazy	is
zero	pleasant	homes
zip	refusal	was

1. Jazz isn't what it was in the days of Dizzy and Fitzgerald.
2. The homes in the zone near the zoo are pleasant, but lack zip.

sh

Unvoiced; tip of tongue raised toward back of alveolar ridge but not touching, sides of tongue are inside upper molars; air directed toward tip of tongue.

Practice material for "sh":

Beginning	Middle	End
shame	bashful	fresh
share	partial	rush
shock	social	wash
sure	session	push

1. She shrugged her shoulders with a bashful expression.
2. The Russian's depression was over after one session with the shrewd shrink.

zh

Voiced; tip of tongue raised toward back of alveolar ridge but not touching, sides of tongue are inside upper molars; air directed toward tip of tongue.

Practice material for "zh":

Middle	*End*
amnesia	barrage
confusion	prestige
occasion	garage
vision	rouge

1. His amnesia caused him great confusion and made every vision seem like a mirage.
2. The businessman's entourage gave him pleasure and prestige.

ch

Unvoiced; blend "t" and "sh" so that they lose their individual identity; tip of the tongue on the alveolar ridge or slightly behind it. The lips are protruded and the front teeth are closed or almost closed; breath passes over tip of tongue.

Practice material for "ch":

Beginning	*Middle*	*End*
chair	hatchet	such
chat	preachy	watch

Beginning	Middle	End
cheer	righteous	each
choose	kitchen	match

1. Rachel Fitch was so rich she didn't know which room was her kitchen.
2. This charmless teacher of our children is preachy and self-righteous.

j

Voiced; blend "d" and "zh" so that they lose their individual identity; tip of tongue on alveolar ridge or slightly behind it. The lips are protruded and the front teeth are closed or almost closed. Breath passes over tip of tongue.

Practice material for "j":

Beginning	Middle	End
jail	engine	age
juice	major	bridge
giant	rigid	judge
joke	imagine	merge

1. The alleged crook obliged the journalist by giving him his age.
2. There is no logic in the legend of John Henry and the engine.

VOWEL DRILL

1. Turn on your tape recorder.
2. Say the sound of the vowel. Be aware of the contact when you say "ee" (deep) for example, feel the front part of your tongue arch toward the hard palate. On "ah" (father) feel your larynx lower and the back part of the tongue arch slightly.
3. Say the sentences out loud slowly.

4. Go through the entire drill.
5. Play the tape back. Listen for the sounds of the vowels. Identify the troublesome ones.
6. Repeat the exercise, concentrating on correcting mispronunciations.

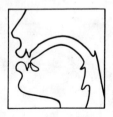

ee

Arch the front of the tongue toward the hard palate; lips are drawn back into a slight smile.

Practice material for "ee":

Beginning	*Middle*	*End*
each	beef	free
eat	dream	he
eel	recent	ski
evening	speak	glee

1. She sees a speech teacher named Steve.
2. The ABC, CBS and NBC News reach millions of people.

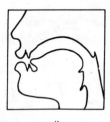

ih

Arch the front of the tongue (a bit lower than for "ee") toward the hard palate; lips are slightly spread.

Practice material for "ih":

Beginning	*Middle*
ill	crib

Beginning	*Middle*
interest	quick
if	sliver
itch	this

1. Jim was sick in the winter and still sniffles.
2. Linda has an avid interest in Israel.

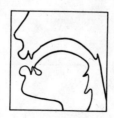

ay

Front of the tongue is arched moderately high toward the hard palate as in "eh," then glides upward toward "ih" position; lips slightly spread.

Practice material for "ay":

Beginning	*Middle*	*End*
ache	grave	hay
aim	phrase	lay
eight	faith	display
age	persuade	pray

1. David's craze for paper airplanes will fade.
2. The trade unions have failed to persuade the newspapers.

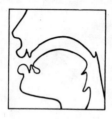

eh

Arch the front of the tongue in the direction of the hard palate, slightly lower than for "ih"; lips slightly spread.

Practice material for "eh":

Beginning	*Middle*
editor	breath
elm	pest
edge	·chef
egg	pleasure

1. Ted checked the validity of the inspector's evidence.
2. Emily is an expert at checkers.

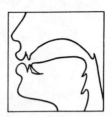

a

Front of the tongue low; tongue practically flat; lips slightly spread.

Practice material for "a":

Beginning	*Middle*
after	drag
add	last
am	rascal
avid	grasp

1. Alice dragged a black bag with her from Hackensack to Alabama.
2. As Andrew grasped Jack's hand, he expressed his gratitude.

uh

Middle of the tongue low; lips neutral.

Practice material for "uh":

Beginning	Middle
up	glove
ugly	luck
until	scrub
us	rough

1. Judd had no rebuttal to the judge's utterance.
2. I trust Lucky has enough fudge to last until Sunday.

ah

Back of tongue low; tongue almost flat, though slightly raised in the back toward hard palate; lips unrounded.

Practice material for "ah":

Beginning	Middle	End
art	father	pa
odd	starve	spa
on	squat	bourgeois
arm	yard	blah

1. It was obvious the slob couldn't carve the turkey.
2. It got too hot for Ma and Pa to stop at the Slavic spa.

aw

Back of the tongue somewhat low; lips slightly rounded.

Practice material for "aw":

Beginning	Middle	End
awe	applause	claw
author	caution	draw
awful	halt	jaw
ought	pauper	saw

1. I bought some awful cole slaw at the store.
2. He stood in awe as the audience applauded and yelled, "Author!"

oh

Back of the tongue higher than "aw"; lips slightly rounded.

Practice material for "oh":

Beginning	Middle	End
oak	afloat	blow
ode	probe	snow
Ohio	clover	glow
own	Rome	portfolio

1. Joseph spoke of the cold snow in Idaho.
2. Don't go home to Minnesota without your portfolio.

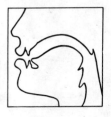

u

Tongue fairly high toward soft palate; lips slightly protruded.

Practice material for "u":

        Middle

butcher	good
crook	full
pussycat	soot
sugar	would

1. Couldn't you be more demure and not put your foot in your mouth?
2. Butchers should be able to fully appreciate good cooking.

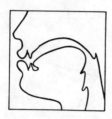

oo

Back of the tongue is curved very high toward soft palate; lips are rounded.

Practice material for "oo":

Beginning	*Middle*	*End*
Oona	booth	crew
ooze	groove	true
oodles	goof	through
oops	rouge	woo

1. Sue blew a groovy blues through the trumpet.
2. Oona had no clue to the true meaning of Proust.

yoo

Similar to "oo," but a more relaxed tongue forms a groove; back of tongue curved high toward hard palate; lips shift from a smile to roundness.

Practice material for "yoo":

Beginning	Middle	End
used	bugle	askew
Eugene	excuse	few
usual	duty	cue
youth	pupil	you

1. Beulah's kitten mewed in a cute, musical way.
2. You can get much amusement from the annual Ukrainian festival.

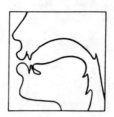

OW

Back of the tongue is low for "ah" sound, then glides upward to "oo" sound; lips move from natural to rounded position.

Practice material for "ow":

Beginning	Middle	End
ounce	clown	allow
ouch	crowd	brow
our	house	plow
out	mouth	thou

1. The clown was drowsy, so he lounged about.
2. Howard allowed the brown cow to plow.

I

Front of tongue is low, as in "a," then glides toward "ih" sound; lips are wide.

Practice material for "i":

Beginning	Middle	End
eyes	behind	fly
Idaho	quite	sky
I'm	child	shy
island	oblige	spy

1. Finally, Mike had time to fly to Iowa.
2. It is unwise to let your child ice skate Friday night.

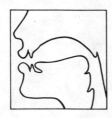

oi

Back of tongue is arched half-high as in "aw," then glides upward and forward to "ee"; lips start somewhat rounded, then widen.

Practice material for "oi":

Beginning	Middle	End
oil	choice	ahoy
oyster	poison	boy
	loyal	coy
	voyage	destroy

1. The loyal voyagers joined the convoy to Troy.
2. Boyd poisoned the oysters with soy sauce.

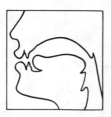

uhr

Middle of tongue tip raised toward middle of hard palate; lips neutral.

Practice material for "uhr":

Beginning	Middle	End
earth	heard	fur
Irving	Persia	blur
herb	squirrel	stir
urge	New Jersey	slur

1. Irma, our furry Persian cat, curled up and purred.
2. Irwin averred that he had earned $30,000 from diverse sources.

er

Middle of tongue lower than "uhr"; lips neutral.

Practice material for "er":

Middle	End
observation	bother
prosperous	inner
percent	lawyer
wonderful	October

1. My father was a wonderful lawyer.
2. The pitcher whizzed the ball to the catcher as the batter staggered.

Pronunciation

Who has never mispronounced a word? I was saying con-tro-vér-si-al until about a year ago, certain I was correct. One day I looked it up and found that the preferred (and in some dictionaries, the *only*) pronunciation is con-tro-vér-shal.

See how you fare on the list that follows.

Words Commonly Mispronounced

Correct Spelling	Wrong Pronunciation	Right Pronunciation
ACROSS	AKRAWST	AKRÁWS
ACTS	AKS	ÁKTS
ACTUALLY	AC SHUH LEE	ÁK CHOO UH LEE (4 syll)
ANTI-CLIMACTIC	ANTI-CLIMATIC	AN TI-CLI MÁK TIK
ANY	INY	ÉHNY
ASKED	AKS	ÁSKT
BECAUSE	BECUZ or BECAWS	BECÁWZ
CATCH	KECH	KÁCH
COMPANY	COMPNY	CÚM PA NEE (3 syll)
CURRENT	CURNT	CÚR RENT (2 syll)
DISTRICT	DISTRIK	DÍSTRIKT
DROWNING	DROWNDING	DRÓWNING
ETCETERA	EK SET ER UH	ET SÉT ER UH
FACTS	FAKS	FÁKTS
FAMILIAR	FMILYUH	FA MÍ LYUR
FEBRUARY	FEB YU AY REE	FÉB ROO AY REE
FIFTH	FITH or FIF	FÍFTH
FOLIAGE	FOLUJ	FÓ LI UHJ (3 syll)
FRIENDLY	FRENLY	FRÉND LEE (2 syll)
GENUINE	JEN YU WINE	JÉN YU IN
GOVERNMENT	GUVUMINT	GÚ VERN MENT
HEIGHT	HITH	HÍT
HORROR	HAWR	HÁWR OR (2 syll)
HUNDRED	HUN DERT	HÚN DRED
INTERNATIONAL	INNERNASHUNAL	IN TER NÁ SHU NAL
INTRODUCE	INNERDOOS	IN TRO DYÓOS
LITERATURE	LIDERCHUR	LÍ TER A CHUR (4 syll)
MAYOR	MARE	MÁ YOR (2 syll)
MIDST	MIST	MÍDST
MIRROR	MIRR_____(1 syll)	MÍRR OR (2 syll)
NEXT	NEX	NÉXT (sound the "T")
NUCLEAR	NOOKYOULUHR	NÓO KLEE UHR
PARTICULAR	PUTICULA	PER TÍK YOU LUHR

Correct Spelling	*Wrong Pronunciation*	*Right Pronunciation*
PICTURE	PI CHUR	PÍK CHUR
PRESCRIPTION	PER SKRIP SHUN	PRI SKRÍP SHUN
PROBABLY	PRAH BLEE	PRÁH BUH BLEE (3 syll)
RECOGNIZED	REKUNIZZED	RÉ KUG NIZD
RECOMMENDS	RECMENDZ	RE KU MÉNDZ (3 syll)
SANDWICH	SANWICH	SÁND WICH
SAW	SAWR	SÁW
STOLE	STOLD	STÓLE
STRUCTURE	SHRUK CHUR	STRÚK CHURE
TERRORISTS	TERR IS	TÉ RO RISTS (3 syll)
VULNERABILITY	VUL NER BIL I TY	VÚL NER A BÍ LI TY (6 syll)
WASHINGTON	WARSHINGTON	WÁW SHING TON

Chapter Eight

FINE-TUNING

I will aggravate my voice so that I will roar you as gently as any sucking dove; I will roar you as t'were any nightingale.

—Shakespeare
A Midsummer Night's Dream

How you express yourself is ultimately as important as the particular words you use. "Now what did you mean by that?" you ask, and proceed to analyze every inflection, every intonation used by the person in question in order to arrive at an answer. Picture this:

John Scott comes home from work five hours late. He opens the door and is greeted by an icy stare from his wife, Joan.

What Is Said	*What It Sounds Like*
JOHN: What's wrong, dear?	(Are you going to nag at me again?)
JOAN: Nothing's wrong.	(I could kill you, you jerk.)
JOHN: Well, you look upset.	(Don't lie to me.)
JOAN: I'm not upset.	(You don't deserve an answer.)

JOHN: Terrific (with cutting sar-
        casm).

The civilities continue for a while. Finally an argument erupts. Later
that night a reconciliation is reached. Epilogue: The next morning, as
Mrs. Scott goes off to work she gives her husband a peck on the cheek
and says what she really wanted to say the night before: "You know I
could kill you for being such a jerk." Only now she means: "But I love
you so much I won't."

The way you say what you say expresses a whole complex of things
above and beyond the literal meaning, such as how you feel about a
situation, about a person or people you are talking to, even how you
feel about yourself. Mrs. Scott's inflections on that unhappy evening
were the inflections of someone trying to project anger yet dignity and
pride. Another person could use the exact same words to convey compassion or even submission.

The great Polish actress Helena Modjeska held English-speaking audiences spellbound even though she only recited the Polish alphabet
over and over again. The gibberish meant something because Modjeska
created a scenario and communicated it with inflection, rhythm and all
manner of vocal diversity. One moment her audience was crying, the
next it was laughing. She moved them by the depth and emotional truth
of the drama she created with sound alone.

If you are to become a truly effective communicator, it's not enough
for your voice to be strong and clear: it must also be expressive. It must
have *variety*, *control* and *flexibility*.

Many of the exercises that follow call for you to exaggerate your sounds.
Do so, even if it feels strange at first. Don't be self-conscious. To strengthen
and stretch your voice, you have to push beyond what is normally required of you. Do this kind of practice in private and don't try to carry
the lessons over into everyday speech immediately. It takes time and
patience to fine-tune the vocal instrument. Once you have, you won't
need to consciously "use" your new skills, because they will be second
nature.

VARIETY

Vocal variety depends on five basic factors: range, pitch, rate, force and quality. Let's take a look at each one in turn.

RANGE

Your range is the span of sound over which your voice plays from its lowest to its highest tone. Most people have a potential range of about two octaves. (An octave is an interval of eight degrees in a musical scale.) Effective communicators use at least one octave regularly.

People in the corporate world often shy away from extending their range. They think a tight-lipped monotone conveys coolness, equanimity and control. They end up sounding dull! Don't fall into this trap. Let your voice use its musical range.

Everyone has his or her particular range. This is why some singers are naturally basses, others tenors and still others sopranos. It is important to explore your entire range even though in reality you will not be speaking on all its notes. Generally we speak on an average of thirteen notes. But practicing your fuller range will give body and color to the range you routinely use.

We should do most of our speaking in our middle range. To find it, do the following exercise.

1. Stand up with your back against a wall, breathe in deeply and then, on an exhale, slowly count to ten while trying to get the back of your neck to touch the wall. Your pitch will naturally lower during the count.
2. By the time you've reached five or six, you're at your median tone. That's where most of your speaking should take place.

Of course the tones should be varied and warm, not monotonous. Think of the late Orson Welles or Barbara Jordan, whose tones caress the ear. You may have lesser vocal endowment, but you can make the most of what you have.

PITCH

Pitch is the musical note you sound on each syllable you make. It should vary automatically as you speak.

Changes in pitch tell us whether a speaker is doubtful or certain, wavering or self-assured, ironical or sincere, asking a question or giving an answer. The more you experiment with changing your pitch, the more expressive your voice will be. (An exercise is suggested on page 218.) *Inflection* is one of the most expressive uses of pitch. It is the changing of pitch within a syllable or word. There are three kinds of inflections: upward, downward and double (up, down and up or down, up and down). *Downward inflections* at the end of a statement, or on a key word, convey certainty and authority to an audience. When you inflect downward you are giving information or advice, not asking for it. Try saying "I think my experience qualifies me for the job" with a downward inflection. *Upward inflections* suggest precisely the opposite: doubt, hesitance, uncertainty, surprise. You should try to avoid using them excessively. If you say "I think my experience qualifies me for the job" with an upward inflection, it conveys an entirely different meaning. Upward inflections are used to ask questions and express doubt. *Double inflections* are used to convey more oblique, complex meanings such as irony, sarcasm, astonishment. Say "oh," making your voice begin up, then go down and then back up like a U shape.

You will have used it in an inquiring way. Now say "oh!" making your voice begin down, then go up and then back down in an inverted U shape.

You will have delivered "oh" with the cutting irony of a sarcastic "No kidding!" We often use double inflections when we talk to children and animals, the few times in life when most people loosen up and make use of their voices' variety.

RATE

Besides variety of pitch there is variety of rate. Rates of speech vary from the breakneck yammer of an auctioneer to the slow drawl of a Deep South tale-spinner. We associate slow, ponderous speaking with slow, ponderous thinking, while fast speech suggests a hyped-up personality. Between these extremes lie several golden means. If your rate of speech is so slow or so fast that it grates on your listener's nerves, you can and should change tempo. (See chapter 6, "Improving Your Voice," for evaluating your particular rate and deciding what to do about it.)

Deliberately varying your tempo can help expressiveness. Wonder, reflectiveness, doubt, confusion, awe and sadness are often reflected in a slower, more measured form of speech. Exuberance, enthusiasm, anxiety, anger, excitement tend to be delivered with more speed. If you experiment with different pacings and rhythms, you'll be able to express yourself with greater impact—provided, of course, that you really mean what you say and aren't putting on an act.

Here are two examples of how an intelligent sense of tempo can be used to produce interesting effects. Read the following passage slowly, lingering on the vowels. Try to use one breath on each sentence to maintain flow, and use warm resonant tones to match the meaning.

My Friends: No one not in my situation can appreciate my feeling of sadness at this parting. To this place, and the kindness of these people, I owe everything. Here I have lived a quarter of a century, and have passed from a young to an old man. Here my children have been born, and one is buried. I now leave, not knowing when or whether ever I may return, with a task before me greater than that which rested upon Washington. Without the assistance of that Divine Being who ever attended him, I cannot succeed. With that assistance, I cannot fail. Trusting in Him who can go with me, and remain with you, and be everywhere for good, let us confidently hope that all will yet be well. To His care commending you, as I hope in your prayers you will commend me, I bid you an affectionate farewell.

—Abraham Lincoln
"Farewell to Springfield"

In sharp contrast, the pace of the following selection from Shake-speare's *As You Like It* invites a sprightly, quick and somewhat staccato delivery. The phrases in parentheses should be said rapidly and lightly on one breath. Rosalind, madly in love with Orlando, teases him with a description of the lovelorn as one who has:

> A lean cheek (which you have not); a blue eye and sunken (which you have not); an unquestionable spirit (which you have not); a beard neglected (which you have not) (but I pardon you for that, for simply your having a beard is a younger brother's revenue). (Then your hose should be ungartered, your bonnet unbanded, your sleeve unbuttoned, your shoe untied and everything about you demonstrating a careless desolation.) But you are no such man. (You are rather point-device in your accoutrements, as loving yourself than seeming the lover of any other.)

> —Shakespeare
> *As You Like It*

There is another aspect of rate which involves more than speed (going fast or slow). It is syncopation, a difficult concept to describe. Synco-pation involves a shifting of stresses, so that a syllable we expected to be weak becomes strong. It's the *off* beat. Jazz and blues are syncopated. Try to recall Ella Fitzgerald's phrasing of:

> "I'm just a lonesome / babe in the woods /
> Oh lady / be good to me."*

You get a sense of color and content more from the manner in which the song is sung than from the words themselves. In speaking, too, syncopated rhythm surprises the listener's ear, changes his expectations and jolts him into awareness. And it averts monotony. The Reverend Jesse Jackson is a master of syncopation. His Democratic National Con-vention speech was full of such syncopated phrases as "Bury the weapons and don't burn the people. Dream!" (and a voice in the crowd echoed,

*_____ means slow
xxx means fast

"Dream!"). By working at syncopated pieces in the song exercise described in the next section, you can greatly increase your ability to speak with rhythmic variety and flexibility.

FORCE

The novice tends to overuse force to convey emphasis. Singling out a particular word for a forceful delivery does little more than call attention to it. Moreover, if you try to express emotions by stepping up your vocal force, you may end up shouting, conveying only a lack of control. Inflecting the word or pausing before or after it is far more effective.

A controlled build-up of force can, however, *express great conviction and draw out the audience.* Moderate contrasts of soft and loud, crescendos or diminuendos can also be very effective as long as they don't sound mechanical. Let the meaning guide you.

QUALITY

The most personal aspect of the voice is *quality*, or timbre. Just as the timbres of flute, oboe, trumpet, violin and organ give each instrument its own extraordinary life and sound, so the quality of every human voice stamps it as unique. Take a look at the film greats of the '30s and '40s. Bette Davis's husky purr, Mary Astor's mellifluous whinny, Cary Grant's smooth-as-Scotch, slightly British sound and Bogey's tough-guy, gravelly growl are etched in our memories as clearly as their faces.

Personality lives in one's voice as vividly as it lives in one's eyes, smile or pout. Confidence, authority and vigor stamp the voice with a different quality than do cynicism, suspicion and hostility. A warm and tender person has a vocal quality entirely different from that of a pompous person.

Temporary moods also leave their mark on the voice. A hollow, slack sound comes from someone who is dejected and depressed, while vibrant, bouncy tones are the sign of a person in an elevated, positive mood. You should think seriously about what sort of quality, and through it what aspect of yourself, you want to project. The self has many aspects and it's best to put forward the more positive ones: warmth, authority and conviction. Much of the work in the next selection is aimed at discovering and developing your own best qualities.

The relaxation exercises suggested in chapter 6, "Improving Your Voice," are important prerequisites for this work. If your muscles are tense, they'll clamp down and resist resonating, and beautiful overtones will be squeezed or destroyed.

How to Develop Variety

According to violinist Yehudi Menuhin, a newborn "carries a sharp memory of the warmth, comfort and safety he knew in the aquatic womb. He also remembers sounds, for even there he responds to voices, to rhythms, and to music. But above all, he remembers the mother's heartbeat. This rhythm unites the developing fetus to this mother, remaining long after he emerges into the light of day. It is impressed upon us like our own identity. We feel its loss and must replace it with other sounds, especially that of our own voice, whose sounds and rhythm are communication."

Re-embark upon that primal quest for sound. A search undertaken in a child's spirit of wonderment and adventure is the surest path to stretching your voice and discovering new possibilities for variety within it. Take no sound for granted, but rather *listen for sounds that spur your imagination*. Absorb them. Reproduce them.

FOUR GREAT VOICES

To make yourself more sensitive to sound, open your ears to all sorts of sounds: waves breaking on a beach, a dog howling, a thunderstorm.

Listen to music and sing along in as many different styles as possible: from Judy Garland to Roberta Flack, from Luciano Pavarotti to Al Jarreau. Try producing the orchestral sounds of percussion, string and wind instruments, and capture the special quality of each.

If possible, study a musical instrument that you particularly like. It will help sensitize your ear, and an acute sense of hearing is as important to the speaker as a fine sense of color is to a painter. If all you can do is fool around with partially filled water glasses, do so by all means.

(Benjamin Franklin made a glass harmonica this way, and Mozart composed for it!)

Listen! Listen to voices you like. The quality of tone, the phrasing, and the tempos stay with you long after you've listened. Eventually they begin to infuse themselves into your speech by osmosis. Here are my choices of four great voices.

Paul Robeson, the singer/actor, had the greatest sound I have ever heard. The aliveness, vibrance, trueness and honesty of tone and the clarity of his articulation were magnificent. When I was a child, I was fortunate to have had aunts who took me to hear Paul Robeson sing. And then as a teenager I ushered at his performances of *Othello*. His sound was so intimately connected to what he was saying and singing. To this day when I play his records, his sound soothes, stirs and satisfies. It's personal, one-on-one, as if he's talking to me. Even with the great range and power he has, I still feel personally approached. It's moving.

Yves Montand, the French singer/actor, has the sexiest sound I have ever heard. Thank goodness for tapes and Walkmans and Yves Montand. They get me through plane travel with my sanity preserved. Yves Montand's sound is as provocative and thrilling today as it was thirty years ago. His use of consonants (particularly the roll of his French "r" sound) sends thrills up my spine. His humor, "joie de vivre" and love for women all come through in his vocalization. It's sheer pleasure on a plane or anywhere.

Ruby Dee, the actress: I remember having my back to the television set and hearing a woman's voice. She was speaking on what seemed like a dull subject—some social issue of no great import to me. But her sound attracted me, and I began to pay attention. I got involved and could hardly wait till the program was over to find out who was talking. There is a musical quality, a perky, insinuating "listen to me" quality in her voice, a pleasantness and authority that command and invite, a warm humanness about her sound.

Zoe Caldwell, the actress: Watching a "Donahue" show several years ago, four women were on a panel, one of whom did not "stop traffic" with her looks. But when she spoke, suddenly her whole being changed for me. An intelligent, personal and important sounding tone reached out and drew me to this woman. She became exceedingly attractive. She sounded cultured, yet real, studied, yet warm, and her sound helped you understand what she was saying. You wanted to hear more.

All of these people worked at and developed their sounds. For instance, Paul Robeson's father encouraged him to recite poetry and speeches, everything from William Lloyd Garrison to Keats and Shelley, from Cicero to Disraeli. His son, Paul Robeson, Jr., told me that he won the debating prizes each of the four years he attended Rutgers University.

In time you, too, can find and develop your sound. And because you've worked to achieve it, it will stay with you.

THE FRANK SINATRA EXERCISE

This exercise expands all aspects of vocal variety at once: range, pitch, rate, force and quality.

I call it "The Frank Sinatra Exercise" because he is a master at phrasing lyrics. The way he lingers on vowels and subtly emphasizes a word, the way he shifts a tone and rushes or delays a beat, etches itself in our ears. Nat King Cole, Ella Fitzgerald and Peggy Lee are artists in their own right as well. I suggest you start with one of these four.

Step 1: Men, choose a Nat King Cole or Frank Sinatra record. Women, select one by Ella Fitzgerald or Peggy Lee. Listen to the record several times, then select one song and write out the words. Now sing along with the recording, trying to imitate every nuance of pitch, rhythm and degree of force as exactly as possible. Repeat until you do it well. At least six or seven times.

Step 2: Gradually wean yourself away from the record until you can sing the song a cappella (without accompaniment). It can take as little as a week, or as long as a month, to repeat the record's nuances and energy. This is training for the ear. So don't give up if at first you sing less forcefully or expressively than you want, and do return to the record for support if necessary. If you are patient with yourself, your voice will eventually achieve an undreamed-of richness. After you feel you've mastered this step, tape yourself and listen!

Step 3: Speak the song using the same words, pitches, rhythms, pauses, inflections and dynamics as you did in singing. The difference is you do not sustain the sound. It's the sound of speech—shorter, more abrupt.

Step 4: Now, preserving the same nuances, change the words of the song. Make them up. Use whatever comes to mind. Vary them each time you speak the song. For example, if you've been singing "My Funny Valentine" with these emphases:

MY FUNNY VALENTINE
SWEET COMIC VALENTINE
YOU MAKE ME SMILE WITH MY HEART
YOUR LOOKS ARE LAUGHABLE
UNPHOTOGRAPHABLE
YET YOU'RE MY FAV-RITE WORK OF ART

you may substitute your own silly lyric, such as:

I LIKE THE WEATHER TODAY
SUN SHINING CLEAR AND BRIGHT
LET'S TAKE A WALK IN THE PARK.
ARE YOU ALL READY TO GO?
I DON'T NEED MY OLD HAT.
LET'S ALL GO STROLLING THROUGH THE PARK.

Though the words and thoughts are simple in themselves, it can be very difficult to retain the melody and rhythm of a song, to imitate the dynamics and quality of the singer's voice, and think up other words at the same time. Yet it's important to practice new words each time you go through the fourth step. What you're doing is stretching your sound to new dimensions, and learning how to transfer melodies and tonal qualities from your ear to your mouth.

After you've worked on a few songs by the artists suggested above, you can move on to more difficult projects: spoken songs such as Robert Preston doing "Trouble" from *The Music Man*, or Rex Harrison doing "Why Can't a Woman Be More Like a Man?" from *My Fair Lady*. You can even tackle spoken text records such as Pamela Brown doing *Lady Chatterley's Lover*, Ruth Draper doing "The Italian Lesson," Richard Burton doing Dylan Thomas's poetry. Select what you find intriguing and vocally challenging.

At the Strasberg Studio, where I originally developed this exercise, a young actor named Henry Holden performed it unforgettably. He walked on crutches because his legs had been paralyzed by polio. For this exercise, he decided to prepare a song whose tonal acrobatics, rocking rhythms and syncopated cadences seemed miles from his personal range. Not only did he master the intricacies of the song, his "sticks" became an extension of himself. He swung them one at a time, above his head and across his body to the rhythm of the song. This helped him pour into his sound all the physical expressiveness his disability prevented him from channeling through his body. It was electrifying.

You will be amazed by what your voice can do. For some, the amazement is at first mingled with uneasiness, so startled are they by the strange sounds emanating from their throats. This is a natural reaction. Remember, as Samuel Taylor Coleridge wrote, "No sound is dissonant which speaks of life." If you shrink away from every unusual sound you utter, you limit your capacity to learn. Like the rancher's wife who serves steak and baked potatoes 365 days of the year but pales at the sight of beef bourguignon, you will thwart your potential development. So practice new sounds and don't be afraid of them.

The vocal variety and control you can learn with the Frank Sinatra exercise can help you enormously as a communicator. When it comes right down to it, most people who are skeptical about the exercise are just self-conscious about their singing. How many children are told to mouth the words of a song because their teacher thinks they are singing off-key? Such unfortunate experiences hamper many adults. After doing the song exercise, one financial analyst said, with tears of gratitude, "I can't tell you what a revelation this has been. As a child, I was told I was tone deaf and couldn't hum a tune." Getting past his early conditioning opened the door to true and varied expression.

This exercise is not a test of how well you sing but how well you listen. More importantly, you'll discover that your speaking voice is a lot more melodious than you had thought. Singing and speaking have much in common. The main difference is that *in singing we sustain the vowel or the consonant,* and link it to the next vowel or consonant in a designated way, while *in speaking we break the flow of the vowels and consonants.* In speaking, too, the rhythm is erratic compared to a song's, and there are no prescribed changes of pitch. But we are dealing with the same vocal elements—vowels, consonants, words linked or cut off from each other, rhythm, melody. And though you don't want to go to the extreme of singing through a discussion, conference or phone call, you do want to nurture the natural lilt in your voice. Eventually, with practice, you will relax into a new and healthy vocal freedom tempered by control.

CONTROL

Your voice can have power, finesse and extraordinary variety, but if it lacks control it will resemble a thoroughbred horse that's never been broken. It will gallop all over the place but get absolutely nowhere. (Consider a boy whose voice is changing: great variety, no control.)

Control does not cancel out variety. It means mastery, not restraint. In communication, voice control can help you negotiate difficult situations and obstacles, just as a fine car can carry you through potentially hazardous driving situations. A controlled speaker has a vocal machine that's tuned fine enough to bear up under stress, exhaustion, even laryngitis! While acting in *Hogan's Goat*, an off-Broadway play, performing Friday night, twice Saturday and twice Sunday, I contracted laryngitis and could not speak after the Sunday night show. Monday morning I had an important singing audition. I still couldn't speak, but I sang like a bird and succeeded at the audition. Why? I was forced to use abdominal and diaphragmatic control to get the sounds out. That taught me a lesson. Be as diligent and strong while speaking as you are while singing, and your voice will respond positively.

Breath control is paramount in vocal control. Say the following passage on one breath through the phrase "oppressively low in the heavens." Now on one breath through "dreary tract of country." And finally, say the last passage on one breath.

> During the whole of a dull, dark, and cloudless day in the autumn of the year, when the clouds hung oppressively low in the heavens,/I had been passing alone, on horseback, through a singularly dreary tract of country,/and at length found myself, as the shades of the evening drew on, within view of the melancholy House of Usher.

> —Edgar A. Poe
> *The Fall of the House of Usher*

Do you hear how the actual meaning of the words is influenced by the rhythm your breathing creates? Change your breathing and you change the impact of the words.

However, breath control is not based solely on being able to get out a lot of words on one breath! It's important to be able to "parenthesize." In the following selection, the line of thought is: "Others may praise what they like, but I praise nothing till it has well inhaled the atmosphere of this river and exudes it all again." Everything else is parenthetical. Those parenthetical phrases have to be said a little faster, with less prominence than the rest, so that your sound moves forward to the completion of the thought. I have marked the poem with parentheses to give you an idea of what I mean. Breathe where you feel it is appropriate.

> Others may praise what they like;
> But I, (from the banks of the running Missouri,)
> praise nothing (in art or aught else,)
> Till it has well inhaled the atmosphere of this river,
> (also the western prairie-scent,)
> And exudes it all again.

> —Walt Whitman
> "Others May Praise What They Like"

Vocal confidence—a knowledge of how to compensate for unforeseen occurrences and a general feeling of control—develops with experience. Give yourself a chance to get that experience. Speak well every chance you get, and reflect on how you sounded afterward. Don't tear yourself down or expect instant perfection. Try to build up your confidence.

FLEXIBILITY

Flexibility is the final element of fine tuning, the harvest you gather from hard work on control and relaxation. When you have trained your speaking mechanism to the point where you control it, and are relaxed enough to permit your musculature to change pitch, rate, force and quality rapidly, you have achieved flexibility.

The goal is to have a lively animated sound. To get that you need to have agility. When you practice fully, strongly and consistently you stretch your range and tone. Then when you speak in daily conversation and/or for professional purposes, monotony and stiffness will be transformed into flexibility.

The cat is a good example of a creature noted for speed, precision and flexibility. The cat owes its gracefulness to relaxation. Relaxation is the key to flexibility.

In chapter 6, "Improving Your Voice," I used the image of bodybuilding as a parallelism of vocal development. The exercises in this chapter are more like vocal gymnastics. Do them with energy, stretch your vocal powers, and your sound will result in effortlessness and ease of response.

Exercises for Variety, Control and Flexibility

The following exercises should be fun, and somewhat surprising! You will discover shadings and subtleties in your voice that you never knew you had. So dig in. Make these a part of your regular practice and preparation.

VARIETY OF RANGE

Here is a counting exercise. Counting from one to ten, attempt to speak as high and as low as possible. The goal is to extend both ends of your vocal range and to acquaint you with the sounds you can produce.

1. Starting on "one," say it as high as possible. Don't worry if it is squeaky and funny-sounding.
2. Descending from one through ten, get your voice to go as low as possible. Make it really basso!
3. Once you've gotten to ten, repeat your lowest note (ten) and then jump immediately to your highest, saying "one" again.
4. Repeat ten (low) and one (high) four times.
5. Repeat exercise three times.

VARIETY OF PITCH

Pitch, you will remember, is the musical notes you sound on the words you speak. In this exercise, the words in the poem have very strong tones, inherent musical tones, in them. The word "deafening" is a deeper, heavier word in meaning and sound than the word "dizzying," for example. As you read the stanza, let the pitch of your voice be shaped by the meaning of the words. Don't hesitate to exaggerate.

1. Read through the poem silently until you are familiar with it.
2. Now say it aloud varying the pitch of the words "rising," "leaping," "sinking" and "creeping."
3. Choose the next four words to concentrate on, and so on.
4. Keep going until all the words are varied in pitch.

> The cataract strong
> Then plunges along,
> Striking and raging,
> As if a war waging
> Its caverns and rocks among;
> Rising and leaping,
> Sinking and creeping,
> Swelling and sweeping,
> Showering and springing,
> Flying and flinging,
> Writhing and ringing,
> Eddying and whisking,
> Spouting and frisking,
> Turning and twisting,
> Around and around
> With endless rebound:
> Smiting and fighting,
> A sight to delight in;
> Confounding, astounding,
> Dizzying and deafening the ear with its sound.
>
> —R. Southey
> "The Cataract of Lodore"

VARIETY OF RATE

Learn to control and vary your rate.

1. Read through this passage from Sheridan's *The Rivals*. Note the short, crisp sentences in the beginning, and the longer, more lyrical ones toward the end.
2. Speak out loud:

ABRUPTLY — My dearest Julia.
           How delighted am I! How unexpected was this happiness! Ah! Julia, I have a thousand things to tell you. I know your gentle nature will sympathize with me, though your prudence may condemn me.

LEGATO — My letters have informed you of my whole connection with Beverly; but I have lost him, Julia!

SLOWLY — My aunt discovered our intercourse by a note she intercepted and has confined me ever since. Would you believe it? She has absolutely fallen in love with a tall Irish baronet she met one night since she has been here, at Lady MacShuffle's rout.

QUICKLY — And since she has discovered her own frailty, she is become more suspicious of mine.

3. Repeat until you are satisfied that you can vary the rate, and control it.

VARIETY OF FORCE

To get as strong a contrast as possible, pull in on the abdominal muscles and diaphragm on the words underlined. Release the muscles and give no force to the words not underlined. This is not an exercise for meaning or interpretation. It is designed for discipline to get as much contrast of sound as possible.

1. Pull in abdomen and make strong sounds on underlined words.
2. Release, and make light sounds on words not underlined.

3. Keep a steady rhythm going—like that of a metronome, or the ticking of a clock.
4. Do not strain.
5. Breathe when you need to.

> <u>Rats</u>!
> They <u>fought</u> the dogs, and <u>killed</u> the cats,
> And <u>bit</u> the babies <u>in</u> the cradles,
> And <u>ate</u> the cheeses <u>out</u> of the vats,
> And <u>licked</u> the soup from the <u>cooks'</u> own ladles,
> Split <u>open</u> the kegs of <u>salted</u> sprats,
> Made <u>nests</u> inside men's <u>Sunday</u> hats,
> And <u>even</u> spoiled the <u>women's</u> chats,
>   By <u>drowning</u> their speaking
>   With <u>shrieking</u> and squeaking
> In <u>fifty</u> different <u>sharps</u> and flats.
>
>   —Robert Browning
>   "The Pied Piper of Hamlin"
>
> <u>Great</u> rats, <u>small</u> rats, <u>lean</u> rats, <u>brawny</u> rats,
> <u>Brown</u> rats, <u>black</u> rats, <u>grey</u> rats, <u>tawny</u> rats,
> <u>Grave</u> old plodders, <u>gay</u> young friskers,
>   <u>Fathers,</u> mothers, <u>uncles,</u> cousins,
> <u>Cocking</u> tails and <u>pricking</u> whiskers,
>   <u>Families</u> by <u>tens</u> and dozens,
> <u>Brothers,</u> sisters, <u>husbands,</u> wives—
> <u>Followed</u> the piper <u>for</u> their lives.
>
>   (Ibid.)

VARIETY OF QUALITY

To keep your sound fresh so that you make people *want* to hear what you have to say, it's important to experiment, stretch, and develop variety. Variety comes from what the text means to you.

1. Practice these three selections, each of which requires a different quality of tone.
    Viola's love cry to Olivia in *Twelfth Night* is a musical and

lyrical expression. Linger on the vowels and almost sing the words, especially the words "Halloo" and "Olivia."

The passage from *Lady Chatterley's Lover* is brisk and somewhat clipped. The words race along image upon image until they come to a halt (and their destiny) on "A man was there."

Robert Frost's "Mending Wall" should be spoken with a deliberateness—a solidity and sureness to begin with, then a wryness when he speaks of "elves." After that there is a steady build as the description of the neighbor heightens to "Good fences make good neighbors."

Think about the content of these selections, visualize the descriptions, and try to make the quality of your sound reflect what you're thinking and experiencing.

> Make me a willow cabin at your gate,
> And call upon my soul within the house;
> Write loyal cantons of contemned love
> And sing them loud even in the dead of night;
> Halloo your name to the reverberate hills,
> And make the babbling gossip of the air
> Cry out, "Olivia!" O, you should not rest
> Between the elements of earth and air
> But you should pity me!

> —Shakespeare
> *Twelfth Night*

She did not go to the wood that day nor the next, nor the day following. She did not go as long as she felt, or imagined she felt, the man waiting for her, wanting her. But the fourth day she was terribly unsettled and uneasy. At last she decided to take a walk, not towards the wood, but in the opposite direction; she would go to Marehay, through the little iron gate in the other side of the parkfence. It was a quiet, grey day of spring, almost warm. She walked on unheeding, absorbed in thoughts she was not even conscious of. She was not really aware of anything outside her, until she started out of her muse, and gave a little cry of fear. A man was there.

> —D. H. Lawrence
> *Lady Chatterley's Lover*

"Something there is that doesn't love a wall,
That wants it down." I could say "Elves" to him,
But it's not elves exactly, and I'd rather
He said it for himself. I see him there
Bringing a stone grasped firmly by the top
In each hand, like an old-stone savage armed.
He moves in darkness as it seems to me,
Not of woods only and the shade of trees.
He will not go behind his father's saying,
And he likes having thought of it so well
He says again, "Good fences make good neighbors."

—Robert Frost
"Mending Wall"

Throughout this discussion of fine-tuning your sound, I have referred to three main factors: variety, control and flexibility, and the five elements: range, pitch, rate, force and quality.

What follows are exercises for even more subtleties of sound. By practicing syncopation, inflection, double inflection, and avoidance of whining, you'll develop even finer-tuning.

A note of caution: Don't try to do all the exercises at one time. Do them slowly, and at a rate at which you can absorb them. And don't immediately try to carry these exercises of voice, articulation and fine-tuning into your everyday speech. The time to carry over an exercise into your nine-to-five day is when the exercise is so much a part of you that it does not intrude on your communication. You shouldn't be thinking about syncopation when attempting to get landlords to stabilize rents. Get to know and enjoy syncopation for and by itself. That may take you six weeks or six months.

SYNCOPATION

Syncopation is unexpected variety of rhythm and rate. The poem that follows lends itself to the use of onomatopoeia: the words sound like what they mean, e.g., "Drum on your drums" should sound like a drum; "batter on your banjoes" should sound like a banjo. "Let your trombones ooze, and go hush-a-hush-a-hush," "moan like an autumn wind" and

"Cry like a racing car" are all images. Use your senses to help visualize, hear, smell, taste and touch what you are saying.

Try being strong, forceful and quick on "Bang, bang you jazzmen, bang all together."

Then start high-pitched and work your way down to the lower pitches on "Make two people fight on the top of a stairway and scratch each other's eyes in a clinch tumbling down the stairs."

Be tough on "Can the rough stuff."

Whisper very slowly on "Now a Mississippi steamboat pushes up the night river with a hoo-hoo-hoooo."

Be slightly more forceful and pick up speed on "And the green lanterns calling to the high soft stars," warm and mellow on "A red moon rides on the humps of the low river hills," and strong and staccato on "Go to it, Oh jazzmen."

Jazz Fantasia

> Drum on your drums, batter on your banjoes, sob on your long,
> cool winding saxophones.
> Go to it, O jazzmen.

> Sling your knuckles on the bottoms of the happy tin pans,
> Let your trombones ooze, and go hush-a-hush-a-hush with the
> slippery sandpaper.

> Moan like an autumn wind high in the lonesome treetops.
> Moan soft like you wanted somebody terrible.
> Cry like a racing car slipping away from a motorcycle cop.
> Bang, bang you jazzmen, bang all together. Drums, traps, banjoes,
> horns, tin cans.
> Make two people fight on the top of a stairway and scratch each
> other's eyes in a clinch tumbling down the stairs.
> Can the rough stuff.

> Now a Mississippi steamboat pushes up the night river with a hoo-
> hoo-hoooo.
> And the green lanterns calling to the high soft stars.
> A red moon rides on the humps of the low river hills.
> Go to it, O jazzmen.

INFLECTION

Inflection is a turn, bend or curve of the voice within a syllable.

This selection combines statements and questions that are inflected very differently.

1. On the final word of each question, inflect your voice up.
2. On the final word of each sentence, and before pauses within a sentence, inflect your voice down.
3. They tell us sir, that we are
                                    ↘weak.
   Unable to cope with so formidable an
                                    ↘adver ↘ sar ↗ y.

                          stronger?
   But when shall we be ↗

                     week?
   Will it be the next ↗

                    year?
   Or the next ↗

4. Choose your own inflections for the rest of the passage.

They tell us, sir, that we are weak—unable to cope with so formidable an adversary. But when shall we be stronger? Will it be the next week, or the next year? Will it be when we are totally disarmed, and when a British guard shall be stationed in every house? Shall we gather strength by irresolution and inaction? . . . The battle, sir, is not to the strong alone; it is to the vigilant, the active, the brave. Besides, sir, we have no election. . . . There is no retreat, but in submission and slavery! Our chains are forged, their clanking may be heard on the plains of Boston! The war is inevitable—and let it come!! I repeat it, sir, let it come!!

                                    —Patrick Henry
                                    Conclusion of Speech
                                    at Virginia Convention, 1775

DOUBLE INFLECTION

1. You've practiced the single inflection, going from a higher pitch to a lower pitch, and from a lower pitch to a higher pitch.

Hell- ↘ o   Hell- ↗ o

Now try   low   high   low

             o
Hell- ↗ ↘ o

        high   low   high
Hell- ↘ ↗ o
          o

That's a double inflection either way.

2. Practice "The Italian Lesson" below. You can double inflect on one word, or on a phrase.

    did
You ↗ ↘ n't   or   A ↘ whole glass of   ter
                                 ↘ wa ↗

3. The goal is to experience more variety.

Yes. And then what happened?... What?... She *didn't*?... *Real* hysterics?... What did you do?... You *didn't!*... A whole glass of water?... What nerve! Well, I've always *heard* that's the thing to do for hysterics, but never heard of anybody *doing* it.... Didn't it ruin her hat?... My dear, how *awful!* What a situation!... My dear, it wasn't your fault. I thought you were most tactful—after all, one *must* discuss things. One must co-operate on any committee—and compromise.... One doesn't behave like that.... Of course, I've always thought her the most im*poss*ible person.... Abso*lut*ely!... and I've always been slightly suspicious that.... What?... You *have*?... No, I've never *heard* it, but I've always *thought* it.... But if that's the case, I think we must just quietly get rid of her.... Exactly—that's what I mean.... Yes, I agree with you.... Mmmm-yes.... I do indeed....

—Ruth Draper
"The Italian Lesson"

COUNTERACT WHININESS

A whine is a nasal, "crying" kind of tone. To counteract it, lower your pitch and aim warm, mellow tones out through your mouth.

1. Read through the following poem to absorb its meaning and delicacy.
2. Say it aloud as warmly and compassionately as possible.
3. Concentrate on the underlined words. They can be difficult to say openly and warmly.

> Speak <u>gently</u>, Spring, and make no sudden sound;
> For in my windy valley yesterday I found
> New-born foxes <u>squirming</u> on the ground—
> Speak <u>gently</u>.
>
> Walk <u>softly</u>, March, forbear the bitter blow;
> Her feet within a trap, her blood upon the snow,
> The four little foxes <u>saw</u> their mother go—
> Walk <u>softly</u>.
>
> Go <u>lightly</u>, Spring—oh, give them no alarm;
> When I covered them with boughs to shelter them from harm,
> The thin blue foxes <u>suckled</u> at my arm—
> Go <u>lightly</u>.
>
> Step softly, March, with your rampant hurricane;
> <u>Nuzzling</u> one another, and <u>whimpering</u> with pain,
> The new little foxes are <u>shivering</u> in the rain—
> Step <u>softly</u>.

> —Lew Sarett
> "Four Little Foxes"

Once you've practiced all these exercises, you might want to increase your sensitivity to language. I have selected three passages that are splendid expressions of our language. Notice how the words are used. Notice the contrast in subject matter, and the uniqueness of style and tone. A new appreciation of language will increase your ability to speak with style.

After you have gone through these once or twice, record yourself. Listen for variety, flexibility and control of interpretation.

Shakespeare

Read in a legato (slow), solemn, ponderous voice.

e.e. cummings

Read joyously, lightly and in a fun-loving manner.

Washington Irving

Read carefully and precisely, always keeping in mind the need to make the words and images (which are so crowded in) clear.

> Tomorrow, and tomorrow, and tomorrow,
> Creeps in this petty pace from day to day,
> To the last syllable of recorded time;
> And all our yesterdays have lighted fools
> The way to dusty death. Out, out, brief candle!
> Life's but a walking shadow, a poor player
> That struts and frets his hour upon the stage
> And then is heard no more: it is a tale
> Told by an idiot, full of sound and fury,
> Signifying nothing.
>
> —Shakespeare
> *Macbeth*

> who knows if the moon's
> a balloon, coming out of a keen city
> in the sky—filled with pretty people?
> (and if you and i should
>
> get into it, if they
> should take me and take you into their balloon,
> why then
> we'd go up higher with all the pretty people

than houses and steeples and clouds:
go sailing
away and away sailing into a keen
city which nobody's ever visited, where

always
      it's
            Spring) and everyone's
in love and flowers pick themselves

                        —e.e. cummings

He was tall, but exceedingly lank, with narrow shoulders, long arms
and legs, hands that dangled a mile out of his sleeves, feet that might
have served for shovels, and his whole frame most loosely hung together. His head was small, and flat at top, with huge ears, large green
glassy eyes, and a long snipe of a nose, so that it looked like a
weathercock perched upon his spindle neck, to tell which way the
wind blew. To see him striding along the profile of a hill on a windy
day, with his clothes bagging and fluttering about him, one might have
mistaken him for the genius of famine descended upon the earth, or
some scarecrow eloped from a cornfield.

                        —Washington Irving
                        The Legend of Sleepy Hollow

Before closing, I'd like to take a look at the relation of voice work to
the work of communication. With this chapter we have reached the point
where the two prongs of my approach converge.

Picture a rainbow. At one end of the spectrum you practice inner
techniques of being real, organizing your thoughts, using a visual guide,
and focusing on delivery. At the other end of the spectrum you practice
the outer techniques of voice, articulation and fine tuning. Gradually
the two processes will become absorbed in you and converge, as they
would in the middle of the rainbow's arc. As you control the content
you will also control your sound. As you respond to your experiences
your voice will respond with variety. The agility with which you react to
what is taking place will reflect in the flexibility of your voice. You need
control, variety and flexibility to mirror that inner life truly.

Continue to develop your awareness and appreciation of sound. Listen! Listen! Listen! To the radio, to the music of the street, "a music which sounds like the actual voice of the human heart, singing the lost joys, the regrets, the loveless lives of the people who blacken the pavements," as Logan Pearsall Smith wrote. And listen to the music of nature.

> Gather a shell from the strown beach
> And listen at its lips; they sigh
> The same desire and mystery
> The echo of the whole sea's speech.

> —Dante Gabriel Rossetti

PART FOUR
SPEAKING UP AND SPEAKING OUT

Chapter Nine

COMMUNICATING NINE TO FIVE

About every other thing nobody is of the same opinion nobody means the same thing by what they say as the other one means and only the one who is talking thinks he means what he is saying even though he knows very well that that is not what he is saying.

—Gertrude Stein
Everybody's Autobiography

For most people communication on the job is essential. Unless you are a solitary writer, artist or researcher, you have to deal with and talk to people all day long. You may have to:

- sell a product—or an idea
- negotiate a contract—or a raise
- conduct an interview—or be interviewed
- motivate a subordinate—or mollify a boss
- run a meeting—or contribute to one

- confer on the phone—or think on your feet
- defuse any number of explosive situations

ON-THE-JOB STRATEGIES

Selling

If you are selling a product, adapt your presentation so that it fills your client's needs in a real way. Get as much information as you can about your client's business before you meet. Be a problem solver.

When Guy Sousa sells advertising time for USA Network to automotive clients he knows they want to reach young men and he knows they want to advertise in a context that makes them feel like men, i.e., sports. So Sousa positions himself as having "without a doubt, the most live coverage of professional sports. We're talking about front-page sports, the things the networks like ABC traditionally cannot afford to do with their prime-time mass appeal orientation. We put on sports events that will target the segment of the male population you want to reach."

Sousa says he tries to listen actively not only to what is being said but to what is not being said. Tones, inflections and hesitations say a lot. "If I'm the one doing all the talking, I'm not getting any information," says Sousa. "Ideally, I want to know that company's 10-K form."

Notice that some people use tactile terms like: "I want to get a handle on this," "I have to get a feel for it." Others use visual terms: "I can't see doing that," "That's not clear to me." Use tactile terms in dealing with the first group, visual terms in dealing with the second. This narrows the distance between you.

Believe in what you are selling. Simple, honest belief in your product's value is the bedrock that will make your proposals strong, real and effective.

However, if your main job is to sell or espouse something for which you have no regard, my advice is not to do it. In the long run, working with artificial enthusiasm and a dishonest attitude takes its toll. Industrial psychologist Dr. Linda C. Jones says that most of her clients seek areas of work they believe in. They've learned that work becomes more meaningful, and they become more successful, when they truly relate to their product and company.

In addition to believing in his product, a good salesperson likes people. Tom Heinsohn, a former basketball star and coach who is now a CBS-TV sports commentator, is also a gold-star insurance salesman who sold $5 million worth of insurance in 1984. Tom knows his voice can sound hard and "gravelly," so he worked to refine his sound and manner. But more importantly, he developed a sales technique that reflects his very caring attitude. When selling insurance, he likes to "sit down and talk with the people about their ambitions for themselves and their families, like sending the kids to college. Once you get the facts, the close becomes relatively easy because it's their situation you're talking about."

Hone your speaking skills, use your best voice and look good so that you come across as personally appealing. If the other person feels drawn to you, he'll be more receptive to your product. Good salesmanship means selling yourself as well as your product or idea.

Know your competition and use what you know to outsell them, to make your product more attractive. Don't ever bad-mouth your competition, however. Negative sell is offensive. It makes you look ugly, and it can backfire. Suppose your client has just bought a lot of the merchandise you're knocking?

To sum up: It's of paramount importance to:
- Know your customer
- Know yourself
- Know the problems
- Know your competition

Negotiating

Gerry Springer, before becoming anchorman on WLWT-TV in Cincinnati, was that city's mayor. He became mayor on December 1, 1976, the day Cincinnati's bus contract expired and the drivers went on strike. Downtown retail sales slumped and tax revenues dried up. Springer said, "I decided that for the city the biggest victory was never to be held hostage again. We had to make sure that the next contract did not run out during the Christmas season. I didn't tell *them* that; I thought that if they knew that's what I wanted it would be the last thing I'd get. So I fought over health benefits and some other stuff. But at the appropriate time I said, 'Okay, but the next contract runs out on January 7th.' By January 7th, the Christmas season is over and it's a slow time. In exchange we fattened up the contract. We gave them a bit, which was all right. It was a compromise."

A compromise, one might add, that benefited all. Gerry Springer knew that the best way to achieve his objective was to reach out to the other parties in the negotiation for mutual benefit. That is always far more effective than getting stuck in a single, unchangeable position that you then try to force the other person into accepting.

A skilled negotiator also organizes his thoughts ahead of time, knowing that a poor choice of words can ruin everything. The chief negotiator in a relocation of reluctant oil company employees committed a verbal gaffe when he said, "For all of you people taking this relocation option, this would certainly make you quite comfortable *by your standards.*" The union, which thus far had been agreeable to everything proposed, took such offense at those words and his condescending tone that they broke off the negotiations. Had the oil company's representative said, "This is a great package. It recognizes your services and the company's debt to you," he would have prevented the impasse that went on for two and a half weeks, cost the company a fortune and almost precipitated a strike.

One way to negotiate smoothly is to do so over a long period of time. Start early while there is no pressure. The following negotiation took place over a period of eight months.

Susan Stein (a pseudonym, as are all the names in this particular example) was the administrative assistant to John Grimes, editor in chief of a major publication. In addition to assisting him in all his day-to-day duties, she supervised all the secretaries and was the office manager for over 100 editors. For the five years they worked together, Susan and John were a good working team.

However, for a period of four or five months, Susan suspected that John was working on a deal for himself and was planning to leave. The uncertainty of the situation made Susan think: "If he's taking care of himself, maybe I'd better take care of myself." So she started looking at her options and decided to try her hand at the copy desk. The challenge of climbing the editorial ladder appealed to her. She took an editorial test and did well on it.

Susan spoke to John about her plan, hoping to get a commitment before he made his move. "Just be patient," he said. "Everything will be fine."

Everything was not fine. John announced his resignation and suggested that Susan talk to the new editor in chief, Joseph Baron. Now she had to start all over again and negotiate with someone else.

Joseph, knowing that Susan was a top-notch administrative assistant, wanted her to work for him rather than go to the copy desk. He tried to talk her out of the copy desk job, saying that she didn't have any editing experience. But Susan countered: "I feel it would be a good place to utilize my five years of experience and my knowledge. I want to get started on a new track."

Susan's confidence came through, but it was not enough to convince Joseph to give her the job. She asked herself why, and realized that though her new boss had told her she wasn't "experienced" enough for the editorial job, what he really wanted was her expertise as assistant to the editor in chief. As the new editor in chief, he needed her knowledge of company systems, her access to information, and her contacts at all levels inside as well as outside the company. They would be invaluable to him.

She began to empathize with Joseph's position. She decided to take a new tack with him. She told him that if he allowed her to go to the copy desk, she would work with him for three months, helping him in the transition to editor in chief and training a new assistant. Following that, he could periodically seek her advice. Patiently but persuasively she was able to win him over to her side.

At each step of the way, Susan talked to herself before she talked to her boss. She was confident of what she had to offer, though at one point she said: "I could have been left with no job at all." As an effective negotiator, Susan did not allow herself to get stuck in an unchangeable position, and she did not force the editor in chief into accepting a nonnegotiable demand. She also trusted her instincts, acted on them and communicated effectively from the inside out.

As Lawrence McQuade, senior vice president of W. R. Grace and Company, puts it: "I think the key to successful negotiating is to solve the other guy's problems for him. First figure out what each party's most essential requirements *really* are, then devise a solution which meets your own essential goals in a way which is compatible with the essential goals of the other."

That's exactly what both mayor Gerry Springer and Susan Stein did.

Interviewing

For the *interviewee*, interviews are a perfect time to prepare a minispeech (see chapter 3, "Organizing Your Thoughts"). You may want to volunteer information, especially with a dry interviewer who is hard to read. With an outline branded into your memory, you'll be ready when asked, "Tell me about yourself."

As you work on your minispeech, frame answers to the following questions and practice them aloud:

- Why do I want to work in this industry?
- Why this company specifically?
- Why am I well equipped for this position?
- How eager am I to work hard?
- Why am I the best candidate for the job?
- What intelligent questions can I ask about the company?
- What are my short-term and long-term goals?
- Why did I leave my previous job, or why am I willing to leave the job I have?

Your résumé has given your credentials. The interview is your chance to show who you really are. During its course make sure you cover the above points and deal with any tough questions by bridging to a statement you want to make. Be concrete. A factually interesting story makes an impression.

On the other hand, there may be times when good listening will be more important than good speaking in clinching the job. John Dunnigan found himself seeking a new job in his fifties after his advertising firm relocated to another city. At one interview, he walked in and found himself "facing a man fifteen years my junior, with a picture of himself and the President of the United States hanging behind him. I discovered that he likes to talk a lot, so the first rule there was to let him talk. I learned later that he said, 'Dunnigan showed a great deal of maturity in the interview.' Well, what I'd really done was listen to his immaturity! But he did what I'd hoped he would do—inflated it into my being a patient person who doesn't break in all the time."

Dunnigan let this interviewer take the lead, a strategy that might also have helped an unfortunate soul who destroyed his chances with a prestigious Wall Street law firm. Interviewer Katherine Loft tells the story:

"This was supposed to be a real star. So a partner and a couple of associates took this applicant out to lunch. To convey a low-key, informal approach they went to a Chinese restaurant where they all ordered Moo-shoo pork [a stir-fried dish that comes with a kind of pancake]. And this person picked the pancake up and wiped his face with it, thinking he was in a Japanese restaurant, where they give you a little hot towel. The partner and associates just choked. This man was never made an offer."

The man might have spared himself embarrassment—and gotten the job—if only he had waited to see what the others did with the mysterious "pancake"!

Here are some further tips to help improve your chances of getting the job:

- As part of your preparation make a list of possible questions you might be asked, like the one suggested above, including dumb, embarrassing and difficult ones, and practice answering them out loud. Most importantly, answer the question: Why would this company want me instead of someone else?
- Try to establish rapport with your interviewer as soon as you sit down. See page 253 for specific ways to break the ice.
- Be detailed when you are asked about your expertise, uniqueness or sense of purpose. For example, if you are asked, "You have on your résumé that you are interested in music—what kind of music?" don't just answer "Baroque" and expect the interviewer to pull out of you the fact that you also play the flute. Volunteer it. Similarly, if you are asked, "How did you get on in law school" don't say

"Fine, a great experience," and leave it at that. Tell what it meant to you, how you changed, what you plan to do now. Talk about a project that was special to you and pertinent to the job you're after.

- Take active measures to guide the interview to what is most interesting about you. For example, ask a question that will lead the conversation toward your areas of strength and special interest: "I understand this company is branching out into video. My masters degree from Syracuse University is in video production. Last summer I worked as an associate producer for a documentary on PBS, and that led me to my interest in communication law."
- Ask questions that suggest you are well-informed about the company and have done your homework. Also ask questions that convey that you know something about the way organizations operate. For example, in a large company you might ask how much autonomy individual business units have to make decisions without consulting the corporate headquarters.
- Be wary if the interviewer creates too cozy an atmosphere. Don't blurt out your own, excessively candid self-evaluation. "I was interviewing a man for our Palm Beach office," said a recruiter, "and some of the things he told me about himself made me wonder if he realized what he was saying. He told me he enjoys his classes but he doesn't like to work hard. This job requires self-motivation!" You can be your honest self and still shape your remarks purposefully.
- Make your last impression count. At the closing moment you might briefly recap your qualifications, then let the interviewer know you are excited about the prospect of working for a company that has so many commendable aspects.

While Paul Sonnenschein was studying for his MBA degree at Columbia University, he spent as much time researching companies and getting ready for interviews as he spent in classes. He took the time to find out about publishing by meeting and talking to people in the industry. He got influential names from Columbia alumni and then called them cold. His network grew, along with his understanding of the field, and by the time he landed an interview at Time, Inc., he was sure that was where he wanted to work.

"I began by convincing the interviewer that I was sure I wanted to be in publishing," he says. "I presented my view of myself, told why it was such a good fit. I expressed my knowledge of Time, Inc., and its competitors, and convinced them that I thought it was the best publishing conglomerate in the world. I did all this without coming on too strong. MBA's especially think they can change a company in five years, that their ideas are better, but I wanted to convince them that I'm also capable of plodding away, working hard. I was being 'aggressive with humility.'"

Paul's tenaciousness and interviewing skill paid off. He is in a job he loves and one that can lead to advancement.

As the _interviewer_, you want the candidates to be themselves, to be so unthreatened that they can forget they are being interviewed. You want them to deal with you in this situation the way they would normally deal with others in their work situation. Dave Francis of Heidrick and Struggles, a leading search firm for Fortune 500 companies, told me that having been a candidate once himself, he knows what the interviewee is feeling.

Many people are frightened to reveal themselves and to let you see their individuality. They have preconceptions of how a person applying for this specific job should act, and they try to project that image. They might even be worried that you'll find their true self unacceptable.

As Katherine Loft put it: "In order to bring out what is in a person, you have to share a part of yourself. Share your interests, feelings, and belief where this is constructive. I enjoy that, enjoy letting people know that perfection does not exist, and they may be afraid but I understand that because I've been afraid too. And to let them know that the people they are interviewing with are human beings who've been in the same position not so long ago."

She tells about an interview with a man who "kept asking me questions like, 'What kind of people work here?'... 'Does it matter very much where you come from?' I kept listening intently for what he might be hiding and finally said, 'What are you asking? I can't answer your question if you don't ask it.' So he said, 'I'm gay and I'm worried that I'm going to be discriminated against.'"

Katherine confronted the issue honestly and directly. "If you make your gayness an issue," she said, "then you may well make people discriminate against you. In other words, it would be a mistake to bring your lover to an office party because this will make it an issue. You're working in a very conservative world."

If Katherine hadn't been tuned in to the subtext, to what he was not saying, she would have been left with a vague feeling that something was amiss and she would have hired someone else. But her sensitive listening and her forthrightness cleared up the confusion. The upshot: She acquired one of the finest antitrust lawyers in New York City for her law firm.

As a good interviewer, you want to be real but at the same time keep an air of transparency about yourself. Keep your own comments fairly neutral and try not to project too distracting a personality. That way, the applicant won't feel he has to "edit" his own personality to fit yours. And remember, too, that you are there to see how a person might qualify for the job, not to find fault. An eminent female doctor was so put off by an interviewer who was giving her a hard time, she said, "You sound as if you don't think I can *do* the job. You're convincing me I don't *want* the job."

In interviewing, it is a good idea to use a visual guide which you can either memorize or copy onto 3 × 5 cards. The following four-step scheme was suggested to me by Ron Knapp of Brissenden, MacFarland and Wagoner, a prestigious search firm in Stamford, Connecticut.

1. Establish rapport and briefly describe the position you want to fill .... 5 minutes
2. Conduct the interview proper, going over the candidate's résumé and asking him to fill in the details and tell of his main accomplishments .... 20–30 minutes
   (Ask to keep it "net"—meaning, stick to particulars.)
3. Describe the company's philosophy/culture, adding more details about the job in question and answering the candidate's questions .... 15 minutes
4. Discuss the candidate's long-term career aspirations and why this might be a potential match .... 5–10 minutes
                                                           45–60 minutes

In about forty-five minutes you can get a good sense of the candidate's abilities, reveal something about your company and determine if this is the right person for the job.

YOUR LOOKS, YOUR SELF

Vain trifles as they seem, clothes have they say, more important offices than merely to keep us warm. They change our view of the world and the world's view of us. . . . Thus, there is much to support the view that it is clothes that wear us and not we them; we may make them take the mould of arm or breast, but they mould our hearts, our brains, our tongues to their liking.

—Virginia Woolf
Orlando

Certainly your professional look should be carefully chosen to mirror what is best in you. Ask yourself: "Does the picture I present reflect my concept of myself? Does it have impact; is it appropriate; is it tasteful?" If you answer yes, then your looks are helping you get your job done.

The goal is simple—to get people to think: "How attractive Jane (or John) looks!" and then get down to the business at hand. If you're overdressed, it's as distracting as being unkempt.

Take your surroundings and your situation into consideration. An art-deco advertising office calls for different attire than a mahogany desk–type law office. A senior corporate executive dresses differently from jaunty, bow-tied Chauncey Howell, who covers the New York City scene for WNBC TV's "Live at Five." Yet, within the structure of appropriateness you can add something that expresses your individuality, such as carefully chosen jewelry, a particular color combination or an unusually textured fabric.

More and more men and women are breaking the mold of the severe "dress for success" business suit. Women who are climbing the corporate ladder are wearing "important dresses that say 'Boss'" says Emily Cho, a New York image consultant. As part of the new relaxed image,

TALK YOUR WAY TO SUCCESS

John F. Akers, president and CEO of IBM, was photographed for *The New York Times Magazine* sans jacket, wearing a bold yellow foulard tie (but with the traditional IBM white shirt!).

Looking good works from the inside out and the outside in. The more inner security you have, the more creatively and freely you can express yourself in the way you dress. And what you wear affects your inner life, your heart, brain and tongue. When you design your physical presence to reflect your real self, you're a winner.

EVERYDAY CHALLENGES

Besides the situations just described—selling, negotiating and interviewing—there are many other communication challenges that confront you in your nine-to-five day. The following situations are typical.

Discussions with Superiors

The Hawver Group survey concluded that the task that managers find hardest of all is selling their ideas to senior management. The situation is often emotionally charged and many psychological factors can come into play: a fear of rejection, a need to impress a parent figure, a perfectionistic streak, not to mention worries about job security in this competitive age. If you are uneasy about approaching your superior, keep reminding yourself that your goal is not to win this individual's approval but to elucidate the issue, get information across clearly and succinctly, communicate your goals or solve a problem. If you don't put your ego on the line you won't end up wasting mental and emotional energy in a battle to protect it. Then no matter what kind of personality you're dealing with—and if you hope to be successful in any career these days you must expect to deal with a great variety on your way up the ladder—your energy will be focused and you'll be able to absorb your boss's ideas while communicating your own.

Needless to say, you must position yourself solidly and your presentation should be top-notch. If you give your superior wishy-washy recommendations backed up by incomplete staff work, he will find fault with it, and rightly so.

But suppose your superior has communication problems of his own? He may be disorganized or a poor listener or give you muddled instructions. In such cases, saying "I don't understand, could you clarify that?" is far better than second-guessing him. After the meeting, send him a confirming memo stating the outcome clearly. An innocent misunderstanding today can lead to chaos tomorrow.

Before your meeting with a "difficult" boss, you might do what George Bush did before his debate with Geraldine Ferraro—namely, think of something you really admire about him. (There must be something!) That way, you will be speaking to him out of respect and warmth, and your regard will color the whole encounter. He will also feel more at ease, making it less likely that he will try to threaten you or inhibit your forthrightness.

Discussions with Subordinates

The young man who mows the lawn for me is nineteen years old. I remember watching him with amusement one day as he shouted into the ear of his helper: "Move faster!" It was a direct, clear, definite command. But how many people can use this tactic with their employees—or would want to? Instructions must be relayed with tact and respect if you want the job done well.

There are times when every manager must deal with employees whose work is under par or whose behavior is in some way unprofessional. To deal with such employees too harshly is to undermine their overall motivation; yet to put off a confrontation until a situation becomes unsalvageable is also unwise. The fact is, you owe your employees an honest appraisal of their performance. How else will they improve? Once a year is a minimum for a full appraisal to be made. That's the time for corrections and/or congratulations. The key is not to be antagonistic but to explain and discuss how the employee can do a better job.

At times you might try the "What If?" approach, which helps people look at things in a fresh way. Say, for example, that a manager is growing increasingly irritated with an employee's long lunch hours. Rather than assuming that the employee is simply irresponsible and lazy, rather than charging up to the worker's desk to "dress him down" publicly, or taking

him aside for a few sharp remarks, the manager takes the time to say
to himself: "What if . . . ?" "What if John is having problems with his
housekeeping and/or child care? [I know his wife works.] Or what if that
back problem is acting up again and he's back to yoga during lunch
hours? Well, I'll just ask." The manager can meet with the employee to
work out a solution to both their problems and end up having strengthened
their working and personal relationship.

If, however, the manager discovers that the employee is being irresponsible for spurious reasons, he can use the "What If?" approach to
say, "I know things are slow right now, so a long lunch doesn't seem to
be of consequence. But what if while you were taking two hours for
lunch today, the chairman of the board had called and asked for a piece
of information I couldn't put my hands on because you weren't here?"
With the "What If?" approach, the employee readily sees the gravity of
his behavior. You help him look at his function from the perspective of
a manager.

Discussions with Peers

There are often a lot of "hidden agendas" in discussions with peers. For
instance, I may be giving a presentation on why I think the company
should be spending $100,000 on an advertising campaign. If I get a
budget approval, it might make my job bigger and more powerful than
someone else's in the room, and he or she may not want that to happen because they might have to work for me, or even be fired. My star
will shine and theirs will fall. People are always competing for the next
level.

Try to figure out what you need to get out of a meeting with peers.
Think back to what we said about Ted Koppel. He knows what he wants
to accomplish and he has the knowledge with which to do it. He knows
how to structure questions to get the information he needs. That is power.
Going into a discussion with peers, he'd never lull himself into a feeling
that "this is only a four-way chat and it doesn't matter what comes out."
He is very careful. And you have to be careful in determining what you
want to get out of your meetings.

You may not have the power to create a certain climate of discussion with your peers, the ability to turn off one person, or get another to speak up. But knowing you don't have that authority, you can still discern the elements that are operating and work with them.

If, for instance, a peer does not come forth with the information you need to help your cause, if he's holding out on you for his own advantage, you can say: "Morris and I have discussed this matter, but I feel he is better able to give you the information." There in the midst of a group meeting Morris will have no choice but to speak up, and the information you need to have shared will come forth.

Much better yet, if you know ahead of time that the meeting is going to be tough, that you may have a detractor that you can't turn off, get to him before the meeting. Talk to him about what you are going to say, and be straight with him. "Look, I know you don't agree with me. Let's talk about what we can and cannot agree on, discuss it now before the meeting and make a deal."

The reason that Ted Koppel is so respected is that he can be genuine while still asserting his power. The two are not antithetical. Lots of people in business, especially in dealing with their peers, think that the only way to deal successfully is if they go "nuclear"—all power—and become a bunch of tyrants. That is not true, nor is it necessary.

Daniel Lawlor, vice president of regional advertising sales for USA Network, is an open, direct and well-liked executive who says: "Without my peer group I cannot get my job done. So I have to make sure that I am never a threat to them in any territorial sense. I somehow have to make them feel that it was through their insights that I made a particular decision, and I let them know how much I value their input."

Daniel Lawlor's positive, productive approach, his self-confidence and his comfort in his level of the corporate structure have come from many years of hard work, awareness, and respect for his peers.

Business Meetings

Meetings of three or more people, such as the regularly scheduled staff meeting, are part of the nine-to-five routine. The person in charge of such meetings sets the course and can make the difference between an inspiring and a profitable regular event or a dull routine to be suffered through. A "group grope" session (where everyone gropes for direction) is a waste of time.

This is what you can do to maximize the effectiveness of meetings:

- Have an agenda. You must have a road map and know what you want to accomplish. Keep the meeting moving clearly toward your goal.
- Be in control and yet invite participation. Be sincerely interested in what people have to contribute. As one vice president put it:

"People feel free to communicate when no one feels threatened and when no one feels that something they say honestly is going to come back and bite them in the ass, or be a problem to them. A successful staff meeting means talking eyeball to eyeball. Each participant must have an opportunity to express his views, or at least be given the option to pass."

And even if you're not chairing a meeting, you can help shape it by the way you contribute, ask questions and listen. Often people give the impression that they are listening when they are really thinking of what they're going to say next. Not only does this lack of attentiveness set the stage for misunderstanding, it undermines spontaneous interchange. Sure, prepare your minispeech ahead of time but also go into the meeting eager to listen to other viewpoints and amend your views if necessary.

Community Meetings

Community meetings are similar to business meetings, but they are even more likely to fall into shambles without strong direction. If you are running the meeting, make sure you work up an agenda and that you keep attention focused on it. You will be dealing with many people who don't know how to stick to the point. They flounder. You have to save them. If a discussion goes off on a tangent, feel free to say: "I think we're getting sidetracked here. Could we get back to the main issue?"

At large meetings held to discuss highly charged matters, angry people in the audience may try to bait the speakers and monopolize the meeting. Taking command under these circumstances requires great diplomatic

COMMUNICATING NINE TO FIVE

skill. In some situations you can restate the angry person's point in analytical terms devoid of emotional language, and then evaluate or debunk it in a noncontentious way. In other situations, you may have no choice but to evict the disruptive person or end the meeting prematurely. If too much time is spent arguing, people will go home wondering why they wasted so much time at that meeting.

If you are a member of the audience, certain skills can help you make a better contribution. First, be brief when you ask a question; at most give yourself twenty seconds. Some people's questions are so long-winded that they only try the speaker's patience and lose the audience's attention.

Whether you are asking a question or making a point, begin by identifying yourself. Give your credentials so people know who you are. If you are at a meeting called to discuss the Indian Point Nuclear Power Plant and begin with "I live in Buchanan, New York, two miles from Indian Point," your remarks will be grounded in a personal reality.

Don't waste time on matters that you and the audience already take for granted. And if you have a personal reason for caring for your cause, don't try to hide it. If necessary, let what is private to you come out in public. For instance, if you think running a red light is a dangerous practice, don't just say: "Much has been said about the hazard of drivers who ignore red lights." One woman's child was dragged for fourteen blocks underneath a car driven by a man running a red light. She started the Stop Traffic Offenses Program, but was having trouble telling her story in public. "You feel a great deal of rage about what happened to your little girl," I told her, "but you're trying to keep a lid on it. The rage is choking you. Let it out! Don't be afraid to let people see and experience what you went through." After understanding the need to express rather than repress her inner turmoil, she was able to let her private agony show itself in public. She used her real self and she moved audiences to action.

On the Telephone

Many otherwise confident people tell me they dread talking on the telephone. Often they are insecure about the impact of their voices or they find the other person's "invisibility" disconcerting. Yet the same oral communication skills that serve you well in other situations will work for you on the telephone. Keep the following tips in mind*:

- Use a full (but not loud), warm sound. If you have a weak, thin voice, talk close to the mouthpiece. You don't want to fade out. Nor do you want to blast off. Some people overreach vocally, piercing the listener's ear.
- Use the first few seconds of the conversation to establish rapport. Opening with cordiality is far more effective than a cold plunge into the business at hand.
- Listen carefully for verbal clues. On the telephone, vocal intonations and nuances take the place of facial expressions and gestures.
- Let the other person know he has your full attention. Don't be abrupt, and keep interruptions to a minimum.
- Outline how you want an important call to progress and anticipate the other person's questions and objections. Have the facts handy *before* you pick up the receiver.
- Don't let speaking into a machine turn you into a machine. Let your enthusiasm, confidence and commitment come through.
- Move the conversation along and make sure the main points are highlighted. You can say, "That's important," or stress a point with inflection or repetition. Taking such measures decreases the chances of misunderstanding.
- Be succinct. Use simple words, short sentences, correct grammar—and get to the point.
- Make sure the other person can tell how you are responding to him. Often people who are quite warm in person sound impatient and cold over the phone. The person on the other end can't see you leaning back in your swivel chair smiling and nodding at his comments. Let him know how you are responding. Put warmth and enthusiasm into your voice. Laugh openly instead of silently. Reassure him.

*Some of these tips are adapted from Helen Bullock's "Working World" column in the *Toronto Star*.

- In a larger sense, your voice has to tell the whole story over the phone because your voice is all that comes through.
- End the conversation on a positive note.

The conference call is one of the trickier challenges of modern life. For maximum effectiveness, it must be as carefully planned as a staff meeting and even more creatively orchestrated. As the call begins, the moderator should address each participant and give each a chance to make a brief introductory remark. This establishes rapport. Identifying yourself before you speak and addressing others by name are crucial when there are more than three participants. The conference call also requires crystal clear articulation. Make an effort to pronounce each word precisely and don't talk fast.

Good phone work is partly a matter of good speaking and partly of good old-fashioned etiquette. For example, I am always delighted to speak to my broker, Betsy Baiker of Oppenheimer & Company, on the telephone. She is an excellent communicator and she usually calls at a time we've mutually agreed upon. Still, she considerately asks, "Is this a good time?" Ms. Baiker has a comforting voice and speaks in simple, clear terms. Often she asks "Is that clear?" in such a way that I don't feel silly saying no. She will patiently go over a point again in other terms, perhaps using an analogy to clarify her meaning. I feel assured and am a satisfied customer because Ms. Baiker keeps working at clarity.

You must also work at conveying an attitude of respect for the person on the other end of the line. As a communications consultant, I sometimes get calls from young journalists who would like to work with me. One day a student called who did not fit one of my criteria for broadcast clientele, which is that they have at least six months' on-air experience. On occasion I make an exception, but this young woman was so whiney, insistent and unpleasant that she virtually conspired in my rejection of her. Had she conducted herself graciously, perhaps asking me to explain my rule and thanking me for my time and thoughts, she would have helped her chances with me and demonstrated a more professional attitude.

You *can* talk effectively to people you can't see. If you have something of value to say, if it relates to the person you're talking to and you have a reason for saying it, you will feel their presence in the room.

The reason talking on the telephone becomes difficult is that you question whether the listener is paying attention to you, or you wonder what his reactions are. Use your sensitivity to make it a personal, involving experience. Concern yourself with the value of your message.

Thinking on Your Feet

"I can always pull off prepared remarks," one executive told me, "but what do you do when a question comes in from left field at a stockholders' meeting and the chairman turns to you to answer it? What happens when you're at a luncheon and someone asks you to comment on your company's interest in conservation? How do you find the words and make sense?"

If you are asked to speak on a subject about which you know little or nothing, don't try to "wing it." Simply admit that you aren't familiar with the topic and offer to speak on a related theme you do know well. "Sanskrit is not my area of expertise, but let me tell you what I know about Esperanto." If it's a familiar topic, start by saying what you do know: "I don't have all the details of the case, but I do know that..." If you stop worrying about what you don't know and just say aloud the one thought you have, other thoughts will follow naturally. You will find that what you know comes through.

On the other hand, you don't want to ramble. Some people think that they do their best when speaking off the cuff. Their confidence may derive from the fact that the anxiety that leads up to prepared speaking is absent under spontaneous circumstances. They "feel" better, so they think they sound better. But were they to read a transcript later, however, they might be shocked to note how rambling they'd been, and how dull.

Though, by definition, you cannot prepare for impromptu speaking, you *can* cultivate a way of thinking that will help you organize your thoughts even as you say them. Essentially, you adapt the methods of prepared speech to the impromptu situation. You quickly assess what is required of you, decide on a main point and then introduce it, explain it and bring it to a close. This structure, similar to the Introduction, Body, Climax and Conclusion of a formal presentation, helps keep you focused.

One night one of my broadcasting student clients, Roseanne Colletti of WCBS-TV, had to deliver a story on-air while it was happening. She had just come out of a courtroom when "The camera and the sound people got the cue to roll. . . . I didn't even have time to collect my thoughts. I wanted to say, 'I'm not ready yet!' But I had to go on."

How did she do it?

"More or less I told the story as it came to me. What stood out in my own mind as important is what I talked about. I took my thoughts in the order in which they hit me, trying to keep a constant thread, trying to tell the story."

When we viewed a playback of her tape, we realized that Roseanne had done a top-flight job. She began with what she knew and followed through with her thoughts one at a time. The same strategy can work for you.

Starting and Stopping

When you walk into someone's office for a meeting, you'll want to break the ice. Unless there's a blizzard going on, referring to the weather seems mundane. Instead, just looking into the person's eyes can be enough to establish rapport. If not, remark on things in the office that attract you: books, posters, mementos. I remember commenting on a leather case containing scissors and a letter opener, sitting on a CBS vice president's desk. He told me it was a gift from his father-in-law, a lawyer, who had displayed it on his own desk for twenty-five years. "Just about the same number of years my husband, a lawyer, had a similar one on his," I said. I had established rapport with the vice president immediately.

You should end the discussion when you've made your points and when you have a general sense that a meaningful connection and communication have been completed. Then make a graceful exit and try to make it memorable by underscoring the personal connection you've made. That might be a formal but heartfelt handshake, a compliment, or a reference to the next time you'll speak together. Make a friendly yet authoritative last impression and ensure a future welcome. That is useful whether you are wooing a client, interviewing for a job, or cementing relations with a boss or colleague.

DIFFICULT SITUATIONS

At one of the traditional New Year's Eve parties the Lee Strasbergs gave, Tallulah Bankhead swept in and saw Marilyn Monroe chatting with Lee's daughter, Susan. In her low-pitched, resonant voice, Tallulah said: "I hate you, dahling, you always take such wonderful pictures!" then audibly whispered in Marilyn's ear, "But at the moment, my dear, you really need some lipstick." A few minutes later Marilyn turned to Susan with a twinkle in her eye and said: "I should have told her it was kissed off."

We've all had moments of afterthought, when the "right words" come all too late. Situations that occur in daily office encounters are rife with "too lates," when you wish you hadn't lost that argument, or panicked, or let that person intimidate you.

When you are confronted with such difficult situations, try saying to yourself:

"I want . . ."

"I deserve . . ."

"I can do . . ."

With these assertions, you strengthen your sense of your right to be where you are, and you remind yourself that you are worthy of trust and respect. Then, if you ask only for what is legitimate and what you believe in, you will find the voice to express yourself. More often than not, people will accord them to you because of your attitude. And if you anticipate hostility or intimidation, you can prepare for it positively so that a hurt ego doesn't get in your way.

Panic

Stage fright and panic are one and the same thing. They flood the system with adrenaline. Your pulse is rapid, your mouth is dry and your knees quaver. You have difficulty vocally because vocal chords tighten up. These are psycho-physiological responses to threat. Here, the threat is audience disapproval. To some extent it's a real threat, for if you don't engage your audience, you are going to have a rough time.

But there may be times when you get up to speak and indeed cannot engage your audience. When this happens, acknowledge your dilemma. "This is a large audience today, larger than I expected. But with your cooperation, we'll make it worthwhile. You can help me by taking your seats, and laughing at my jokes." If you admit that you're in a tight spot and allow your humanity to come through, you touch off a response in the audience. Once that occurs, a lot of tension is eliminated.

The next best insurance against panic is preparation. If you suffer from panic or stage fright, a one-minute presentation could call for as much as thirty-to-sixty minutes of work beforehand. Yes! Whether you are negotiating a raise or introducing yourself spontaneously at a meeting, you should plan what you want to say and how you want to say it. Plan, but not so rigidly that there is no room for flexibility. When you are wedded to a rigid format you can't handle an interruption, and even an unexpected question can throw you.

During your preparation verbalize your ideas in different ways. Use your minispeech to practice bridging from different questions. Build in flexibility. If what you want to say is grounded in you clearly, you're going to be able to handle interruptions, digressions and questions, and still stick to your road map.

And remember, panic passes. Don't hold on to it. Let it go, and it will go. Another suggestion: take a moment to compose yourself. Focus on your breathing process. Use your diaphragm. By dealing with this tangible, you lessen tension from the inside out. You also support your tone, which gives you a stronger sound.

A member of Mothers Against Drunk Driving (MADD) was interviewed on the radio with a panel of other people. The first question was directed at her: "How do we deal with this problem?"

"Even though I expected that question, I panicked," she told me. "I thought the interviewer was going to start with the traffic officer and instead he started with me. I practically choked on my words. Then, when I started talking, I was using too many words, struggling, trying to think my way through. The shock threw me completely. I kept drawing blanks."

The woman from MADD may have expected the question, but she had neither framed a detailed answer nor practiced it out loud. She also had the naïve idea that the reporter would begin where she wanted him to. When he didn't, she was thrown off balance. What she might have done to regain it was *work with* her surprise instead of against it. Had she turned around and said "I thought you were going to start with someone else, but let me try to answer...," the extra time gained by saying these words would have helped her find her way. It is another instance where being real is your best policy. If you deny what you are experiencing you are certain to feel tongue-tied, but if you work with your panic as part of the reality, you'll be better able to recover your equilibrium, and accomplish your task.

Intimidation

James Thompson went in to ask his boss for a raise and a promotion. He had been working for two years as a public information specialist and felt he deserved more money than a newly hired peer. "He knew I came in there to talk about money so right away he said: 'About the money issue. I want to tell you right off the bat I can't afford to pay you any more than I am paying you right now.' He took the upper hand right from the start. He became the aggressor."

James let him take control and thus put himself on the defensive. He could have said: "Wait a minute! I haven't gotten two words out and you're telling me no! Please listen to what I have to say first." This would have preserved his right to state his case. Instead: "All the things I'd planned to tell him got confused in my head," he said. "I found myself stuttering, trying to pull myself together, unable to formulate my words."

At a time like this your best option might be to confront the other person with what you feel is happening. Tell the antagonist: "I'm beginning to feel intimidated. Are you saying I'm not qualified for this position? Not working hard enough?..." Quite often the other person will back down. If, on the other hand, he says: "Yes, I guess I am telling you that," at least you'll know where you really stand.

It's enormously important to project confidence when someone tries to intimidate you, otherwise the intimidation can grow and begin to dominate the exchange. James was able to marshal his forces, because: "At one point he said something just crass enough to make me regain my composure. He said: 'In relation to what everyone else is making, I think you're making what you should be.' Which was the lowest salary! It got me so furious that I came right back at him and said: 'I think you're wrong and I think you should review what everyone is making.' He respected that. And because I stood up for myself he said: 'Okay, we'll review it.'"

For some high-powered individuals, intimidation is a consciously chosen tactic, a part of their working style. As New York's mayor Ed Koch has written: "I don't get ulcers. I give them." But some bosses wish they knew how to be less intimidating. They realize their brusqueness only cows people, turning them into disgruntled—and less productive—employees.

If you think this is the case with your boss, you can be frank with him. "Your brusqueness takes all the pleasure out of working with you. The next time you take exception to one of my reports, could you try to advise me calmly and with respect for the good work I've also done?" We have much to learn from our bosses, but occasionally they can also learn from us.

Hostility

Hostility often takes you by surprise, as it did with a woman we shall call Harriet, who holds a public policy position in a Midwest state department of health. Before Harriet was appointed to this particular post, she was invited to teach a graduate seminar by one of her mentors. She was well prepared and eager to teach the class.

At the second session, the mentor challenged Harriet on a number of points in severe tones. In front of everyone, she treated Harriet like an uninformed student rather than the instructor. This was shocking, demeaning and as Harriet said: "I was devastated."

She started to cough, and couldn't stop for several minutes. For about two years after this incident, every time Harriet made a presentation she would do well until about three-quarters of the way through; then she would have a coughing spell. We traced it to a moment when she anticipated the question-and-answer period and interruptions from the audience. The coughing spells continued until we worked through Harriet's anxiety.

What could Harriet have done about that initial act of hostility? To collect herself, she might have taken a drink of water. (It's smart to have water handy, not only for catches in the throat.) Then she might have said something like: "You all know Professor Engle. She is my former teacher and the one who invited me to head up this seminar. I've always respected her opinion. Professor Engle, would you like to come up and tell us what you think? I have a lot more to say, but please feel free to take over for a few minutes." Then the onus would have been on Professor Engle to make her point, and if she did, it would have been a positive insertion that Harriet could pick up on when she resumed her lecture. If the professor didn't make her point, she would have lost all credibility, and Harriet, without having to force a confrontation, would have remained in control of the class.

In some situations you can restate the hostile remark, letting both the person who said it, and yourself, hear it and evaluate its impact. Most people don't like to be thought of as hostile and are disturbed to learn they are coming across that way. They may quickly back down. Even when they don't, you will have gained a moment of reflection, shown the audience that you are a statesman and underscored the mean-spiritedness of the remark.

Be mentally prepared for the possibility of hostile opposition, and remember that your audience will recognize the hostility and root for you if you keep cool and maintain control. Remember too that your responsibility to your audience is greater than to one hostile person who is probably behaving badly for reasons that have nothing to do with you. Months later, Harriet and her colleagues began to realize that her mentor was becoming mentally unstable and needed to seek professional help.

Laying your cards on the table is another way of dealing with hostility. Acknowledge points of difference up front, but also suggest that it is worthwhile to hear you out. James C. Miller III accomplished this in the introduction of his speech quoted in chapter 3: "Organizing Your Thoughts." "My objective today is to convince you that continuation of the FTC authority over the professions is in your best interest. If I succeed, I will deserve to be called Houdini. If I fail, at least I hope to clear up some of the misconceptions that apparently form a basis for much of the current opposition by professionals to FTC law enforcement."

Where possible, head off a confrontation with humor. It clears the air of tension and helps your opponent see you in a human, real way. Try to get beyond distorting emotionalism to what is really at stake. "Steel loses much of its value when it loses its temper."

Humiliation

"It was Christmastime," recalls Charles, a graphic design artist. "We were on our way to an office party, laughing and having fun, joking about the fact that Richard had been fifteen minutes late and I had been fifteen minutes early that day. I told him he could have my fifteen minutes. There was no real meaning to any of this.

"Suddenly Oscar, my boss, told me that I had better keep my fifteen minutes, implying that with all the errors I've made I should be giving time to him instead of someone else. The shock of that comment coming in such a serious tone, and such a nasty way in the middle of such a happy time, was too much. I said: 'I do stay later. I do make up for occasional errors.' But he kept going on, implying that I make errors too often, that I couldn't possibly make up the time. Then I got angry. I said he always had to put something right under his thumb and squish it right down to the table, and I made a gesture like that. He said if I didn't like it I could go and find another job. This kind of thing just pops up out of nowhere."

Humiliation is an emotional response you can control. Your pride is hurt, but if you have enough self-esteem you can throw the hot potato right back and not get burned. If Charles had said the following he might have saved himself distress: "Fine Christmas spirit you're showing! Why don't we discuss this some other time?" He would have avoided a public confrontation, defused the situation, and projected his own maturity and confidence.

Another tactic is to leave the scene. After a while you'll gain a new perspective, and may realize the person who tried to humiliate you is just a jerk. It's also likely that the person will let you know later, in some manner, that he feels sorry about his behavior.

At a later date and in less charged circumstances, Charles confronted his boss "in a stern voice, not angry, just definite." (He had practiced

out loud over the weekend with his wife.) He told him: "What I want
to do is keep moving forward, not backward." Then, as he recalls, "I
pointed out a situation where he had given somebody else a little design
job that was so minor, but was something he hadn't even bothered to do
for me yet. I told him I thought that was unfair. He was much less
qualified than I to do it. After I talked to him about that, he gave me
three things to design. He started keeping me informed, and educating
me more."

Indifference

One of the most frustrating situations is trying to communicate with
someone who is indifferent to you. As George Bernard Shaw wrote in
The Devil's Disciple: "The worst sin to our fellow creatures is not to hate
them, but to be indifferent to them; that's the essence of inhumanity."

First realize that indifference is often a mask for something else.
When I was teaching at Brooklyn College, one day I noticed a distracted
student. I couldn't get his attention. Finally, I asked him outright why
he wasn't listening. It turned out he had a terrible stomach ache! There
the indifference was simply part of the circumstances and not to be taken
personally.

When someone is genuinely indifferent to what you're saying, you
have to try to find out why. You might have come to discuss the Mideast
crisis when your listener has learned that his life savings are at stake
due to the failure of his hometown bank and he couldn't care less about
the Mideast.

Often indifference is a mask for personal prejudice. Susan Flaherty,
a sales rep for "a very conservative company," says of her peers: "They
don't look at me and say: 'Oh, hell—female.' With some of them it's
'Oh hi, Sue,' pat-on-the-back and then they dismiss me."

She runs into the same problem in the course of her sales work. "In
Boston [her home town] women are everywhere in sales. Down here in
the South, the dealers don't take me seriously. 'Oh sure, get her in here,
she's our token female.' Much like the token black."

The key to handling indifference is realizing that you must analyze
your listener just as you do when organizing any set of remarks, as
discussed in chapter 3, "Organizing Your Thoughts." It is up to you to

figure out where the indifference is stemming from and to find a way to get the person to focus on the substance of what you're saying.

Interruptions

Some interruptions are positive in nature, because the interrupting person has something valuable to contribute. Give him the benefit of the doubt. If you are well prepared, an interruption shouldn't throw you. It may even help you develop your own statement.

If a pattern of interruption occurs, it could be for one of two reasons. The person interrupting may be trying to undermine you by preventing you from finishing what you have to say, or he may be so involved in his own ideas that he can't stop talking. In either case, keep cool and be polite. Act on the assumption that the interruptor isn't doing something hurtful. You might say: "If you let me finish, you can tell me what you think."

Some people interrupt to show that they can get and maintain the advantage. They break into your statement before you are finished in order to throw you off course. One woman told me her law partner often uses this ploy, to test her skills at responding. He'll interrupt her with a barrage of abrupt questions: "In other words, are you telling me...?" "Does this mean that...?" "So you're saying that..." His rapid-fire questions are designed to lead her to a conclusion she may not necessarily hold. She's trying to respond to one question while the next comes flying at her. She solves this problem by refusing to fire back quick answers. "When you stop talking, I'll answer you."

There are other types of interruptions. It's dismaying when a person you are conferring with takes phone calls. Instead of dwelling on your annoyance, use the time to go over your notes or clarify your next point. Concentrate, too, on where the discussion left off so you can pick it up again without missing a beat. Assume that you can always use the time, and the interruption won't throw you.

Remember, healthy self-assertion and belief will engender respect. Say to yourself:

"I want..."

"I deserve..."

"I can do..."

• • •

Some say that working in an organization is like engaging in sports, an analogy that invites us to conceive of our nine-to-five challenges as hurdles in a race or tackles on the football field. In this view the purpose of every encounter is winning.

But there is another way to think of our workday endeavors. Instead of the game of football, we can think of the art of archery. The superior archer trusts in the skills he has acquired and concentrates fully on the moment. In so doing he is able to bypass the nervous, needy ego and tap into his best potential. Then he doesn't so much shoot the arrow as release it, and because of his centeredness and his skill it arcs to its target.

If you feel uneasy about some aspect of your job or find that you lose your self-control in difficult situations, remember the archer. With careful preparation as your foundation, you can proceed confidently. You are neither a winner nor a loser. Like the archer, you have a purpose and you can think of yourself as the instrument of that purpose. When others try to deflect you from it with interference or personal attacks, you can remain firm. Let your communication flow through you. Focus, and you'll be on target!

Chapter Ten

MAKING THE MEDIA WORK FOR YOU

A cool medium, whether the spoken word or the manuscript or TV, leaves much more for the listener to do than a hot medium. If the medium is of high definition, then the participation is low. If the medium is of low intensity, the participation is high. Perhaps this is why lovers mumble so.

—Marshall McLuhan
Understanding Media, 1964

Five years ago the XYZ Company was up against the wall. It was looking for a larger company to take it over and solve its problems. But XYZ had no buyers. So XYZ's board of directors did the only thing it could. It hired a new chief executive, who set about trying to save the company.

The new president realized the company had been losing shares in all its markets and that tough new competitors were spending a great deal of money to advertise and promote their products. He launched a new marketing campaign, designed new packaging, made improvements

263

in his product and took it to the marketplace for a last try. A few years later the company was back in the black.

Reporters from a national business show heard the story of how the XYZ company had come back from near death and called the president to find out how he did it. The president was wary of the media and decided not to cooperate. He was doing well, he figured, and would leave well enough alone.

Here was a man who was spending $100,000 for a thirty-second commercial for his product (plus $10,000 a month to retain his public relations people) turning down a free four-minute spot on a widely watched news show. Why? Because he didn't know how to use the media.

Television, newspapers and radio get their information through hundreds of interviews with thousands of people like you, me and the president of the XYZ Company. And that's the way the public gets its information. Here's what *Broadcast Magazine* said in a special report titled "The Fifth Estate Is Bullish on Business News":

> Business journalism and business programming have become businesses themselves, with more stations, more networks, and more cable channels betting that there is money to be made in reporting on money.

> The three major broadcast networks' morning and evening newscasts, their producers say, are now reporting more business news—spurred, they add, by the public's increased sophistication and interest in the economy.

Business is news. If you are a successful executive, the chances that you'll be called upon to meet the press are very good. Your ability to deal with the media and make it work to your advantage will be a key factor in the success of your job or cause. It's my hope that as you learn about the media, you'll seek opportunities like the ones described here to deliver your message.

Let's start with television and consider the amazing variety of situations that you as a company spokesperson might face.

TELEVISION

LOCAL AND NETWORK NEWS

News stories that are reported on the day they "break" or happen are called "hard news." Stories that could be reported at almost any time are called "soft," or feature, stories. "John DeLorean was indicted for fraud today" is hard news. A profile on John DeLorean is soft news, a feature story. "Ted Turner made a bid for CBS today" is hard news. "Ted Turner of CNN, how he founded it and made it grow" is a feature story, or soft news.

It's likely that you could be interviewed for either type of story. Be prepared.

Reporters of local news will be relatively young, rushed and not as well informed as they want to be. They are often required to cover up to three different stories in one day. Network reporters never work on more than one story a day and therefore are much better prepared. Here are examples of the questions each might ask:

Local Reporter: "We heard that RELY tampons cause toxic shock. What is toxic shock? Does your product cause it?"

Network Reporter: "An FDA report says your product testing was inadequate. Two national consumer reports say you have withheld key facts from your tests. A major medical study disputes your test results. Please respond."

DOCUMENTARIES

Local mini-documentary. You may find yourself involved in one of those multi-part series that local stations produce, usually aimed at "Sweeps" (the four periods every year when the local audience is measured). A local mini-doc takes time. These people may be around for a while, and they may come back for follow-up interviews or additional background shooting.

For example, a reporter goes to Boeing to do a story on the history of the American aircraft industry. She's there not just for that day's news headline, which might be "European Airbus Challenges Boeing Planes in Their Markets," but for an explanation of how that company got to where it is; whether it's vulnerable to strong competition; what some of the considerations are that airlines make in buying planes—price, fuel efficiency, etc. The mini-doc has a statement to make. The news story doesn't.

Network documentary. You probably won't find yourself involved with a network documentary unless you or your company are central to the issue being examined. If you are, you may get the feeling that you will never see the end of the taping or filming. It can take six months or more to produce a major documentary.

PUBLIC AFFAIRS

Public affairs broadcasts on national and local television are similar. They usually have a panel format and a reasonable amount of time to discuss the subject. Topics range from the reopening of a nuclear plant to a threatened strike by postal workers.

On the national level such shows as "Meet the Press," "This Week with David Brinkley," and "Face the Nation" are prestigious, and only CEOs or national public figures are likely to be invited as guests. However, local broadcasts, such as "Eyewitness News Conference," "Face the State," and "Let's Find Out," are eager to have good discussions on current issues and very often need participants to fill the time.

TALK SHOWS

There are two varieties these days: syndicated talk shows such as "Donahue" and the "Merv Griffin Show," and local talk shows. (NBC's "Tonight" and CNN's "Larry King Live" are among the very few network talk shows still in existence.)

Local talk shows run the gamut from personality formats to information formats. The host or cohosts set the tone. A celebrity host almost always dominates his show. The guests are the spokes in the wheel and the host is the hub.

If the talk show leans toward the information format, then your message and your personality are important. The host or hostess will play second fiddle to you. You will have the opportunity to dominate, and may be encouraged to do so.

MAGAZINE SHOWS

The grandfather of all magazine shows was the British Broadcasting Corporation's "24 Hours," a nightly program that occupied the equivalent of the U.S. "Tonight" show time slot. "24 Hours" reviewed the day's news in depth. CBS News producer Don Hewitt took the format and developed "60 Minutes," the CBS News weekly magazine that has become the most popular (and most profitable) network broadcast in U.S. television history. It's one competition is ABC's "20/20."

If you or your company is the subject of an investigative story on "60 Minutes" or "20/20," then your life is going to be very interesting. The first contact you get might be from a researcher, embarking on the early phase of story preparation. The researcher works with a producer and they are probably both beginning to learn about the subject and/or you. What you say and how you handle yourself can be crucial at this point. It's just as important for you to interview them as it is for them to interview you. Ask them what they know. Ask them what role you will play in their story, and try to divine their approach.

Anticipate questions, prepare your answers, be prepared for a lump or two if they are deserved, and never, never count on bad news staying hidden. Count on the bad news coming out and be prepared to deal with it. Honest mistakes honestly admitted can make you a hero. Even dishonest mistakes, honestly admitted, can be expunged.

"Evening Magazine," produced by the Westinghouse stations in San Francisco, Pittsburgh, Boston, Philadelphia and Baltimore, and its syndicated twin, "PM Magazine," produced at other stations around the country, are lighter fare. Feature stories, personality profiles, and helpful hints are their stock-in-trade.

If you are a high-profile figure in a glamour industry such as publishing or fashion, you are an ideal candidate for this type of show. Just remember that news standards do not apply here. Staging and clever editing are permitted. Information may be at the mercy of production values. These shows have been dubbed "bubble gum for the eyes," and you must be clear in your own mind as to whether or not appearing on one of them is in your own best interests.

FINANCIAL BROADCASTS

Financial shows, or news broadcasts, can offer a real opportunity for the businessman to introduce or explain his product, his service or his position on a business issue. Mark J. Estren, senior vice president in charge of programming for Financial News Network, says: "When I created the 'Nightly Business Report' for National Public Television, there was virtually no business news on TV, and most people in the industry dismissed business as being 'hopelessly non-visual.' Today, so many people have learned how to visualize business and economic news that there is business programming everywhere, not only on the network level but on many local TV stations."

There are several types of business television broadcasts. First there are economic news stories, such as those seen on network news shows, or on local stations. These might discuss federal tax plans, international trade barriers or foreign countries' debt to the U.S. banks. The purpose of these stories is to explain a complicated issue and its effects on individuals. Your interest in appearing on these might be, for example, to talk about how a new tax plan might affect your company, or how excessive foreign debt makes it tougher for little businesses or entrepreneurs to get financing for their enterprises.

Next there are special interest business shows. These include programs such as CNN's "Moneyline," "Nightly Business Report," "Wall Street Week," or FNN. These target an audience with a more sophisticated knowledge of business. Appearing on these programs could help you introduce your product or explain the major competitive advantages of your service.

Finally, there are *consumer* shows, such as "Taking Advantage" and "Moneyworks." Stories on these can give you a chance to talk about what you do. This could attract new customers, distributors or users of your product or service.

In any of these financial stories or shows, you have a chance to reach the public. Take advantage of the opportunity.

Business professionals are beginning to move into the reporting field; yet at present you may still find yourself confronted with a lay reporter assigned to cover business. Whether you face this reporter on radio, on TV or in print, the problems are the same. You may be talking to a reporter who does not understand business. The worst kind are the reporters who think they understand, or have made up their minds what the story is before they do the interview. In any case be prepared to carry the interview, and to explain matters that you consider elementary. If you have an opportunity to speak with the reporter before you are interviewed, try to find out how well informed he is and adjust your approach accordingly. Don't take umbrage at an uneducated reporter. Be patient and help him understand.

You will also be helping the television audience to understand. In fact, no matter what the reporter's background, assume that your audience knows little if anything about your business. Even the "Wall Street Week" show attracts unsophisticated viewers. You should anticipate questions, avoid jargon, and rehearse brief, simple answers. Go ahead and run the risk of oversimplification. It beats a long, muddled, wandering answer that no one understands. If you are about to oversimplify, say so. Tell your audience and tell your interviewer: "This is an oversimplification but the basic truth is..." Why is it that the experts seem to come across better on "Wall Street Week" than on most other business programs? If you listen carefully to Louis Rukeyser's questions and the questions of his regular panelists, you will understand. They never let a guest get away with an incomprehensible answer.

The following is a good example of an obfuscated and then clarified response to a reporter's attempt to get information.

The president of the company: "It was necessary for us to redeploy our assets if we were going to survive." (Obfuscated)

The Reporter: "What do you mean: 'redeploy our assets'?"

The president: "Take the money that we have, and use it for something new." (Clarified)

If you are going to be a guest on a business show, be sure to find out if you are the only guest. Is a competitor going to be on with you? Are you one member of a larger panel? Will you get to ask questions? How long will you be on? What colors are the set and background? Who is the audience? Is there a live audience? Is the show live or taped? The general principles of preparation always apply.

PRINT

Daily newspapers. Let us say that hundreds of employees are picketing your plant, protesting the recent mass firings of fellow employees. The daily reporters are on the scene. They want to know why these people were fired, how they were told and how they were chosen. They want to know if more people will lose their jobs, how much notice they'll be given and what kinds of benefits they will receive with severance.

When the daily newspapers cover a story such as this, they report the story to a general audience, from a generalist's viewpoint, albeit with some financial information.

Specialty newspapers. Reporters from a specialty newspaper, such as the *Wall Street Journal,* will also scurry to the scene of such a story. But their reporters will be asking slightly different questions. They are going to want the financial story. Their readers are fairly sophisticated business people. The *Wall Street Journal* will want the numbers, will want to know how the company got into trouble, how its position is different from or the same as other companies' positions, how it is doing better or worse on the job. The *Wall Street Journal* wants to know if management will change, if stock prices are forever ruined, if recovery is in the planning or even possible.

Local newspapers. Local papers, like the *Nashville Tennessean* or the *Denver Post,* are papers that have a specific audience, the people who live in their areas. They are interested in details that affect these people personally. They want to know the names and addresses of the people who were in the fire, whether the local school auditorium will be used to collect food for them, how their fellow citizens can reach them with further assistance.

News magazines. Newsweek, U.S. News & World Report and *Time* are high-caliber publications with large circulations. Their reporters do exhaustive reports. Despite the somewhat breezy tone of the articles produced, the reporters file pages and pages of information on their subjects. Fifty pages of research may go into a three-paragraph story. But you may well not think it's worth your time to talk to them. If you can, find out how much of your information they're planning to use in the final story.

Business news magazines. Fortune, Forbes and *Business Week* make no secret of the fact that their readers are well educated, sophisticated, affluent executives throughout the world. These are highly motivated readers with good foundations in business and economics. You expect the journalists who are writing for this kind of audience to be solid, informed, intelligent, top-flight interviewers who know what questions to ask and what answers to expect. They may come looking for the news story, but they will end up reporting much more than you disclose. They will reach out for all possible sources to back up or refute your story. They have to put events in perspective. If these magazines just reported the news, they would be no more than newspapers. They are after stories of more depth, and if you don't supply the information, they'll get it elsewhere.

Fortune frequently starts with some type of premise in question form. Just look at some titles for its stories: "Is Business Taking on Too Much Debt?" "Can GM Manage It All?" "Guess Who's Bought Whoops Bonds?" *Fortune* began a June 1983 feature story with the news that:

> Timex doesn't discuss its affairs, and for more than a year rebuffed *Fortune*'s requests for an interview. Former executives, whether from lingering loyalty, ingrained habit, or fear of risking their severance payments often, but not always, refused to speak.
>
> Ultimately, alerted to *Fortune*'s calls to former officers and worried about the possibility of a one-sided account, the company offered up its worldwide vice president of marketing and sales for an interview. Eventually the chairman joined the group.

This article went on to report what the chief executive said, what the marketing vice president said, along with lots of quotes from former employees and miscellaneous other sources that *Fortune* had been collecting. You can't help wondering if the article would have taken a different course if the management had agreed to come forward sooner. What made the magazine think the company had something to hide? What inspired them to spend money digging up evidence against the management? Once again, it is usually not a good idea to refuse to talk to the press.

Specialty magazines. Specialty magazines would include *Entrepreneur*, *Inc.*, and a host of other trade magazines. These magazines may come after the same story as newspapers or other magazines will, but they are looking for a bit of a twist in their reports. *Inc.*, for example, is a business magazine that focuses on the small business. The reporters from *Inc.* will talk about your company, its products and its customers' opinions, but they will also want to know how you started and how you will keep up a small business. That is the core of continuity throughout the magazine. It is the appeal for their readers—small business owners and managers.

Entrepreneur's reporters are looking for items of interest to entrepreneurs and would-be entrepreneurs. They want to offer some advice for success to these people. Do you have any?

Read the magazine and you'll see the angles.

Unlike TV reporters, print reporters needn't rely on anything more complicated than the telephone for the average story. When a reporter calls your office and wants to interview you right away, do not feel obligated to comply with his request. Instead, make a date for later. This buys you valuable time to prepare your remarks. When you will be speaking as a corporate representative, it is also wise to work out your comments with your boss or your company's public relations people.

If a secretary screens your calls, he or she should know how to buy this preparation time for you. She should also make sure she gets the name of the reporter's publication and finds out what she can about the publication's readership and the reporter's objectives.

RADIO

There are approximately ten thousand radio stations in the United States. If you're in Los Angeles you can listen to about one hundred different radio stations.

You may be asked to contribute to a local news or talk show by being interviewed in person or over the phone. That's one of the advantages of radio. It's easier to get and give news because you don't need the elaborate trappings of a TV station.

A trip to the radio station is quite different from an appearance on television. In a radio studio it's just you, the host, an engineer and a microphone. Think of that microphone as your link to your audience. In radio it's your voice alone that communicates. Your words have to say it all; clarity, expressiveness, imagery are critical.

The Interview

To give a successful interview, you must think of yourself as a one-man or one-woman show. It's a mistake to approach an interview with an attitude of dread or submission, ceding all control to the interviewer. Prepare to take control yourself if it should become necessary.

In chapter 3, "Organizing Your Thoughts," you learned to shape your thoughts into an introduction, body, climax and conclusion. This format also works for an interview. Both brief and extended interviews are constructed like minispeeches. After you've been introduced, make your most important point right off the bat. No matter what the first question is, find some way of bridging to your central message. This way you are certain your central message will be conveyed. Use the rest of the questions to elaborate on your initial statement. Then, as the interview winds to a close, and if time permits, try to build excitement to a climax, and restate your main point.

In general there are four basic steps to prepare for any kind of press interview. They are:

1. KNOW THE OBJECTIVES—YOURS AND THEIRS

As soon as you are asked to be interviewed, find out as much as you can about the objectives of the reporter. What kind of story is he or she doing? For example, if you are a middle manager in a cosmetics company, you might ask if the reporter is doing a story on the cosmetics industry, a profile of your company, a report on new makeup trends, or product differentiation.

Who else might appear in the story? Will there be spokespersons from competitors? Will other people in your company be speaking? Will your customers or employees be interviewed? What angle is the reporter taking to discuss the subject?

You must know the angle of the story if you are to prepare for it well. Try to write one sentence that describes the reporter's objectives. Now you are ready to determine yours.

Your objectives must be stated in positive terms. To say "I want to avoid controversy" is not a positive statement. Here are some examples of the positive objectives/directions you might take.

If you are Howard Rothberg of Allison Software Corporation: "I want to discuss why my company is putting out the best computer software."

If you are Ralph Nader: "I want to explain how oil prices are determined by oil companies."

If you are representing a toy store chain: "I want to show how we have changed our line of children's toys to make them safer."

2. PLAN YOUR MAIN POINTS

Once you decide on objectives, write out a list of facts, ideas or opinions that support your objectives. For example, an objective for a Continental Airlines executive might be: "I want to explain why our airline must ask its employees to take a pay cut."

The main points toward this objective might include the following:

a. "Deregulation has increased competition in the airline industry and has led to lower fares."

b. "Fuel and labor costs have continued to rise while revenues continue to go down."

c. "The resulting crunch has forced Continental out of business. It cannot go on operating this way."

3. WRITE A LIST OF POTENTIAL QUESTIONS

Once you've analyzed what the interviewer wants and what kinds of things you want to get across in your interview, begin to make up questions you might be asked. You may even be able to provide these questions to your interviewer in advance. In many cases, the busy interviewer appreciates knowing the areas you want to cover as long as you don't force your ideas on him.

Ask a friend, a spouse or a co-worker what kinds of questions he thinks might be asked by a reporter. Try to field them from your friends. Tell your practice partner not to hesitate to ask stupid, rude or tough questions.

4. PRACTICE ANSWERING THE QUESTIONS

If you don't have anyone to practice with, use a tape recorder and/or a video recorder. As you play it back, imagine how it will sound in the real interview. After these rehearsals, you'll approach the interview with the confidence of someone prepared to meet any eventuality.

When you practice answers for a television interview, recognize that a TV news reporter will most likely have to edit your statements into twenty-second "bites" of information that contain the central points. (This does not apply to public affairs or talk shows, though "bites" from these broadcasts are often used later in news programs.) Frame your answers in complete sentences or "headlines," using simple and clear language within a twenty-second framework. Avoid jargon and industry terminology that will not be readily understood by a general audience.

Here's an example: A doctor is asked to discuss the point at which people should contact a doctor during illness. Obviously there are hundreds of cases he could talk about, but since he has just a few seconds, a "bite," he could reply: "If a fever persists, if there is no sign of improvement within a few days, or if you are in a great deal of pain, call your doctor."

Though the examples that follow focus on the television interview, they also apply to other media.

To help make the interview as successful as possible, *supply your interviewer with background materials*. A good press kit might include an annual report, copies of several past articles published about the company or yourself, a brochure of products, descriptions, your biography, and perhaps a copy of a recent speech of yours that discussed the topic of the interview. Another point to remember is to supply a phone number or a follow-up reference in case there are more questions before air time, or in case some other source contradicts what you have said. Don't risk being unavailable in the event of a follow-up call. Somebody else might answer for you.

I believe *it is the responsibility of the interviewee to get across the main points* he or she wants to make. Marshall McLuhan once said to an interviewer in Canada: "That should be the subject of a separate show. I don't think we should spend the precious moments here on something that requires a big treatment." He was trying to keep the interview on course to develop the points he wanted to make. You may not have McLuhan's outspoken self-confidence, but if you have prepared properly, you will be able to maintain focus. Moreover, you will be eager to express and share your views.

Give the interviewer your unlimited attention and respect. Listen with interest and patience, acknowledge questions with direct answers, and *bridge to whatever point you want to make.* Here is an example:

Reporter: "Isn't it true that your company is trying to cheat its employees by asking them to accept a pay cut?"

Eastern Airlines representative: "Far from cheating them, we're trying to assure them they can keep their jobs and that the airline can stay in business [the answer]. We plan to cut *all* our expenses and become more efficient [the bridge]. Our people will no longer be employees; they will be owners. We're giving them stock shares instead of raises [the point made]."

Overall, it's best to approach your interview with an attitude of civilized grace and gentle good humor (the demeanor of a Ronald Reagan or a John F. Kennedy). The ultimate goal is to get something dynamic going between you and your interviewers. This means you need to speak with excitement and candor. If you are the subject of an extended interview, you can even ask questions yourself. Ask the interviewer what he would do in this situation. Doesn't he agree with this point? What does he think of that one?

When Jacobo Timerman, author of *Prisoner Without a Name, Cell Without a Number*, appeared on "Bill Moyers' Journal" to talk about Argentine Nazism, he took the initiative. "You see," he said to Moyers, "after being under so many hours of interrogation and torture, every time I have a meeting with somebody I don't know, or an interview with journalists, this syndrome of interrogation comes back to me and I prepare psychologically for this interview by saying: What is he going to ask me? Is he a friend? Perhaps Mr. Moyers is working for the secret service of Argentina. Is he going to question me about this? Should I say I saw the killing of somebody, or shouldn't I? How's he going to use it? Probably I don't know English well so he's going to confuse me. Why should I go? I prefer not to go."

In Moyers, Timerman faced a figure who echoed the fearful interrogations of his past. By admitting that, he focused the audience's attention on what was happening right then in the studio between the two men. The immediacy he established made for riveting viewing. Moyers couldn't help but respond to his guest's candor. In the most moving part of the discussion, Timerman asked a question that caused Moyers to admit something and, in turn, Timerman made his own revelation:

"Let me ask you this, Mr. Moyers. These days the president of the Jewish Community of Argentina is here in the United States lobbying in favor of the Reagan administration and against me."

MOYERS: "How do you explain that, Mr. Timerman?"

TIMERMAN: "It is not the Argentine government who is making a statement about the situation of the Jews. It is not the Argentine army . . . it is a Jew, afraid, worried, who comes and quietly says to everyone, 'It hasn't happened yet.' This is the proof of anti-Semitism. It is the best proof. Don't you think so?"

MOYERS: "I've never had to be a survivor. I've never had to live surrounded by hatred, suspicion, paranoia and the threat of persecution. So I just cannot tell you what it is like to be tortured, I cannot tell you what it is like to be the leader of a community that is besieged."

TIMERMAN: "And at the same time, Mr. Moyers, I cannot tell you how it is to be free."

Timerman, a newspaper editor and interviewer himself, a man who knows a great deal about the subject, used the question/answer technique with Moyers to arrive at a deeper, more poignant understanding of his life in Argentina.

You can draw your host and audience in as David Halberstam, author of *The Powers That Be* and *Breaks of the Game*, did when he appeared on the "Tomorrow" show with TV newsman Tom Snyder. Halberstam said things like, "Good move, good move!" "That's an excellent question." "Yes, that's really the central point." Such comments help to establish rapport between the host and you.

At first glance, establishing rapport with your interviewer and taking subtle control of the interview as Timerman did may seem to be contradictory. The key is doing what's appropriate at the time. Obviously you can't let your efforts in warming up your interviewer distract you from making a goal-related point with each answer. The more you seem to know what you are doing, the more he or she will respect you.

In all interviews, your ultimate goal is communication with an unseen audience. Although you can't see the viewer, listener or reader, you still need to use all the devices of good communication: personal anecdotes, vivid analogies, and statistics that are striking and easily grasped. I cannot overemphasize the importance of these attention-getting devices. Michael Korda, author and editor in chief of Simon & Schuster, says: "If you want to have a best-selling novel, go on TV and tell one personal anecdote. That will do it." So whenever possible, tell a story. Keep it crisp and to the point, use humor if you can, and you will engage your audience, put your host at ease and increase your likability.

Most interviewers are genuinely interested in getting and giving information, but often they are also looking for controversy. If you forget that, you run the risk of being taken off guard and saying something damaging. At the very least, you may get sidetracked and leave out the crucial information you are there to convey.

THE STUMBLING BLOCKS

Here is a list of potential stumbling blocks, and tips on how to leap over them.

Loaded preface. If the preface to your interviewer's question contains a slur, such as, "Over the past five years your company has consistently lobbied against the ERA. What are you doing about hiring women and minorities?" Defuse it as quickly as possible to block further questions in that vein, then bridge to a point you want to make: "To be exact, we lobbied against the ERA briefly because of its association with certain groups which our board of directors found objectionable. If you look at our hiring record over this past year, you'll see a dramatic change. We have completed construction on four new plants. Approximately 40 percent of the new employees are women! We're glad to have the opportunity to hire them. We're on the move!"

Try to anticipate loaded prefaces and prepare countermoves in your practice sessions.

The either/or question. Here your host asks you to agree to either one alternative or another. "Will the President cut back taxes or try to balance the budget?" If the truth is either the first or the second alternative, say so. If not, you don't have to choose either one. Say neither is true! You're not taking a multiple choice test.

The "suppose that" question. Once in a while an imaginative host asks how you would handle a hypothetical situation: "Suppose," he might ask a weapons manufacturer, "the United States sent troops to El Salvador. Would you support the move?" Don't be conned into this sort of thing. "I can't answer that hypothetical question. I find it to be an outrageous assumption."

The stupid question. If your host asks you a stupid question, be big about it. Don't correct him in an obvious way, but in the course of your answer clarify whatever he muffed. You will get your point across, and your graciousness will register with the audience.

The irrelevant question. If the host asks an unpleasant question but one that is germane to the discussion at hand, you must address it. But many a host will ask an irrelevant question that is provocative and/or inflammatory just to jazz up the show. The best way to deal with these questions is either to respond with humor or to ignore them with a comment such as: "I don't think that's the point of the discussion."

The stab-in-the-back question. You may criticize your opponent's position, record or credentials. But never question his motivation, character or devotion to his cause. In other words, don't stab him in the back! Hosts may tempt you sorely with remarks such as: "What did you think about Mr. X saying this about you?" Unless you're sure Mr. X did indeed "say that" about you, don't comment. Or preface your remarks with: "It's hard to believe that Mr. X said that, but if he did I really can't agree with him."

The digging-up-the-past question. In the past, if you or your company have taken a position inconsistent with your present one and you are asked about it, answer honestly and directly. Admit the discrepancy but make sure you clarify the present position.

The deadhead question. Every now and then you will encounter an interviewer who really has not done his homework. He may ask you about the wrong company, or the wrong issue, or call you by the wrong name. In this case, bridging comes to the rescue. Politely and unobtrusively correct the error in the question: "I'm sorry, Ms. Smith, but I work for Adcom Company, not IBM..." and then bridge to your main point, "but Adcom does have a new product, and it is more powerful and less expensive than our last computer offering."

These basic strategies can make you a polished interviewee who won't be caught off guard or made to stumble in public.

Remember, you can always refuse to answer a question, but you have to at least imply a reason. If there is a topic you are not free to discuss, tell your interviewer beforehand if you think it's likely to come up. He may respect your wishes. After Suzette Charles took over the Miss America crown in 1984 from Vanessa Williams, who had to give it up because of her nude photo layout in *Penthouse* magazine, Ms. Charles was constantly being asked: "Do you think Vanessa Williams was wrong in posing for those photos?" Her response on a TV talk show was: "I'd rather not answer that question. Vanessa and I are friends. It's a delicate and sensitive subject that I'd rather not talk about." If the interviewers persisted (as some did), they began to look bad. It is all right to refuse to answer the question; just make sure the audience understands why. "No comment" leaves a bad impression no matter what your reasons are.

TV and Radio: On-the-Air Savvy

As soon as you enter a TV studio, you are "on." It is not always clear when the camera is hot, so consider it hot the moment you enter. Observe, but don't get involved in the activity around you. The floor director signals the host. (He won't signal you.) The host speaks to and listens to the director in the control booth, so he will not pay full attention to you. Time is uppermost in everyone's mind. Signals are passed back and forth. Don't be distracted. Just concentrate on how you plan to use the time allotted to you.

If you are not already seated when the camera lights up, you must make an entrance, and the way you do so makes a significant if subliminal impression. It's good to project an image of controlled energy. Don't come across as either too eager or too timid. Walk confidently from the door to your seat, sit comfortably and securely, and face your host. Don't look at the floor. You can look eye-level out into the studio audience, if there is one. Look pleased to be there. Smile.

Don't play to the camera. Forget about the camera! Talk to the host or to the other panelists. When someone else is speaking, look at him or her. Don't look up, down or sideways. These glances give the impression that you are uncertain and/or suspicious and evasive. Rivet your eyes on the person speaking to you.

You can, however, glance at notes if you've brought them. Do so as unobtrusively as possible. You don't want your notes to come between you and the person you're speaking to. So, don't arrive with a huge stack of unwieldy papers: 3×5 or 5×8 cards are best.

Have a key fact written on one side of each card. You can keep them in your hand and flip rapidly through the stack to reach a desired point of information when you need it. Don't be afraid of the time this will take, particularly if you are quoting someone or using a statistic. It gives your interviewer and your audience a sense of comfort and trust to know that you are prepared, and glancing at a card is a good-natured, human gesture with which they can identify.

Be careful about nodding while you listen or try to assimilate a question. On camera this can be interpreted as agreeing to what is being said.

Perspiration is a natural, normal result of being under pressure and hot lights. If you have to wipe your forehead, do so. Don't pretend you're not perspiring if you are; the camera could be right on top of you and it looks dreadful if you have sweat running down your forehead and are doing nothing about it. Just calmly, inconspicuously use a handkerchief to mop your brow.

The important thing is to feel good about yourself and what you are doing, physically as well as verbally. If you do, you'll come across as trustworthy and authoritative.

Don't think the show is over because the credits are rolling on the screen. The audience's very last impression of you is the one they'll be left with. Many people believe Ronald Reagan clinched the 1980 election by a simple gesture of friendliness after his debate with Jimmy Carter. He walked over to the President and shook his hand. It's a good idea to continue talking as the credits flash across the screen even though you won't be heard. Take the initiative and reach over to ask the host a question. Shake his hand if you've finished the interview. The audience will feel that it's caught a glimpse of the real behind-the-scenes you, and will be reassured to find that you are at ease, polite and in command.

Likability counts for more than anything else on television. If viewers like you, they will listen to you. And long after what you have said has faded into the dim past, they'll remember "how you came across," what kind of "vibes" they got from you, and they will judge the import of what you said through those impressions.

If the show has been taped, the crew may ask your permission to shoot some "reversals." They want to film the interviewer asking his questions a second time from different angles. This gives the editor more options, helping him to develop continuity and add variety by intercutting shots of you and your host. Without them, your appearance may be cut short and the segments may seem choppy. Insist on being present while the reversals are shot. Then, if the interview seems to be going in a way that alters its overall thrust, stop the cameras. If you wait until the crew has its reversals under wraps, any objection you make is likely to prove futile.

YOUR TELEVISION IMAGE

When you are dressing for an appearance on television, you must keep in mind the piercing eye of the camera. Simplicity is the key. On TV you don't want to wear anything that will distract the viewer from what you have to say. You also have to avoid certain colors and prints that "jump" on the small screen. Here are some tips:

For Women
- Choose strong blues, greens, grays, wines, earth tones. Don't wear black, white, red or pale pastels.
- Wear a matched suit or a dress in one solid color for a sleek line. Avoid stripes, prints, plaids; they jump.
- Choose a comfortable skirt length, with enough fullness to drape well when you are seated.
- Avoid shiny fabrics and glittering jewelry, both of which glint blindingly on the TV screen.
- Make sure that your hair is carefully coiffed and doesn't hide

your face in any way. If you dye it, remember that TV lights are merciless with dark roots, so get a touchup.

• You'll need to wear more makeup than usual. Shading and eye makeup must be artfully applied and colors must be subtle—no aqua eye shadows, frosty blushers or slick lip glosses. It's worth it to hire a makeup pro if you need help.

For Men

• Wear a well-tailored suit in a deep color such as navy, brown or gray, and make sure that your tie and lapel widths reflect the current fashion.

• Select a quality tie in a quiet design that won't jump on screen, and a blue, rose or beige shirt—never a white one.

• Think texture. Suits made of nubby wools or other "touchable" weaves look rich on television.

• Avoid busy stripes, plaids or herringbone tweeds.

• Don't wear short socks that expose skin when you cross your legs.

• Men should also avoid bright jewelry, including tie bars.

• Take care with your hair. Consider a blow-dried style for a neat, contemporary look. If you are bald, you can powder the shine from your head, but don't be self-conscious. A bald man can look attractive and authoritative on television. Joe Garagiola is a good example, as is Marvelous Marvin Hagler.

• Men, you too need makeup in order to even out skin tones and define your features. And makeup keeps you from fading away if you're fair. Get professional help if you need it.

YOUR RADIO PERSONALITY

"Broadcasters are looking for something to talk about every day," says Charles Osgood, radio and TV newsman. For that reason, you may be asked to do more radio than TV or print interviews. There's a lot of radio around, and logistically radio is easiest to do. You can pick up a phone and do an interview from home or wherever you happen to be.

The format for radio interviews is basically the same as for television. Once again, your four-step preparation is in order, and you must add your television insight to arrange your major points into "bites" of information. Keep your statements to "twenty" seconds. Radio reports can be even briefer than television stories, so make sure you time your deliveries during your practice sessions. Remember, too, that without pictures any little "ehs," "wells," "you knows" and "I means" will stand out and hurt your performance. Work with a tape recorder to rid yourself of these bad habits if you have them.

Call-in shows are popular on radio. If you find yourself on one, a caller may spout radical views or uninformed opinions and try to draw you into an argument. Don't be taken in. You can't change such a person's mind, and you risk tarnishing your own image if you become argumentative. Acknowledge their right to their opinions, make your own point briefly and hope the host will go to the next caller as soon as possible.

A few radio stations employ hosts who specialize in insult and invective, offending their callers and guests alike. There is a simple piece of advice on this. If you are approached to be the guest of one of these disagreeable personalities, don't accept. It's a no-win situation. You would not be asked on the show if there were no controversy. If the host threatens to say that "you refused to appear," invite him to do just that. You have more to gain by refusing than by accepting.

A final practical consideration is a *tape*, audio or visual, of the interview session. You have a right to tape any interview you give but no claim to the tape the interviewer is making. In some cases the program director or producer of a television or radio show will give you a copy of the version that is aired if you request it, but you can't depend on that. You should at least audio-tape the interview. It's your insurance against irresponsible editing.

The TV or radio interview may exert a certain degree of performance anxiety, but it is actually the press interview that requires the most thorough preparation, in most cases. The reporter will probably have considerable background; your business will be his beat. Your preparation should follow the four-step guideline, but go into greater detail and be ready to discuss the nuances, the subtle implications of issues. Do another kind of homework as well. Read through a few back issues of the newspaper or magazine, paying attention to the quotes in a pertinent story. This will give you a good idea of what kind of quote will be in the next issue—yours!

As with other interviews, give the reporter a backup *press kit* including a professional black-and-white photo of yourself if you are to be prominently featured in his article. Work at establishing rapport with the reporter, and let him know that you will be available if he needs to ask further questions or clarify information.

The Media and Your Message

The world of the media offers wonderful opportunities for you to deliver your message, be it for a cause, a product or a service. Here is how four people, in four entirely different situations, found a way to make the media work for them.

One of my clients had a persistent problem with airport noise and asked to be included in the agenda of her neighborhood association meeting. "I did something that proved to be the best thing I ever did in my life," she says. "I told them that I had been speaking to my neighbors and we had written proper authorities and received no satisfactory response. And then I played a tape of the noise and people couldn't believe it. Their mouths fell open. I got a call two days later saying not only are we going to bring this up, but we'd like you to come and speak at a city-wide council of neighborhood associations meeting.

"I went to the meeting and found the press there. I was very nervous, because all of a sudden this was turning into a political action. This noise issue was assuming a life of its own. But I made my statement and I played my tape again and the press loved it. The next morning it was in the papers, and there were radio and TV people on my front doorstep, saying: 'Would you play that tape again?'

"After that we formed an airport committee of the neighborhood association. I really had to do my homework. I knew how many flights went over and how many new airlines had been given space at the Albany airport in the past nine months, and I knew that the decibel level over my house was equivalent to six roaring locomotives coming down the track at sixty-five miles an hour. We not only asked for a meeting with the FAA but with the county authorities as well. Then I wrote and called every reporter and every TV station to make sure they were going to be there. And when the FAA and the County Authority representatives walked into this meeting there were literally banks of reporters there.

The officials had to take us very seriously. I had pictures from the front pages of the local newspaper ten years ago, of an airplane that crashed two blocks away from my house, and I held them up. The press loved it. There on the evening news was the clipping, the tape recording, and a video-tape of the meeting. We really got some momentum going."

A new landing system at the airport is now under construction.

The activities of corporations can be newsworthy also. If you are part of a business news story, and are as prepared as Continental Airlines' Chairman Frank Lorenzo was on September 24, 1983, it's easy to make the media work for you.

On that day, Continental Airlines filed for bankruptcy and announced to 12,000 employees that they were fired. The company then offered to re-hire 4,000 workers at half their former salaries and with greatly reduced benefits. Continental's "asked-backs" were in a tough position. They were faced with a choice of joining the crowded ranks of America's unemployed or working the same job for half the money. As you can imagine, outcries were intense—from the workers, the unions and the employees of other airlines who could see the writing on the wall if this ploy worked for Continental.

Chairman Frank Lorenzo painted a clear picture for the press. He explained:

"Continental has been forced into bankruptcy by high labor costs. Deregulation has increased competition in the airline industry and has led to lower fares. Fuel and labor costs have continued to rise while revenues continue to go down. The resulting crunch has forced Continental out of business. It cannot go on operating this way."

The articles about Continental's bankruptcy filing were accompanied by charts that showed the rising costs of fuel and labor, directly related to the decreasing airfares in the industry. These numbers showed it was impossible to continue such a declining cash position. Lorenzo had given the press the information, and he'd conveyed it in a clear and organized series of easy-to-understand steps. There was no double talk, no industry or financial jargon, no technical explanations. Simple sentences told his story.

In addition, Lorenzo seized the opportunity to explain Continental's intention to become the largest discount carrier in the country. Using his own bridging technique he also did a quick advertisement for a new

$49 fare to twenty-five markets. The press reported his explanation and went on to tell everyone about Continental's new offer. The telephone lines were swamped the next day with callers making reservations.

The Continental Airlines story ended up as a press interview well handled in a tough situation.

Sometimes individuals misjudge the media altogether.

Richard Viguerie, president, The Richard Viguerie Company, felt that the conservative point of view was not getting across in the major media (i.e., the commercial networks, the *Washington Post*, *Newsweek*, etc.); yet for many years he had avoided the press, believing it was too liberal to be trusted. Then he changed his tune. He started talking to reporters and realized to his surprise that the press gave him a fair shake. Conservatives and businessmen often complain about the media. But here is one of the leading conservative spokespeople in the country saying: "They will be fair. But you've got to talk to them." Viguerie tells how it happened:

"In the mid-70's, a *New York Times* reporter called. My advisors said I wouldn't talk to him. But I figured: 'Even if I'm a little boy now, if I want to be a big boy someday I've got to learn how to play with the big boys.' The reporter spent three hours with me. It wasn't an article my mother would have written but it was decent and fair.

"After that, I realized I needed someone to help educate me about the media. I hired a young man who had worked in the Nixon-Ford administration. Conservatives needed to know how the media worked, their deadline pressures, how they viewed things. One day, he made a lunch date for me with Mary McGrory [liberal, syndicated columnist now with the *Washington Post*]. I panicked. Why should I have lunch with her? My advisor said it was a good idea, so I did it.

"Mary and I had lunch for three hours. I didn't want her to leave. It was delightful and we've maintained a cordial, respectable relationship ever since.

"Today I have more friends in the media than in politics. I play poker with nationally known figures in the media on a regular basis. I enjoy the relationships. And that's true of many of my conservative friends as well. We get along fine. It's not an adversary relationship. But it didn't come easy. We had to work at it."

Now Viguerie also has a syndicated column in 1,120 newspapers. The medium he once disdained has become a forum for his own views. "To get my message across, I had to learn to do things differently," he says.

The following is a prime example of just how helpful the media can be.

In 1984, Aetna Life Insurance Company found that the U.S. spent $1 billion a day on health care. Of the $1 billion, about $2 million was accrued through fraudulent overcharges. So Aetna created a fraud squad to investigate and prosecute those people who filed insurance claims for amounts in excess of what was really charged.

One of the reasons for doing this was to catch the perpetrators. Another was to publicize the fact that the people at Aetna were aware of these frauds and that they intended to prosecute. They wanted to educate the public about what these overcharges were costing and alert people to the fact that these overcharges are criminal and will result in prosecution. So Aetna notified the press:

"We knew we had a hot story that day," says Judy Hyfield Starr, Corporate Communications. "We are the largest insurance company in the country so what we say carries weight. And our story was consumer-oriented so it was easy to interest the nation in it."

Letters were sent out to a select list of editors in the electronic media and print. One medium parlayed into another: the *Journal of Commerce*, the *Wall Street Journal*, *Business Week*, the *Los Angeles Times*, etc. Ms. Starr sent out this message:

"We want you to do a story on the Fraud Squad. We'll give you examples of people who have cheated insurance companies, and we'll arrange for you to interview James Garcia, who is in charge of the Fraud Squad. He's a middle manager who investigates claims that look suspicious."

Mr. Garcia's aim was to alert people to the fact that when they received funds they were not entitled to, they were stealing. By submitting fraudulent claims, they were committing a felony punishable by five years in prison and/or a $5,000 fine. Mr. Garcia states: "In the first week that we went into the area calls came in like crazy to our field claims office to report fraudulent discrepancies. We have a 100 percent conviction rate at this point of what we turn over to law enforcement officers."

•   •   •

There is no single "right way" for you to get your message across, whatever the medium. Writing this book, for example, has taught me how to put my life's work into the written word. And that in turn has strengthened my resolve to "broadcast" it, to tell people about it. Each of us has to find his or her way to share knowledge and experience with others, to get our message out. After reading this chapter, I hope you feel as I do, that the media are there to help us do it.

YOUR
"POCKET GUIDES"

The motto of the Boy Scouts of America: "Be prepared."

If there is one thing you have learned in this book, it is that good communication takes time and effort. Whether you are making a presentation to your boss, introducing the guest of honor at your club, or giving the speech of a lifetime, you must organize your thoughts, create and mark a visual guide, and rehearse. When you take these measures, you approach the meeting room or the dais with a confidence that holds you steady, and everything you say rings with clarity, response and aliveness. You speak well, you touch your listeners, you make an impact.

As stated in chapter 9, "Communicating Nine to Five," a good rule of thumb is 30 to 60 minutes of preparation for each minute of speaking— and major presentations requiring a lot of research demand even more time. Of course, when your schedule is hectic or when you are called to speak on short notice, you won't be able to carve out the optimum preparation time; nevertheless, it is crucial to take *some* time, even if it's just to put your thoughts in order, jot them down on a 3 × 5 card, and practice them quickly with the "mute out loud" technique.

The following "pocket guides"—set up in chart form so that you can duplicate the pages you need and carry them with you for practice anywhere and anytime—present five preparations intended to help in any speaking situation or media appearance.

You must have a roadmap. The one that follows is a re-cap of chapter 3: "Organizing Your Thoughts." If you prefer, design your own guide, but do include the essential parts: the Introduction, Body, Climax and Conclusion. And keep your listener in mind. You want and need response.

Outline for Organizing Your Thoughts

CHOOSE AN OBJECTIVE
  Arouse Instinctive Drives
    Survival
    Ego
    Pleasure
    Altruism
ANALYZE THE SPEAKING SITUATION
  To Whom Are You Speaking
  Who Else Will Be Speaking
  The Occasion
  The Place
  Your Personal Stake
PLAN YOUR THOUGHTS
  Finding Material
  Using Tools
  Deciding on a Length
  Selecting One Main Point
STRUCTURE
  (Minispeech)
  Developing the Body: Tell Them
  Choose a Format:
    Topical
    Chronological
    Comparison/Analogy

STRUCTURE (cont.)
  Mixed Time Frame
  Problem Solving
  Gestalt
  Developing the Climax
  Developing the Conclusion:
  Tell Them What You Told Them
    Summary
    Motivational
    Application
    Dawn-of-a-New-Day
  Developing the Introduction:
  Tell Them What You're Going to Tell Them
    Seize Attention
    Establish Rapport
    Tell Them What You're Going To Tell Them
STYLE
  Be Yourself
  Incorporate:
    Clarity
    Flow
    Focus
    Highlights
    Humor: Own

THE HALF-HOUR PREPARATION Your boss calls to tell you he needs a report at an impromptu meeting later this morning, or you are asked to offer a toast at a dinner party tonight. The Half-Hour Preparation is designed to answer your needs in a crisis.

Half-Hour Preparation

Outline Your Thoughts	Mark Your Copy	Bring Life to Presentation	Practice
Intro	Underline	Determine Intro:	Out loud
Body	Circle	Get attention	or
Climax	Slash	Establish rapport	Mute out loud
Conclusion	Pause	Tell what you're going to tell	for:
		Think up an anecdote or memorable example to illustrate your main point	Clarity
		Determine climax	Response
		Set conclusion	Aliveness

THE THREE-TO-SIX-HOUR PREPARATION A speech or presentation of three to six minutes will require three to six hours of preparation, and this guide will help you get the most out of those hours. Use it to prepare for:

- A speech of introduction
- A welcoming speech
- An award acceptance speech
- A speech to present an award
- A presentation to the boss
- A job interview in your field of expertise

Three-to-Six-Hour Preparation

First Hour	*Second Hour*	*Third Hour*	*Fourth Hour*	*Fifth Hour*	*Sixth Hour*
Analyze situation Set objective Determine message	*Set Structure* *Block Thoughts* *Review*	*Flesh Outline* *Set Road Map* *Choose Format*	*Refine Your Style* *Review*	*Mark Your Guide*	*Practice Out Loud*
To Whom Where When Why What	How: Outline Introduction Body Climax Conclusion Gather Facts Review	Talk into tape recorder Indentify: Introduction Body Climax Conclusion Establish content of: Introduction Body Climax Conclusion	Use your language Look for: Clarity Flow Focus Highlights Review	Underline Circle Slash Pause Record—play back Clean up road map to make it legible	Emphasize Identify audience Focus on: 1. Clarity 2. Response 3. Aliveness Prepare Q & A

THE THREE-TO-SIX-DAY PREPARATION This guide is designed for speaking events of roughly five to ten minutes and situations that are somewhat more complex than those in the previous preparation. Each day's task is broken down into six time-efficient steps that will help you prepare your remarks with care and deliver them with practiced ease. Use this guide to prepare for:

- A fund-raising speech
- An explanatory report (e.g., for a product, an issue, a tactic)
- A how-to-do-it speech
- A dinner speech
- A short political speech
- A job interview in a new field

Day One: Organizing Your Thoughts

Analyze Situation	Set Objective	Determine Message	Set Structure	Block Out Thoughts	Summary
1. To WHOM are you speaking? 2. WHERE and WHEN will you be speaking?	WHY are you speaking?	WHAT will you say?	HOW? 1. Outline introduction 2. Outline body 3. Outline Climax 4. Outline conclusion	Gather materials: Facts Arguments Reasons Background, etc.	You have outlined the information and developed your objective. Now sleep on it

Day Two: Structure and Style

Flesh Out Basic Outline	Set Up Road Map	Choose Format	Use Style	Refine Your Style	Summary
1. Write down thoughts 2. Talk them into tape recorder	Identify and circle: Introduction Body Climax Conclusion	*Introduction:* Attract attention Establish rapport Tell what you're going to tell *Body:* 1. Topical 2. Chronological 3. Comparison/ Analogy 4. Mixed time frame 5. Problem solving 6. Gestalt *Climax* *Conclusion:* Summary Motivation Application Dawn-of-a-new-day	Use *your* language	1. Clarity 2. Flow 3. Focus 4. Highlights	Have a cleanly typed copy ready for tomorrow.

Day Three: Marking Your Visual Guide

The Form	Mark Outline for Key Words & Thoughts	Mark It for Rhythm/Pacing	Mark It for Response	Record & Play It Back	Summary
Decide if you want to deliver your remarks from: A complete sentence outline A phrase outline A key thought outline	1. Underline key words 2. Circle key thoughts	1. Make slashes 2. Make arrows	1. Write PAUSE 2. Write APPLAUSE and LAUGH for responses	Change markings if need be	Road map: must be easy for you to read

Day Four: Practice the Delivery

Record for Clarity	Record for Response	Record for "Aliveness"	Record Focusing on All Three Factors Simultaneously	Q and A	Summary
Emphasize key words and key thoughts	Picture to whom you are speaking	Ask yourself: What does this mean to me?	1. Clarity 2. Response 3. Aliveness 4. Play back and evaluate	Prepare for Q and A at end of presentation	Try to find a willing ear to practice on

Day Five: Practice the Delivery with a Friend/Friends

Absorb the Presentation	Dress Rehearsal for Friends	Set the Stage	Ask for Reaction	Make Adjustments	Summary
1. Memorize the first and last lines 2. Make a mental picture of the structure	Before your friends arrive go back to your visual guide with the edits you've made	Set up what you may use or need: Podium Conference table Desk Chairs Props V/A	1. Clarity: What did I say? 2. Response: Where did I lose your interest? 3. Aliveness: When did I seem phony?	After your listeners have left, practice again.	You've gotten to the final stage

Day Six: Fine-Tuning

Relax	Get Yourself Ready	Set the Stage	Rehearse Out Loud	Relax	Summary
Do the warm-up exercises in chapter 6: "Improving Your Voice"	Dress yourself as you will appear when you make the presentation	1. Arrange the podium, etc. 2. Look at yourself in the mirror to check posture, flow of garment, hosiery, hemline, jacket bulge, etc.	Rehearse in your attire and with props in the setting you prepared	Take a break	You're ready! Tomorrow, allow 30–45 minutes before you "go on" to: Check all equipment Relax Review Rehearse out loud one more time

THE SIX-WEEK PREPARATION This guide is for the major speeches of your career, when you will want to invest a significant amount of time for preparation. By spreading out the process of discovery, you allow your unconscious intuitions and sensibilities to surface. You also give yourself more time to research your subject, develop anecdotes, etc.

Because these speeches run twenty to forty minutes, and demand a lot of you in terms of phrasing, pacing, response and aliveness, taking extra time to rehearse is especially important.

Use this guide to prepare for:

- A commencement address
- A convention address
- A lecture
- A speech to a professional association
- An involved demonstration using visual aids

Week One: Organizing Your Thoughts

Analyze Situation	Set Objective	Determine Message	Set Structure	Plan Out Thoughts	Summary
1. To WHOM are you speaking? Relationship Occupation Background Potential Future	1. WHY are you speaking? Formulate objective in one succinct sentence	1. WHAT will you say? One central point Two or three supporting points	HOW? 1. Outline the introduction—tell them what you're going to tell them	1. Gather materials: Facts Arguments Reasons Background, etc.	By now you have a good idea of what your presentation will be like. You have outlined the information and developed your objective
2. WHERE and WHEN will you be speaking? Size of audience Place Who precedes and follows you?	2. What will motivate your listeners? Survival Ego Pleasure Altruism	2. Select subject according to time allotted	2. Outline the body—tell them 3. Where might the climax be?	2. Use tools: Tape recorder Scissors Scotch tape	Now sleep on it. Let it roll around in your head
3. Who else will be there? 4. What is the occasion? 5. What is your stake in it?	3. Link your objective with their motivation		4. Outline the conclusion—sum up what you told them		Next week you will put together a draft

Week Two: Structure and Style

Flesh Out Basic Outline	Set Up Road Map	Choose Format	Use Style	Refine Your Style	Summary

1. Write thoughts
2. Talk it into a tape recorder
3. Write a complete draft or
4. Edit your writer's remarks
	Identify and circle:
	Introduction
	Body
	Central Point
	2 or 3 supporting points
	Climax
	Conclusion
		1. Introduction
		Attract attention
		Establish rapport
		Tell what you're going to tell
		2. Body
		  1. Topical
		  2. Chronological
		  3. Comparison/analogy
		  4. Mixed time frame
		  5. Problem solving
		  6. Gestalt
		3. Conclusion
		Summary
		Motivation
		Application
		Dawn-of-a-new day
			1. Use your language: "Is this what I really want to say?"
			2. Imagine talking to a friend
			3. Use your humor
			4. Insert A/V aids
				1. Clarity:
				Correct grammar
				Simplify language
				Active voice
				2. Flow:
				Vary length of sentences
				Move back and forth
				Transitions
				Recurring phrases
				Repetition
				Alliteration
				3. Focus
				4. Highlights:
				Special interests of audience
				Create curiosity
				Controversial questions
				Striking facts
				Statistics
				Quotes
				Definitions
				Analogies
					You have created a working copy of your presentation
					Have a cleanly typed copy ready for next week
					You will record it and work on your delivery

Week Three: Marking Your Visual Guide

The Form	Mark Outline for Key Words & Thoughts	Mark It for Rhythm/ Pacing	Mark It for Response	Record & Play It Back	Summary
1. Make three copies of the clean transcript you have from last week (it's good to have extras) 2. Decide if you want to deliver your remarks from: A complete sentence outline A phrase outline A key thought outline	1. Underline key words 2. Circle key thoughts 3. Check to see if the underlined words are: Nouns Verbs Numbers Comparisons 4. Only 2% to 5% should be underlined	1. Put a slash where you want to breathe 2. Put an arrow where you want to continue from sentence to sentence	1. Write PAUSE between sections of presentation—Intro.—Body—Climax—Conclusion 2. Write APPLAUSE and LAUGH where you want those responses	1. Did you verbalize the markings? Key words emphasized? Key thoughts stand out? Rhythm and pacing varied? Did you give the listener time to respond? 2. Do you want to change the markings? Do so	This week you have solidified your road map, your guide. It must be easy for you to read. Now you are ready to use it to instill your presentation with your personality and commitment

Week Four: Practice and Delivery on Your Own

Record for Clarity	Record for Response	Record for "Aliveness"	Record Focusing on All Three Factors Simultaneously	Q and A	Summary
1. Think your presentation through as you say it out loud	1. Rehearse using objects in a room (a chair, a lamp, etc.) as a stand-in audience	Ask yourself: 1. What does this mean to me?	1. Clarity 2. Response 3. Aliveness 4. Play back and evaluate	1. Encourage Q & A throughout the presentation	This week you have taken your presentation from its beginning to its (almost) final form
2. Emphasize key words	2. Picture whom you're speaking to	2. What thoughts am I thinking?		2. Prepare for Q & A at the end of the presentation	You've made it come alive out loud
3. Subordinate less important words	3. Give one thought to one person	3. What associations am I making?		3. Make a list of possible questions you might ask	Now try to find a willing ear or two to practice into
4. Make your key thoughts stand out	4. Imagine how he might respond	4. How do these associations affect me and my listeners?		4. Make a list you can suggest should no one ask you any	
5. Play back to evaluate	5. Take command	5. Play back and evaluate			
	6. Imagine environment				
	7. Playback and evaluate				

Week Five: Practice and Delivery with a Friend/Friends

Absorb the Presentation	Dress Rehearsal for Friends	Set the Stage	Ask for Reaction	Make Adjustments	Summary
1. Memorize the first and last lines 2. Make a mental picture of the structure. Know the main points and sections of the body. Memorize the overall structure, not each word 3. Paraphrase the presentation out loud. Find new ways to make the same points 4. Record and play back 5. You may find a new or better way to make your points, adjust your guide	1. Before your friends arrive, go back to your visual guide with the edits you've made 2. Practice out loud once more before the curtain goes up on the dress rehearsal	1. Set up what you may use or need: Podium Conference table Desk Chairs Props V/A 2. Seat your friends 3. Give the presentation	1. *Clarity:* What did I say? Did I make my points? Were the supporting points well defined and expressed? 2. *Response:* Were you interested all the way? If not, where did I lose you? 3. *Aliveness:* When did I seem phony? Were you moved, involved, amused, provoked?	1. After your listeners have left, practice again 2. Record and play back, concentrating on improving the weak spots 3. Take a break	You've faced an "audience." It's different from speaking to yourself You've gotten to the final stage

Week Six: Fine-Tuning

Relax	Get Yourself Ready	Set the Stage	Rehearse Out Loud	Relax	Summary
Do the warm-up exercises in chapter 6: "Improving Your Voice" Clear your mind Get physical exercise	1. Dress yourself as you will appear when you make the presentation 2. Make preparations for hair, makeup and all accessories 3. Make adjustments in appearance if needed	1. Arrange the podium, table, desk, chairs, etc. 2. Prepare props, V/A, etc. 3. Look at yourself in the mirror to check posture, flow of garment, hosiery, hemline, jacket bulge, etc. 4. Do not practice your delivery in front of the mirror.	If possible, use a videocorder and camera; if not available, use a tape recorder: 1. Rehearse in your attire and with props in the setting you prepared. 2. Play back and evaluate: Clarity Response Aliveness	Take a break. Do something entirely different to clear your mind	This week you went through the final stages of rehearsal. You're ready?! Now, allow 30 to 45 minutes before you go on to: Check all equipment Relax Review Rehearse out loud one more time. *Be a detective; look for clues and response from your audience at all times*

GEARING UP FOR TV

This four-step plan will take you through a successful TV appearance: Research, Preparation, Interview and In the Studio.

Step One: Research

Investigate the Show	Investigate the Audience	Investigate the Host/Reporter	Investigate Participants	Make Contact	Summary
1. What format does the show have?	1. Is there a live studio audience?	1. Who is the host?	Who else will be there? Competitors Customers Employees	1. Contact the show's production assistant; introduce yourself.	Find out everything you can about the nature of the show. Watch it, if possible. Read reviews of it.
2. Is it live or taped?	2. If so, how large is it and what is its role and character?	2. What is his point of view or general bias?		2. Ask any question you have about the show.	
3. How long will you be on camera?	3. Who is the viewing audience?	3. What are his strengths and weaknesses?		3. Ask if you can be provided with a list of questions ahead of time (if it's a news broadcast they will probably refuse)	
4. Are you the only guest or part of a panel?	4. Does the audience expect to be: Informed? Entertained? Stimulated through controversy?	4. What kind of story is the reporter doing?			

Step Two: Preparation of Your Material

Define Your Objectives	Write Out Questions	Prepare for Controversy	Create a Minispeech	Practice Bridging	Summary
1. Write your objectives in one succinct sentence 2. List the main points you want to make 3. Fill in facts, ideas, opinions, etc., that support your objectives.	1. Write a list of five to ten questions you would like to be asked 2. Contact show and offer them the questions to help them prepare for the interview	1. Begin to generate a list of tough or embarrassing questions you could be asked 2. Know how to deal with: A loaded preface Either/or questions Stupid questions Stab-in-the-Back questions 3. If there are going to be other panelists, think about the kind of tough questions they might ask	1. Turn your objectives into three to five short statements you want to leave with the audience; each should be 15–20 seconds in length. 2. Take your central message and formulate it as a 3–10 minute minispeech so you can be a "one man show" if necessary. 3. Practice talking your minispeech out loud. Record and play it back	1. Using the list of difficult questions, begin to practice bridging from them to your main points 2. Incorporate anticipated questions into your minispeech	You've begun to work on your delivery—you will be better able to handle whatever surprises come up as you practice out loud Keep time limits in mind Be clear Be concise

Step Three: The Interview

Your Responsibility	Take Subtle Control	Use Attention-Getting Tactics	Prepare Props Prepare Yourself	Rehearsal	Summary
1. Get your message across	Get activity going between interviewer and yourself:	Anecdotes	1. Decide if you want to use any props	1. Rehearse out loud and create an interview with chairs, tables, sofa, etc.	Keep fine-tuning your minispeech and anticipating questions. Practice and plan. Look and sound your best
2. Don't expect Host/Reporter to:	Be candid	Humor	2. Check with show to make sure they will be usable	2. Practice entering and sitting down	
a. have read your book	Ask questions	Statistics	3. Plan clothing	3. Visualize host and the initial meeting	
b. studied your company	Phrase rhetorical questions	Analogies	4. Get haircut, or plan style	4. Do a run-through asking yourself questions and giving your responses	
c. ask the questions you suggested	Draw your host out	History	5. Plan makeup	5. Always keep time in mind!	
d. avoid controversy	Establish rapport	Quotes		6. Be prepared to take subtle control	
		etc.			

Step Four: In the Studio

Before the Show	Demeanor on Show	Your Physical Self	You and the Host	Your Mental Attitude	After the Broadcast
1. Remember, you are "on" from the moment you leave your home or office	1. Enter confidently. Don't look for the camera. It will find you	1. Sit up. Slightly forward	1. Think of yourself and your host as partners: "keeping the show on the road"	1. Maintain good humor	1. As credits roll, continue talking to the host. Take the initiative, if necessary
2. Arrive at the show ½ hour before the scheduled time	2. Focus on the interviewer and other participants	2. Keep hand gestures moderate	2. Know your objective	2. Be personal; be real	2. Leave follow-up information: Phone number Address etc.
3. Bring notes	3. Use 3×5 or 5×8 cards for notes	3. Do not nod or laugh unnecessarily	3. State your key thought in a 15–20 second bite	3. Avoid jargon	3. Ask for your audio or video copy of the show
4. Bring tape for associate producer to dub the show		4. Talk to the host or panelist	4. Speak to the host and other participants	4. Don't bluff. State what you know clearly. Admit what you don't know	
5. Get comfortable. Concentrate on yourself		5. Look at host and panelists when they are speaking			
		6. Do not look into the camera lens. (It may be the wrong one)			

AFTERWORD

Speaking is no problem, right? You do it all the time. You have something you want to say; you have somebody you want to say it to; you say it. It's as simple as that.

Look at the people around you, in a restaurant, let's say. They are talking with one another. Their faces are animated. Their expressions and gestures come naturally. They are engaged in one of the most enjoyable of human activities—conversation with another person. Or persons. Two, three, four people at a table, no problem.

Ah, but what if it's three or four hundred people? What then? Then it is called *public speaking*, and something awful happens. The face that was so animated becomes stiff. The eyes that were so expressive stare blankly into space. The hands that gestured so effectively now hold the rostrum in an iron grip. The voice, once warm and compelling, becomes cold and mechanical. It's as if the words on the page were passing through the speaker's eyes and out his mouth without passing through his brain.

The same affliction befalls people speaking before television cameras and into radio microphones. They say things they would never say to another person in real life, and say them in a way that they would never really say them.

Lilyan Wilder knows—because she has made it her business to find out—how to identify and deal with the impediments that turn public speaking into something other than regular old-fashioned talking to somebody.

Testifying at a hearing is talking to somebody; delivering a commencement address is talking to somebody; broadcasting a news report is talking to somebody. Somebody is out there. Somebody wants to know what you have to say. You have to be aware of that somebody. You have to give that somebody a break. That is what the Wilder method boils down to.

—Charles Osgood

INDEX